The Camp-Fires of the Everglades

A Florida Sand Dollar Book

The Camp-Fires of the Everglades
or
Wild Sports in the South

by Charles E. Whitehead

Foreword by Lovett E. Williams, Jr.

University of Florida Press
Gainesville

Library of Congress Cataloging-in-Publication Data

Whitehead, Charles E. (Charles Edward), 1829–1903.
   [Wild sports in the South]
   The camp-fires of the Everglades, or, Wild sports in the South / by Charles E. Whitehead;
foreword by Lovett E. Williams, Jr.
      p. cm.
   Reprint. Originally published: Edinburgh: D. Douglas, 1891.
   ISBN 0-8130-1089-6 (cloth). — ISBN 0-8130-1095-0 (paper)
   1. Florida — Description and travel — To 1865. 2. Everglades (Fla.) — Description and
travel. 3. Natural history — Florida. 4. Natural history — Florida — Everglades. 5. Hunting
— Florida — History — 19th century. 6. Hunting — Florida — Everglades — History —
19th century. 7. Seminole Indians. 8. Whitehead, Charles E. (Charles Edward), 1829–1903
— Journeys — Florida. I. Title. II. Title: Wild sports in the South. III. Title: Campfires of the
Everglades, or, Wild sports in the South.
   975.9'39 — dc20   91-95
                                                                                                        CIP

   The University of Florida Press is a member of University Presses of Florida, the
scholarly publishing agency of the State University System of Florida. Books are selected for
publication by the faculty editorial committees of Florida's nine university presses: Florida
A&M University Press (Tallahassee), Florida Atlantic University Press (Boca Raton), Florida
International University Press (Miami), Florida State University Press (Tallahassee), University
of Central Florida Press (Orlando), University of Florida Press (Gainesville), University of
North Florida Press (Jacksonville), University of South Florida Press (Tampa), University of
West Florida Press (Pensacola).
   Orders for books published by all member presses should be addressed to University Presses
of Florida, 15 NW 15th Street, Gainesville, FL 32611.

THIS VOLUME IS DEDICATED,

WITH FEELINGS OF THE PROFOUNDEST

RESPECT AND VENERATION

TO THE

BIG BEAR OF THE WAKASSARE RIVER,

AND THE

FRIENDS WHO WERE IN AT

HIS DEATH.

Contents

Full-page Illustrations	ix
Foreword, by Lovett E. Williams, Jr.	xi
A Note on This Edition, by Dolores Jenkins	xiv
Preface [to the 1891 edition]	xv
1. Turkey-Hunting	1
2. The Camp Fire	8
3. A Bear in the Camp	22
4. The Dangers of Fire-Hunting	30
5. The Plantation House of "Far Away"	36
6. The Panther's Cub	46
7. The Deer Hunt	54
8. The Fireside at "Far Away"	66
9. The Still Hunt	73
10. The Florida Pocahontas	89
11. The Florida Pocahontas—*continued*	99
12. The Battue on Bonda Key	110
13. The History of an Old Friend	123
14. The Drowned Lands	130
15. The Skin of the Tiger-Cat	150
16. Supper	154
17. Home Again	165
18. The Burial	177
19. Indian History	183

20. A Bear in Difficulty   188
21. Turtle-Spearing   193
22. Tarpon-Fishing   198
23. How We Conquered Halleck Tustenuggee   208
24. The "Painter" in the Pig Pen   218
25. The Sand-Hill Crane   227
26. Poke Receives a Cur'osity and Tells a Yarn   232
27. Woodland Choruses   242
28. Life in the Light-House   249
29. Tracking the Enemy   253
30. Smoking Out the Enemy   260
31. Besieging the Light-House   266
32. Mike and Tiger Tail Play Chess   275

Full-page Illustrations

Bonda Key—Moonlight Scene   *Frontispiece*
Breaking Up Camp, by H.R. Poore   10
The Hunters' Camp Fire, by P. Frenzeny   14
The Bear at Bay, by H.R. Poore   26
Negro Quarters, by P. Frenzeny   38
The Panther's Cub, by P. Frenzeny   50
The Deer Hunt, by P. Frenzeny   61
A Wild Shot, by H.R. Poore   85
The Florida Pocahontas, by E.W. Deming   100
The Drowned Lands, by H.R. Poore   137
Among the Wild Ducks, by P. Frenzeny   146
The Leap of the Tarpon (*photograph from life*)   200
Watching the Manatee, by P. Frenzeny   204
Old Spanish Church of St. Augustine, by P. Frenzeny   255
    (since burned) (*from a photograph*)
Departure of the Tribe, by E.W. Deming   268
The Last Climb, by W.L. Sheppard   272

* * * *The vignettes in the text are the rude efforts of the author.*

Foreword

by Lovett E. Williams, Jr.

THE SETTLERS WHO HAVE COME TO FLORIDA in the last quarter of the twentieth century would never guess what Florida was like only a few years before their arrival. A short trip back in time would find the same people and language and way of life described in *Camp-Fires of the Everglades*.

In the mid 1800s, the setting of *Camp-Fires of the Everglades*, Florida was the new home of a few rugged pioneers and a small number of Seminole Indians who lived close to and off the land. Both the settlers and Indians were immigrants from other parts of the rural South, namely Alabama, Georgia, and the Carolinas, and both hunted wild game and fished extensively for their subsistence. The native Indian inhabitants of the peninsula had been extinct for more than a century, and there was much competition between the recently arrived Seminoles and white settlers for the land and game claimed by them both.

But the dangers to settlers and travelers were probably no greater in early Florida than anywhere else in pioneer America. The Seminole Indians became hostile only when on several occasions the U.S. Army attempted to move them to Oklahoma. The difference is that Florida remained a frontier long after all the eastern and most mid-southern states had been settled. While the Old South was prospering and posturing in its culture of cotton and tobacco plantations, the Florida peninsula remained untilled, covered by swamps of giant cypress, hammocks of cabbage palm and live oak trees, and flatwoods of mature pine that were inhabited by unique and abundant wild animal and plant life. Florida was a land of infertile soils, hot climate, malaria, high humidity, biting insects, and little economic activity. The only places in Florida that showed any evidence of civilization or prosperity were a few port cities on the coast. The state was speckled with army forts about every fifty miles along the major trails and inland travelways. Today many local places are named for forts from the era of the Seminole wars.

Camp-Fires of the Everglades captures many aspects of earlier Florida landscapes and the prevailing attitudes toward the Seminole Indians. It contains good descriptions of some of the peninsula's wildlife and the methods by which it was hunted. Florida of that period is appropriately depicted from the perspective of an extended hunting trip, for it was indeed a land of wild hogs, deerhounds, swamp cabbage, and dugout canoes. The panther, wolf, and black bear ranged throughout Florida and were taken for granted. Deer, wild turkey, sandhill crane, white ibis, and waterfowl were abundant and important food items. Hunting was a convenient and reliable source of everyday food. Resourcefulness, self-reliance, and skills of survival were crucial to the people then; and these traits had to be adopted, or at least adequately imitated, by the visitors who got off the steamships to travel in the interior of Florida. Water was everywhere. Extensive drainage had not yet occurred, and the streams were a major means of inland transportation by canoes propelled by paddles and arm power.

Camp-Fires of the Everglades says more about the rustic style of outdoor living and hunting in nineteenth-century west-central Florida than it says about either camp-fires or the Everglades. In fact, the small hunting party in the book never quite got to the Everglades proper. The primary setting is in the wooded swamplands and hammocks along the coast of west-central Florida from the Steinhatchee and Suwannee rivers southward to Tampa Bay and inland to near Lake Okeechobee with excursions farther south to the northernmost Florida Keys and northeast to the St. Johns River near the east coast. Most of the adventures took place on and in the vicinity of the Withlacoochee River.

The descriptions of the landscape and wildlife are sometimes insightful, but the book's best parts are the fanciful Florida tales retold by the author and the vivid descriptions of life in a Florida hunting camp. Some of the stories are exaggerations, as admitted by the author, but they add much to the adventure and, in their way, reveal something about the backwoodsmen in Florida, who, then as now, would gladly pull your leg if you left it sticking out.

The small matters I might question, such as a casual mention of a sycamore tree on the Steinhatchee River, which location is actually several counties south of where the sycamore is known to have grown in the 1800s, do not detract from the book's overall authenticity. Other misstatements are few and can be attributed to the several years that intervened between the happenings and the author's writing about them. The author did a good job of naming and describing the local plants, especially considering that he was not a botanist and was writing for a general audience. He must have taken good notes, had a good memory, and gotten much help from his educated traveling companion "Doctor" Pollock.

Besides the good Doctor, who was a source of much philosophy and sophisticated information during this adventure, there was Mike, the swamp-wise, seldom-spoken, unschooled hunter, guide, and Florida Cracker who is the hero of the story. Mike wore leather clothing and knew his knife and gun, the land, the wildlife, and the Indians. I have met a few Florida backwoodsmen with some of Mike's personal traits and skills. The Negroes in the party were there to skin game and assist as needed and were only minor actors—a role for them that was true to the time. There were also a dozen dogs without which hunting would have been much more difficult and probably less successful.

I read this book with the critical eye that the author anticipated when he wrote in the Preface that "the Author has carefully striven not to offend the keen observation and long experience of his hunting comrades at the South, whose eyes will scrutinise these pages ..." To that I can only say that I, myself a hunter, naturalist, and sixth-generation Floridian, find no shortcomings of authenticity in *Camp-Fires of the Everglades* that are not more than offset by its overall value as richly informative entertainment. I am sure that Charles Whitehead's southern hunting comrades had no complaints either. An outsider like Whitehead can sometimes describe things well because, as a traveler, he has a basis for comparison that natives often lack.

Charles E. Whitehead (1829–1903) was a successful New York attorney and sportsman and an educated and cultured man. *Camp-Fires of the Everglades* was his only book, but he translated from the French a book about African hunting and presented an oration before the Delta Phi in New York City in 1855. He was known for his support of the arts and was active in the child labor movement of the day. His will included significant bequests to the Children's Aid Society, the YMCA, and other social welfare organizations for the poor and underprivileged.

Whitehead is a master of the American writing style of the late nineteenth century, and I have kept you from him too long already. It is fitting that the University of Florida Press would bring back into print and make available to us this rare account of an outdoor adventure in Florida that can never happen again.

A Note on This Edition

MR. WHITEHEAD'S BOOK has gone through several changes of skin. It was published originally in 1860 by a New York firm, Derby & Jackson, a smallish book, nineteen centimeters in height. Its title was *Wild Sports in the South: or, The Camp-Fires of the Everglades,* and it contained a few lackluster prints typical of the "popular press" art of the period. When it was reissued in 1891, with the titles reversed, it fairly blossomed into a beauty of the bookbinder's art, deep glossy green cloth covers, royal octavo in size, and with marvelously detailed collotype plates (here reproduced as halftones) by various artists and vignettes drawn by the author.

Charles Scribner's Sons held the copyright for the revised edition of 1891, but officially the book was published by David Douglas of Edinburgh and printed at the Edinburgh University Press. Douglas specialized in an array of hunting and sports volumes for the gentlemen of leisure of that era. A later American edition, issued from New York City by Field and Stream in 1897, is virtually the same in appearance except, of course, for the title page bearing Field and Stream's imprint.

The reader may wonder why so much British spelling appears in our edition. We have reproduced the text of the 1891 Scottish edition, with all its archaic usages and spellings and occasional inconsistencies. But examination of the 1860 American edition reveals that Whitehead already tended to favour/favor British spellings over today's American spellings: more instances of "colour" than "color," "spectre" rather than "specter," and so forth. Noah Webster's spellings evidently did not hold complete sway in mid nineteenth-century America.

Dolores Jenkins
Associate University Librarian
University of Florida

Preface

SOME OF THE SKETCHES contained in this volume were contributed by the Author to the journal *The Spirit of the Times;* some have since been floating about in other papers; while others were also published in New York in 1860, under the title of *"Wild Sports in the South."* So much it seems necessary to say, lest the reader should regard these "twice-told tales" as lacking in originality.

Nothing more is claimed for this volume than that it contains reminiscences of an actual hunt, and some adventures in the peninsula of Florida that happened many years ago, and counterparts of tales, some of them then told and since remembered, some of them fancied, such as frontier hunters tell when assembled at night around their camp-fires.

The Author does not ask that each story shall be regarded as having occurred literally as written; but he believes the spirit of the tales, the portraits of the frontier characters, the description of natural scenery, and the fragments of Indian history, to be correct. Much of the Indian history may be found in *The Exiles of Florida,* a historical work written by Joshua R. Gidding, and published in 1858. The basis of the Florida Pocahontas is recorded in the history of Garcilasso de la Vega, one of the early Spanish chroniclers.

The Author has carefully striven not to offend the keen observation and long experience of his hunting comrades at the South, whose eyes will scrutinise these pages, by any allusion to natural history which is not exactly true. As years go by nature and out-of-door life seem more and more attractive, and even the memory of the woods and waters is the sweetest of the author's possessions. Trusting that others may enjoy these recollections half as much as he has enjoyed the experience, he offers them to the public.

The sketch of the Leap of the Tarpon is from an instantaneous photo-

graph taken by Otis A. Mygatt, Esq., an experienced fisherman. That of the
Manatee, at page [207], is from the pencil of Mr. Wycliffe Taylor, London,
drawn from nature, and for the full-page illustrations the author is indebted
to Messrs. Poore, Frenzeny, Deming, and Sheppard.

                                                              The Author

June 1, 1891.

CHAPTER 1

Turkey-Hunting

"O flourish, hidden deep in fern,
Old oak I love thee well,
A thousand thanks for what I learn,
And what remains to tell."
—*Tennyson*

A GOODLY SIGHT IS A TREE! Its trunk, supporting a thousand branches that interweave the blue air with their tracery; lithe to the wind, stubborn to the storm, the pillars bend but do not break, in the leafy aisles of Pan's cathedral. Its roots, far-reaching, with tiny fibres probe the earth for moisture, and send the life-blood through the arteries to the fragrant blossoms and the topmost leaves that "clap their little hands in glee with one continuous sound." To its shadow not only the beasts of the field come for shelter, but millions of insects seek a home under the folds of its bark, or weave their cradles in its rocking boughs. On its branches the birds build their nests, and in its hollows the squirrel and the hooting-owl conceal their young, and the wild bee stores its sweets, while both day and night the buds breathe their perfume, and the wind, the leaves, and its feathered guests, chant an anthem of praise.

How it doth delight the heart to look down the forest, where trees of every form stand in countless numbers, and their shade, with its twilight, makes a new climate, where new flora gem the sheltered earth, where parasite plants and vines festoon the trees, building corridors gay with flowers, or purple with clustered fruit where the moss takes the place of grass, and the last year's leaves fill the hollows, where the wild bird and game make their home, and gambol in the unrestrained indulgence of natural instincts! To this scene add the brook filled with leaves, the open river tenanted with aquatic birds, and making vistas in the woods, and, lastly, the deep blue of the sea, fringed with the white of the breakers, and

1

complaining of its limits, and you will have the view that is to be met in the woods of the Florida peninsula.

"There simmer first unfaulds her robes,
And there the langest tarries,"

bringing in her train the fragrance of the earth, with the colours of the sky, decking her tallest trees with flowers proportioned to their grandeur. There the lakes and rivers are broad, and teem with curious animal life, and the birds of the air are painted with blue and crimson. There the queen lily rides the lagoon, curtained with drooping moss from the live oaks, and there the earth is so prolific of her fruits that there is abundance for all the crowded forest. No single life is forgotten, and the minute insect that feeds on the pollen of the tiger lily, lives as abundantly as the alligator that takes his toll from the whole animal creation.

Thus from year to year have the seasons come and gone; animal and vegetable life has reached its limit of years, has fallen and decayed, and wealth that would have enriched a nation has only formed the subsoil for another age, and none had seen the wonders of that inner forest that was barred by nature and the Seminole from the civilised world.

Under such a wood, near where the Stinhatchee River empties into the Gulf of Mexico, at Deadman's Bay, a hunter's camp was pitched years ago. Hunters and negroes were all still buried in dreams, and the weary hounds lay stretched around indiscriminately among the sleepers. No tent was raised, for the elements required none, though a screen of boughs had been built as a break-wind, and to keep the reflected heat near the fire. Here and there were scattered accoutrements, or the relics of the last night's meal, feathers of birds, skins of beasts, antlers of deer. The serried leaf of the palmetto fringed us around like a hedge, and above us spread the tassels of the pine-trees just discernible against the morning sky. Once in a while a bird twittered in the trees, now and then a sound like dropping rain was heard, where some animal shook the dew-laden branches. All else was still, save the quiet murmur of the sea on the beach, some little distance off. Its low roar lulled the sleepers; but the thought of game moving in the early hours awakened me, and, taking my rifle, I sauntered down the bank of the river. The air was clear and cool, and all nature seemed to be coming forth to salute the day. The quail whistled in the distance, and a mocking-bird on the summit of a pepperidge tree poured out his volume of song. The grey and fox squirrels leaped from bough to bough, or half descending the great trunks of the oak-trees, challenged with pert gestures the passers-by. Long trains of cormorants sailed overhead to their feeding grounds, and with measured beat the ibis and heron were slowly passing seaward. Flocks of ducks were feeding on the margins of the river, and the various tribes of woodpeckers, jays, and hawks, flitting among the trees; but none of these excited attention: they were rather the constant sights that one sees without regarding. At length the gobble of a turkey came faintly on the air. I have heard that sound often before, but one can never listen to its first clear note without a flutter of delight, that I verily believe is greater than that of its sweetheart, as she listens from the jungle to this the loud love-call of her mate. It apparently does not strike the ear, but the heart, and then tingles outward through every nerve. There may be something in this of early association, but it is one of the pleasantest that a man has in this world, and which so often makes him rich when he has never a sou. I stopped short and listened for a repetition of the sound, to tell from what direction it came, and also for any answer that might come back, as by directing my course toward the latter I could intercept the cock when he should take his course. The hundred little beings that talked around me in their various tongues were all speaking. Yet I could hear no cluck of hen, or responsive gobble of the younger cocks of the brood. Again the call was repeated. First a low chuckle, and then the rich guttural vowels poured out in a hurried volume. It domineers over every other sound by reason of its peculiarity. There is no manner of representing it in language, though the negroes have a song that ends in a turkey chorus, which might be written thus:—Chug-u-logga, chug-u-logga, chug-u-logga-chug. In the liquid negro *patois* it is not dissimilar. Having taken the bearings of the turkey by his sound, and estimated his distance, I ran on ahead, during a time equal to the interval between his calls, and then stopped and listened. In a moment the call sounded through the woods near me. I walked carefully forward, awhile sheltering myself behind clumps of alders and trunks of trees, and then waited and watched attentively. Again the note sounded, but it seemed in the air. I cast my eye upward, and there, perched on the dead and topmost boughs of a scyamore, from whence he could overlook the surrounding forest, stood my friend. His erect and slender form was drawn up to its full height, his little head turned quickly to the right and the left as he surveyed the forest below him, lit up by the same early sun that was burnishing his own glossy breast. I could imagine the view he was eyeing, and it must have been the conscious pride of a chieftain viewing his native heaths and hills that drew his form to such stately proportions. From where he sat he

3

overlooked river and lake, broad lagoon, and hundreds of low-lying islands; he saw savannahs covered with reeds and osiers, and shady with tapering canes, where bred the crab, and trailed the snail and centipede; he heard the pattering rain of pecan and of beech-nuts on the upland, and saw the pawpaw bear its luscious fruit; shady glens invited to repose, and in fancy's eye his lazy harem lay beneath those trees, shuffling with their wings the white sand of the hummocks that bounded the sea. All this he saw, and then swelling his throat, he sent forth his call, herald of the morn, and gathering-cry of his clan.

Raising my rifle, I took aim and fired. A half-uttered gobble was suppressed, and spreading his wings he sailed away in a slanting direction. "Missed," I ejaculated, as I saw him skating along like a hawk. Just then, without an indication, he rolled over in the air and came crashing through the boughs of the pine trees to the earth.

I ran to my prize. His heavy beard and long spurs showed him to be an old gobbler, probably one of those lonely birds that, expatriating themselves from their flocks, wander about in self-doomed celibacy. Throwing my game over my shoulders, I returned to camp and to breakfast, well contented with my success.

If the reader is desirous of knowing what is a wild turkey, by turning to Audubon's, Wilson's or Bonaparte's Ornithology he will discover it to be of the gallinaceous order, with conical papilla on the forehead, neck corrugated, beset with cavernous caruncles, frontal caruncle blue and red, and with scutellate toes, scabrous above and papillæ beneath, etc. After pondering on this description he may suspect that his ideas on the subject may be rather confused, and doubt if he would be able to sketch the bird from the description given.

Let him imagine a full-grown black turkey-cock of the domestic species, with a much smaller head, made shy and cautious in its movements, restless with its head and neck, high stepping over obstacles with its red, bare, sinewy legs, and erect, slender, and game-like in its bearing. Its eye is full and soft, with a hazel iris. The wild turkey is to its barnyard kinsman what the racehorse is to the carthorse. See him in the early morn as he stands on some elevation and welcomes the dawn, and announces to his family his movements for the day. His scarlet wattles lie pendent on a neck that one moment curves like a swan's and in another is erect like a crane's; his comb is a soldier's plume; his eye is full and hazel black, gleaming with something of a human look from his shapely head, which is covered by the wrinkles of skin and a few scattered hairs, and tinged with blue and red.

His neck swells very gradually to his body, and is burnished with a gloss of bronze and gold, that varies with every light. There is no pomposity or clumsiness about his air; on the contrary, his whole manners are those of an accomplished gallant.

See him among the hens. Their gentle looks are on him, and they follow his unspoken directions with perfect readiness. They ramble hither and thither as fancy leads them beneath the wild plum-trees, picking the stray fruit that has ripened before its season, and fallen to the ground, or a russet persimmon or a choice pecan-nut shaken down by last night's wind. Their leader casts his eye from side to side, scanning everything that moves. Now a caressing love-note is uttered to his favourite hen; then, drawing himself to his full height, he gives a glance of scrutiny into the woods ahead of him, where the slim pine-trees open an extended vision. Passing a rotten stump, with a stroke of his leg and claws he tears down the rotten bark. A half inclination of the head defers to the nearest hen a curd-white grub that has rolled out from the wood, and with a low cluck of acknowledgment she picks it up. Now with one foot half raised, he searches for the cause of a sudden noise. Ah! it was only that opossum, and the turkeys care little for him when they are in a flock together, and now in passing he leaps up and catches a beetle that was crawling in a bush above him, now a may-apple, then a spider or plethoric tadpole stranded in the hollow of the receding waters, all are appropriated. At length they reach the banks of a river; there is a little hurry among the young hens. They don't like large streams: there are alligators and garfish in the water, and wild-cats and eagles prowling around the banks, yet the river is to be crossed, and they are not half so good at flying as they are at running. Indeed they would walk round the head of it, had they not learned that all Florida rivers connect, in some way, one with another. As it is, they walk up and down a little while on the high bank, clucking and purring, with an occasional pick at some misplaced feather, just as an old lady smooths down her apron before expressing any decided opinion. The cock may occasionally spread his fan if the sun shines brightly where he stands, and utter his loud thrumming sounds like the roll of a drum. He has eyed for some minutes a low-limbed juniper-tree, standing near, and presently, after much examination, flits into it. Up go the hens in succession, and from the juniper they all fly to the upper limbs of a dead cotton-wood standing hard by. There is a continuation of the cluckings and notes of preparation, and then with the gobbler in the van, they launch themselves out in the air, and with broad extended pinions float in a slanting direction across the river, landing on the opposite side, at the edge of the underbrush, and are immediately lost to view. If the cock sees danger he lowers his body to the height of a chicken's, and, followed by his harem, runs through the brush, with a speed and silentness that renders pursuit futile unless by a fast and trained turkey-dog.

I remember a pretty incident in connection with a turkey hen demonstrating a knowledge of character on her part.

I had taken my stand on the end of St. Rosas Island, off Pensacola, to watch for deer that the hounds were driving. After my arrival a turkey hen came skimming to the ground, and presently walked toward a knoll of grass a few yards from my place of concealment. Her anxious look and her feigned attitude of indifference immediately showed that she was near her nest, and taking a pocket spy-glass I carried with me to watch the water channels, I presently saw her settle herself down among some low willows, until nothing but her head appeared.

Shortly afterward a fox came by, and coming across the trail of the turkey he turned short about, and throwing up his sharp nose, scented the different spears of grass the bird had touched, and then taking up her trail, commenced following it slowly and cautiously toward where she was sitting. With noiseless foot and undulating body he wound along in the trail, when suddenly, to my surprise, I saw the turkey hen leave her willow clump, and returning on her own trail, walk directly toward the fox. She picked hither and thither, in a nonchalant manner, and when within some ten or fifteen yards of her enemy, who had crouched in the sparse grass when he first saw her coming, she diverged slowly to the right, and the fox, as she turned aside, recommenced his crawlings, keeping his eye on the bird, and leaving the trail he had been previously following. In this way they progressed some hundred yards in a direction contrary to her nest, when coming near a low tree, with a soft chuckle, which seemed to say, as plain as accent could make it, "What a fool you are!" she flitted up in the tree.

The fox being then on open ground, at once knew himself discovered, and rising from his crouching position, after one or two longing looks, and a whimper of disappointment, trotted over the sandhills and was lost to sight.

The wild turkey is trapped under a crib made of cross sticks, with a ditch dug under one side. A string of grain is laid for some distance, coming down under the ditch and into the crib. The turkeys with their heads down, eagerly picking up the grain, walk down the ditch and into the crib. The grain finished they lift their heads. Finding themselves confined, they are frightened, and never lower their heads again, and never find their way out. To ensure success, the woodwork of the crib must be open work, and the turkey is always seeking to escape through the openings at the top, and never looks at the hole by which it entered.

CHAPTER 2

The Camp Fire

"Under the shore his boat was tied,
And all her listless crew
Watched the grey alligator slide
Into the still bayou."
—*Longfellow*

"TURKEY-BUZZARD?" sarcastically cried my friend and hunting comrade, Poke, as, returning to camp, I laid my game down, and seated myself by the blanket that was serving for a table, and around which Poke, the hunter Mike, and the two negro boys were busy at their breakfast.

"Spring turkey?" inquired Mike, in delicate allusion to the age of my bird.

It was generally the habit of the party to quiz each other at every success, and even mishaps were treated as sources of amusement.

"Da is har nuff to pizen all Floridy," said Scipio Africanus, raising the long tassel of beard hanging at the turkey's breast.

"Pooh!" said Poke, "I don't believe in that nonsense; it wouldn't kill a cat."

"Jis you try him, da's all; ya cut em up fine, and put um in de grog or de bread, and you's done for. Din't ole Ma'm Lize, on de Robinson place, take off Maussa Robinson? She be real nigger witch! Ole man, he took sick, and all ee doctors in Swanna couldn't cure him all winter; spring cum, he die ob turkey beard. Dat's Gospel!"

"You nigga mussen come cooking 'fore our fire, or we be habin' turkey beard too," retorts Cæsar, as with his black muscular arms, bare to the shoulder, he elbowed his darky brother aside to put a dish of meat before the party.

The sight of the smoking food brought every man's thoughts and fingers to the subject before him. The huge roll of cookery smelled good,

8

but was by no means comely to look at. As layer after layer of green leaves were pulled off, there presently rolled out what might have been a pig in civilised life, but which we immediately recognised as an opossum. His skin and hair adhered to the wrappings that had been bound around him, and which kept him from the ashes and the burning coals, and nothing now remained but the steamy fat little carcass that would have made a vegetarian forego his creed. Added to this there was a venison steak and some corn-bread, and Poke had a canteen of whisky hid away (the sensual dog!), and we feasted like kings, or rather as kings are supposed to feast, with great good-humour and monstrous appetites, which kings rarely have. Each one pulled at the 'possum, or cut strips from the venison, as he liked, and as fast as one cake was eaten, another would be ready on the stone in front of the fire. Beyond the circle sat the hounds, awaiting, with plaintive attitude, the stray bits that were tossed them from time to time; and joke, and tales, and future plans, were one by one rehearsed with laugh and hopeful wishes.

Poke was a jolly fellow. A critical judge of character might have said he was a little lazy, but none of us were critical, and who could blame a man who never lost his temper? His face was like an orange, so full and gentle, and the soft flaxen curls that clustered tight around his head were like a child's. A shrewd observer, he never saw a leaf changing colour but he inquired the reason, and with his gentle air read human character with facility. He seemed to know everything, medicine, and the arts, and the commonest little handicraft, and the greatest human theories, and he would discourse up to his waist in a miry slough upon the beauties of some aquatic plant as gracefully as in a parlour on the colour of a painting. His acquaintances call him Doctor, for he had studied medicine at Paris; the newspapers call him the Honourable Mr. Pollock, for he had once been appointed bearer of despatches to Russia; we called him Poke. Poke was short in stature, and ready to talk. In this respect he was the counterpart of Mike, or Michael Hone, or Mike the Spook, as he was termed by different classes of people. Mike was gaunt, though not over tall, slow in his motions, and very quiet in whatever he did. There was no pretension or ostentation about him, and so far did he carry this negative virtue, that he never mentioned himself if he could avoid it, and no one could tell his intentions or anticipate his motives until the act was done. A leather dress, and a leather cap, the same coloured shoes and belt, with a blue flannel shirt, buttoned in front by two polished alligator's teeth, was the invariable costume of the hunter. Once he had a cabin at Tampa, where he would come and go with such uncertainty that he obtained the name of Mike the Spook. Thence, at eve-

ning, when the settlers with anxious eye regarded the forest that environed them, dreading the whoop of the Seminole on every wind, Mike would flit into the shadow, and be gone a month or more, appearing again on the limits of the peninsula at Fort Dallas. The great interior wilderness was his home, and in its solitudes he had acquired his taciturnity. His voice was low and musical. He might not speak for hours, the indication of his finger and the expression of his countenance being sufficient for all ordinary language, yet when he did, his tone was as effective as a command. The villagers at Micanopy called him Injun Mike, and said they never saw him come or go but in a storm, and they, hunters as they were, seemed afraid of his strong will and arm.

Mike acted as our guide. He had undertaken it partly from a liking for me, and partly, as I suspected, from mere curiosity to see the Doctor and myself in the woods, for he would sometimes sit by the hour in his silent way, watching our motions and conversation. He never added a word, but if his opinion was asked, and the subject one that had been in the range of his observation, he answered the querist in the simplest manner. There he sat by the fire that morning; I remember him as if painted before me. His mahogany face wrinkled in kindly lines, and his chin covered by a long, thin beard. He was smoking in the Spanish fashion, rolling cigarettes from dried leaves across his knees, and his quizzical eye wandered over us with a considering look, as though we were children. A big black and dun hound, with a melancholy face, stood beside him; it was said either of them could track a bear by the scent. He had acquired the Indian habit of inhaling smoke for some minutes, and then driving it out of his mouth and nostrils in dense volumes, as a whale fills his lungs with water, and then spouts it into the air.

The negroes, Scipio and Cæsar, regarded him with feelings of respectful veneration. He excelled them in all their own handicraft. He knew every tree in the woods, and its uses; the habits of wild game, vegetable poisons, and the best manner of cooking; he could swim, ride, hunt, and shoot better than they. He had a close acquaintance with the Indians, and, the boys said, with the devil, and therefore there was a superstitious awe in regard to him, that was exhibited to no one else.

Besides the two negro men, we had two half-grown negro boys, whose arcadian simplicity of attire befitted the primeval woods. They were sleek and merry, worked when they were watched, and slept under one blanket, with their heads covered and their legs bare. They were called the Cherubs.

Besides the human members of our party, there were a dozen dogs of

11

high and low degree. Mike had two; they were long-eared, sad-looking hounds, with melancholy eyes. The negroes had four or five. The Doctor had one, Wag by name. If he should be regarded through the Doctor's eyes, he was a Gelert in courage, of the sagacity of a fox. But any one else in speaking of him would have called him a rusty mongrel, with an elfish disposition for mischief.

It is beyond the scope of this story to describe the toils and successes of each day in the campaign which had commenced that morning. Scenes of hourly interest to the actor, and adventures which to the hunter and naturalist would be beyond expression exciting, might be dull to the reader. Therefore, in a long winter's trip, that extended from the Suwannee River almost to Okechobee Lake, I can only recall those scenes that remained most strongly in mind after the lapse of months, and which sometimes, when the brain is most active, will reappear in dreams, with the wash of waves and the music of hounds, and the frantic rush of the chase. Yet there are many little minutiæ of an extended hunt to explain, as they form the regular duties of camp life.

After the breakfast has been despatched, the one sauce-pan, one soup-kettle, one coffee-pot, and four tin coffee-cups, and tin plates, are neatly cleaned, the two little vagabond horses are caught and led up with leading ropes around their necks. They are vicious, ragged-looking little beasts, but invaluable as pack-horses. On their backs we strap a couple of blankets folded in half; over that a little open framework, in which, and to which we may fasten anything that is to be carried. This novel pack-saddle resembles a kitchen chair turned upside down. In it is put the little box containing our salt, pepper, vinegar, cloves, lard, all little matters, but of great use—we familiarly call the box "the kitchen"; a sack of onions, one of bacon, a small keg of powder, a bag of shot, another of bullets, caps, needles, thread, scissors, etc., then a joint of venison, or a turkey, or any article of food, the Doctor's trophies, skins of birds, skulls of animals, or strange flowers or sketch-books. Then the coffee-pot, frying-pan, etc., are hung on the perpendicular legs of the saddle, two axes are strapped to the sides, and the ponies move off after making two or three malicious kicks at the dogs and bystanders. Mike leads the van with a cat-like motion, his long rifle lying on his arm, and followed by his dog. The negroes and the ponies bring up the rear. We passed for the most of our time through an open pine-country with a sandy soil. Here and there a grove of closer vegetation could be seen, and now and then a pool of water, surrounded by oaks and cypress, but generally the long vistas of slender trees would only be interrupted by some climbing plant, or the high knolls that traversed the country, following the general course of the drainage of the water. We only made one march a day of about six hours, and then selecting some spot for the beauty of its location, or the abundance of its game, pitched our camp, built our fire, turned out our ponies, and made ourselves as much at home as though we never expected to change. There were many days that we never broke camp, for the great abundance of game would entice us to stay, and then our resting-place gradually assumed a comfortable appearance. A tent of boughs carpeted with skins, a substantial fire, a well-stored larder, a pine slab table, and the Doctor, half reclining, smoking his pipe, and watching the frying joint, lest Wag should steal it, formed an agreeable picture of contentment in low life, and made one marvel how few are the necessaries in this world essential to happiness.

Several times we had our privacy intruded upon by our rustic neighbours during our absence, and once in a way that ruffled our good-humour. The camp had been left at early morning as usual, and from the ridgepole of our tent was suspended a sandhill crane, recently killed, and waiting for a cooking. In returning, toward the dusk of the evening, the negroes had separated to drive in the ponies, and the Doctor was leading the van, and talking of his bird, the sandhill crane, which at that season of the year was fat and delicate. The fire had gone almost out as we came up to the tent, but by its light we could see the little matters around in their usual condition. The Doctor laid down his gun against a tree, and, stooping down, walked into the tent. At that instant there was an aspirated growl, Poke was hurled over on his back, amid a cloud of feathers, and a big wild-cat came dashing out over his prostrate body.

"Oh! ah!" sputtered the Doctor. "Catch him! stop him! The wretch has eaten my crane!"

The dogs yelped; a flying shot was fired, and with two or three rapid bounds the cat leaped up into a huge magnolia tree growing hard by, and with a corkscrew motion was soon lost to sight in the dense foliage that extended far above the level of the surrounding trees.

On entering the cabin, I found Poke disconsolately sitting on his blanket, with the head and bill of the crane in his hand, the sole relic the cat had left him for his supper.

It was a pleasant hour in the old woods when our day's travel was ended, we had pitched our tent and drawn up around our gipsy camp while the huge fire flickered and crackled and lit up the green dome of the woods.

The tree trunks, for a long distance around, were lighted into rugged distinctness, and behind them remained the wall of shadow. The evening meal was eaten. The negroes had curled themselves to sleep, and the rest of the hunters, settling themselves down to the easiest positions they could invent, drew forth their pipes, the universal solace to the wanderer. The dogs still mumbled their bones around the fire, with an occasional wrangle over some breach of canine etiquette, and the two ponies appeared once in a while, when the flame blazed brightly, munching the wild grass that grew around.

It was the hour for meditation, and the mind, composed by the fatigues of the day, the glowing light, and the soft climate, wandered back through misty years. My cheek felt the free wind of the north; my eyes filled with moisture; I thought of home, and then I heard "zee-zee-zee-zip!" Ah, misery! what a mosquito! And then there is another—has been sitting on my cheek for ten minutes and I didn't see it. And now that I am listening I hear them on every side zee-zee-zeeing all around me, and every moment taking a nip. Oh, I see how it is! I forgot to light my pipe. There are Poke and Mike in undisturbed dreams of tobacco and glory, smiling faintly at my convulsive slaps. Now my pipe is lighted—no more nips; blessed pipe! Why are mosquitoes created; and what do they feed on when they can't get blood? Please answer me an oft-repeated thought, sage frequenters in southern swamps.

"Do you know what an alligator is?" drawled out the Doctor, after he saw me fairly roused to the comfort of the pipe.

"No; do you?" I replied.

"Not precisely, but I came very near knowing to-day. I was stooping to gather a strange flower on the bank of the river, when the earth caved in with me, and let me down with a fearful thump upon an old alligator that was sunning himself beneath. He gave a snort and plunged into the river, and if he was half as frightened as I, he will never come ashore again."

"Pooh, man! why didn't you take him by the legs and lay him over on his back?"

"Oh, I hadn't the time; he wouldn't wait."

"Doctor Poke was up the bank before the alligator could see him," said Mike, in a low quizzical voice.

"Oh Poke! for shame, to decline a fair fight!" said I.

"Who wants to fight with such a huge dragon? Not you, I warrant!"

"Whar your pup alligators?" said Mike to the Doctor.

"Bless me, I forgot them!" exclaimed the Doctor, diving his hands up to his elbows in his capacious pockets. Out came bits of thread, seeds of plants, little tin boxes, claws of birds, and finally two or three young alligators, about the size and shape of small daggers. They were of a mottled chocolate and yellow colour, and feeling the genial effects of the fire, commenced scrambling around like tortoises. The Doctor, with a hand on each knee, regarded them with unfeigned delight, and Mike, between his puffs of tobacco, looked on the scene with a quirk in his cheek.

"Reptilia, Loricata, oviparous, amphibious," enunciated the Doctor.

Just then one of the little animals inserted his nose under Cæsar's neck, as he lay snoring by the fire, and commenced wriggling himself into the woolly retreat.

"Bress de Lord!" shouted Cæsar, springing to his feet; "whas am dat yer pizen little varmint—what fur yer cum here, hey?"

Seeing our laughter he shook himself, and going to the other side of the fire rolled up again like a ball, pulling his blanket over his head, and went to sleep as soundly as before.

"Do you see that alligator's tail?" said the Doctor, as he pointed with the mouth-piece of his pipe at the caudal extremity of one of the little brutes as it lay on the warm sand. I admitted that I did, because I saw the Doctor was in a humour to talk, and I did not want to contradict him.

"Now tell me why it is that this animal should have such a big tail for so small a body, when any one knows he can't wag it with any pleasure?"

"Couldn't say, Poke."

"Can't you imagine, then?"

"Ornament," I blandly suggested.

"Ornament, indeed! Now, I have been studying these mammalia to-day. Mike and I went down Black Bayou after bear tracks, and I saw he was going farther than I fancied, so I sat down to watch the alligators lying on the opposite bank. I then noticed that an alligator, when he came to the bank and heard the others grunting in the reeds, climbed up as far as he could go with his short legs, and then bending his tail under him, against the beach, by that means, with a single jerk, threw himself up on the bank. Now, therefore, as these animals live chiefly on streams with low perpendicular banks, as they, by this example, do mount the bank with the assistance of their tail, and as nothing was made for naught, ergo, their tails were made to climb banks with."

"As these animals frequently scratch themselves with their hind feet, and as nothing was made for naught, ergo, their hind feet were made to scratch themselves with."

"That is sheer malevolence," retorted Poke. "You try to take away my cane and don't offer another."

"I did. I consider the tail an ornament, of as much use as the tail of a mouse or a turkey gobbler."

"And why should so cruel a monster, hidden in these solitudes, have his person decorated?"

"And why should the flowers bloom in the ever-glades with the same glory of colour as they do in the Tuilleries gardens?"

"There you go again. You are never kept down to the practical bearings of nature. I warrant you that these negro boys would coincide with me, and give the true reason. Cæsar! Cæsar! you sleepy-head. Explain to us the use of an alligator's tail."

"Wha's dat, maussa?"

"What does the alligator do with his tail?'"

"Suck um in de winter."

"You fool—you know better than that."

"Da' so fur true, maussa. Mars' Poke, nebber see picaninny 'gator in de egg, just gwine to hatch, hey? Den he see little 'gator wid his tail in his mouf, and when he cum out de egg den he take tail out of he mouf and eat hop-toads , and debil-bugs, and sich like, till winter cum on, and den he curl up in de mud and suck tail again till hot wedder."

"There, Doctor, you have it, an explanation by a child of nature! I hope you are content."

"Cæsar, you're a fool!" said the Doctor sententiously.

"Cæse ain't no fool nudder," interposed Scipio, raising his curly head from behind his comrade. "Ef he don't pickle young 'gators, he sees 'em and knows sum'en or nudder."

This retort was hailed with a volley of applause, and even Mike smiled at the Doctor's discomfiture.

Scip, evidently elated with his success, continued: "I knows 'gator from time I picaninny. I knows 'gator tail's good to eat. Course he suck 'em. 'Gator's science varmint, und when he roars in de spring-time he knows what he roarin' 'bout; ain't no fool, nudder, and makes speech wiser'n the judge in 'lection times."

"What does he say, Scip?"

"Mauss ask ole Aunty Foko what he say. She's got witch roots, and she knows how to talk 'gator. She stay out all night in Oke'fnokee swamp, 'gator neber so much as looks to her. She tell me what 'gator say to his picaninnies."

"Don't maussa, ketch me tellin' 'bout 'gator and dem little 'gators layin' da wid ears wide open. 'Morrow mornin' they'll be in de ribber, und ole 'gators know all 'bout me."

"Well, we will stop that, by carrying them away." So the little eaves-droppers were taken by the tails and dropped into the nearest watercourse, and the superstitious negro looked all about him with a suspicious glance, rolled over to a more comfortable attitude, and commenced his story:

"Yer see Aunty Foko's Guinea nigger, cum ober from Cuba, but after her boy ben sold away she don' work no more, and tuck to de swamp. She be older'n Cæsar an' me, boff togedder, and her hair a'mos' white. She know de pizen roots, and she know all de woods, an' day an' night be all de same to her; an' she know medicine to trow huntin' dogs off de track, an' nobody kin ketch her. An' she tell dis child all de 'gator say, an' so I knows. 'Gator lay he eggs in de sand, and den when dey hatch out some blazin' hot day little 'gators cut streeks for de water right off; da's all seen of 'em till night. Night cum, an' ole 'gator dat keep watch crawl on de sand-bank, an' he find little 'gators all hatch out. Den he turn round and commence to croak little: nuffin pays no 'tention to 'im. He croak little louder, nuffin come; den he stand up on his toes and he roar like all natur. It makes de water bile. Toreckly young 'gators cum, an' ole marm 'gator cum, an' dey all stand dere togedder, an' ef de moon is shinen it's real savage fur to see 'em. An' de ole 'gator he takes de chair, an he tell 'em, and dis jes what he tell 'em, I knows it's so, and so does Aunty Foko:

"'You chillen, yer great fools! you tink you sumt'in an' you ain't nuttin. You live half de time on land, t'udder half time in bayou, an' so you ben't smart in nudder. You be so loggish-like in de water yer can't ketch fishes, and yer got such little legs on land yer can't come up to nuttin. Now yer must larn, and when you've larnt den you'll know sumpsin. And I'm gwine to give you a teacher, and he's de possum.'

"When de ole 'gator says dis all de chillen dey larf, for dey knows what possum is, for dey seed 'em a pokin' long the b'yous, and dey's clined to de pinion dat possum's a fool. But de ole 'gator growls 'em down an' den he say—

"'Possum, he great animal; not kase he fast, for he bery slow; not kase he strong and kin fight, for he bery weak; but kase he's sly. Ef he sees anytin' cumin he make b'lieve sleep an' ketch 'em. Ef he's get ketched heself, he make b'lieve dead, an' dey lets him go. Now ye all play possum.'

"Den ole 'gator send all de picaninnies back in de water an' dey grow bery smart. An' dey learn to lay in de hog parf for sumsin to cum long nice, an' den gobble 'em up. An' dey roll in de mud till gets all kivered, an' den cum outen in de sun to get dry, an' nobody take 'em for 'gator, an' would

18

cum an' sit right down on 'em, an' den he grab 'em. An' after a while he gets so he lays side to de water, little piece back along de hog parf, an' when anyting cum along de bank, he hit him a slap wi' his tail an' knock 'em in de water, and den he slide in after an' eat 'em up, an' de only ting he won't hurt 'tall is de possum. Possum nebber gits ketched 'tall, an' dat am a fac.' "

Before the negro's fable had ended, one by one his auditors' pipes had gone out. The fire had burned low, and shadows, not parlour shadows, but huge ghostly shadows, went and came among the forest aisles as the fire flickered high and low. In Scipio's legend I remembered my first experience with alligators, and as it is of a kin with the legend I will describe it:

I was visiting a friend some years ago who lived on one of the many banks of the Alabama on the Gulf coast, and whose plantation was intersected by several little creeks. One of these inlets was quite near the house, and the morning after my arrival, while dressing at my window, I saw a large alligator crawl out of the water and settle himself down on the grassy bank on the other side of this creek. Between the house and the creek was a rice field, and the rice bank built along this inlet intercepted all view except from the upper part of the house, so I would have an easy approach.

I seized my double-barrel shot gun, loaded with the heaviest shot I could find in my room, descended the stairs, and made my way across the rice-field to the rice bank, and there lay my prize on the other side of the narrow creek, wholly unconscious of his fate. He was a huge beast, with scales glistening in the rising sun, and his big yellow eye shining like a golden pippin. After a moment's survey, and a mental congratulation that there was a creek separating me from the monster, I took aim at the largest part of his body and fired. I heard a splash in the water, and when the smoke cleared away the waves showed me the spot where my friend had disappeared, and after waiting some time to see if he would float ashore dead, I gave it up and went back. As I entered the house a dozen grinning rows of teeth appeared at the kitchen window, where the negroes were enjoying the spectacle of my skill in hunting.

At breakfast my friends questioned me about my shot, which they had evidently heard of from the servants, and I learned, for the first time, that I could only kill the alligator with a ball, and even with that it was no certain matter. I also was informed that this particular alligator had frequented that spot for several years, and was well known on the plantation by the name of John Bull.

The next morning as I rose I incontinently cast my eye over to the bayou, and there, in the full enjoyment of the glories of the sunrise, lay my yesterday's acquaintance. It did not take me three minutes to get into my clothes and down to the rice bank. I saw the grinning waiters at the door, but I did not care, for I was armed with rifle and sure of my game. I took a rest on the high bank, and sighting for a big chocolate spot on his side, I fired away. A wheeze, like a plethoric alderman, came from across the creek, and with a mighty splash the animal slid into the river, and the dark waters closed over him. I knew I had not missed him, but, as he did not rise, I supposed him dead at the bottom.

"Well, Charlie, my boy, how's the shooting to-day?" was the hearty salutation of my host as I took my seat at breakfast. A suppressed giggle, behind me, informed me that the negroes were enjoying the joke, and I had to explain by assuring my friend that the alligator was dead at the bottom of the river.

"How's that, Johnson? Do you think you can find his body?" said my friend to his huntsman, as he came in to get his orders for the day.

"Find his body, sah? Yes, sah, easy nuff find his body, sah; he body crawled up on de bank before de gememan dun gwine in de house, sah."

Every one laughed, and I did not forget the mishap until I became engaged in shooting, in which we spent the day. The next day was a repetition of precisely the same farce, except that the conduct of the servants became quite extraordinary, laughing outright, as I went across the rice-field, and the little nigs came out of the cabins in crowds, and crowed with delight.

"Well, Charlie, my boy, how's the shooting to-day?" became a stereotype question at the table, and "tough as an alligator, hey?" one of the commonest comparisons.

At last my patience and visit were finished together, and as I was being pulled out to meet the Mobile steamer in my friend's canoe, manned by eight as good oarsmen as ever pulled a blade, in passing by the head of the creek a heavy splash was heard in the water, and my friend whispered to me, loud enough to create a chuckle among the boatmen, "There's your target, you have left behind."

The alligator builds a nest of broken sticks and reeds of a conical shape, and about three feet above the water. It resembles in appearance a musk-rat house, and is anchored in the shallow water of the swamp. The eggs are pure white, elongated, and of equal size at both ends. They are distributed all through the nest, sometimes to the number of a hundred. The heat engendered by the sun, and by fermentation, hatches out the young, which are about six inches in length, and when hatched they immediately take refuge in the shallow waters. When young they are prettily barred in yellow and chocolate colours, and provide for themselves the moment they are hatched; and the mother, who during incubation constantly lies by the nest, then leaves it and seeks other enjoyments.

On Sapelo Island one winter day the negroes were draining a pond when they found an alligator ten feet in length, buried in the mud, hybernating. They hitched a log chain around his tail, and, fastening the other end to the traces of a team of mules that was employed in the work, drew the animal out of his retreat, and proposed to pull him up to the house. The friction of the warm sand revived him, and he spread out his feet and commenced to pull in the other direction. The mules turned their heads to see what stopped their progress. They gave but one look at their load, then jumped as only a mule can; the traces broke, and the mules ran one way to their home, while the alligator ran the other way to his home in the bayou.

CHAPTER 3

A Bear in the Camp

"I'll pitch my tent on dis camp ground
 A few days, and a few days,
Till I give old Cuff anudder round,
 A few days, and a few days,
  Wake, snakes, day am breaking."
   —*Negro Ballads*

AFTER ONE OR TWO DAYS of quiet southward travel, sometimes verging toward the seaside, sometimes turning into the back country, we came one day on the banks of the Wakassare River, a deep, black stream that empties into the Gulf. No fording-place being near, we halted preparatory to crossing the river—an everyday exploit in travelling a new country, traversed by sluggish streams.

Picture to the eye of fancy a camp, with all its accessories of rustic comfort, its bright fire, its feeding ponies, called "Marsh Tackies," dogs, and hunters under the pine woods. Before it, a close hummock of tangled vines, and tall trees bordering the bank of the river, and the long vines pendent from the branches. Beyond this leafy barrier, turbid with the gleanings of swamps, with whirl and glassy eddy, the dark tide of the river moves onward to the sea, trailing with it the floating skirts of moss that cling to the trees. On the far side a dense canebrake arises from the low bank, from whose fastnesses, as the shadows settled on the view, came forth the quacking of ducks and the booming of bittern.

On such a scene we looked one afternoon, and forthwith began our preparations for crossing. Selecting from the fallen pine-trees one or two logs of medium size, we cut them in uniform lengths, and dragged them to the water's edge, where they were bound in couples with grape-vine withes. After having made several couples, they were gently launched over the drifting wood and tangled roots that cluttered up the side of the river, and were all connected together with a rope, and then tied to a tree. This was our ark, and on it were placed, first of all, the powder and other ammunition, and Mike, as captain, and a negro as crew, each armed with a long pole and a rude paddle, began the first trip. First fastening the end of a long rope to a tree on the shore from whence they started, they poled out until the depth of the water prevented them from touching the bottom, and then with the paddle slowly worked their way to the opposite bank. Then commenced the difficulty. The tall canes grew down into the water, and presented a barrier to the entrance of so obtuse a vehicle as a raft; and though they might be pushed aside sufficiently to effect an entrance, they would spring up on every side, and hedge the pioneers in an enclosure as tight as a bird cage. To meet this difficulty, Mike sat down on the bow of the raft, and with a hatchet cut away the reeds, as the negro poled the raft, until a narrow lane was cut through to *terra firma,* and the men landed with the munitions. Here selecting a sturdy cabbage palmetto, they fastened the other end of the rope securely, thus making a taut line entirely across the river, and throwing away both poles and paddle, by means of the rope pulled back to the shore from which they started.

Next came the ponies' turn, and with much coaxing, and some pushing and pulling, one of their equine highnesses was brought on board the raft and pulled to the other shore, where, when he was loosened, he quickly disappeared in the reeds. Sometimes we made him swim by the side of the raft, but it was a dangerous attempt in large rivers on account of the alligators that were tempted to nibble at the legs so invitingly paddling above them.

The third trip brought the other pony, who, by his obstinacy, came near breaking up the raft; and, finally, I rowed over with the balance of the camp equipage and the dogs, that had to be tied up at the beginning of the operations, to prevent them swimming, which, had they attempted, they would have certainly been lost by the rapaciousness of the alligators, that even in the early fall were still very active in all the rivers.

Lastly the raft was sent back empty, with Scipio to unfasten the end of the rope. He, after casting off the rope, pulled himself leisurely ashore with the slack line, and taking off the rope that had been used in the construction of the raft, he followed us back from the river to where we had pitched our camp for the night, after clearing away the fallen leaves and sticks that there should be no harbour for snakes.

While coming through the canebrake, Mike, with an indication of his finger, and a quiet smile, pointed out the plantigrade track of a bear impressed in the soft mud; his huge paw left a print as though a man had walked by on his knees. The Doctor stepped around his mark rather suspiciously, and, I noticed, looked back at it as though suspecting his bearship might retrace his steps. The dogs were still tied, and they threw up their noses and whined, but it was too near night, and we would not let them loose. The marsh was alive with ducks, and the white egret, with his long crest, arose near us with a croak of surprise. Indeed, the whole bottom was trodden up with the tracks of deer, turkey, and the smaller game that find refuge in these close coverts.

After making our camp, and as the darkness drew its curtains around us, shutting in the bright firelight, and shutting out the void of darkness beyond, all the natives of the forest and river lifted up their voices in concert. Each bird or beast that dwelt in these heavy brakes uttered his individual note, and while smoking one's pipe, lying by the fire, the mind amused itself listening to the confused cries, and distinguishing them one from the other. The ducks quacked and fluttered in the marsh, the raccoon's plaintive call sounded its decrescendo from the wood, the honk of the heron, the shrill clatter of the rail, the mournful howl of the wolf, ascended in turn, or in a confused medley, now low, now high, as the wind rose or fell, and all up and down the river the bellowing of the alligator domineered over other cries with its huge volume of noise. Then there were other sounds that played low accompaniments to the bass of the river. The occasional twitter of a bird, the drops of the chinquapen nut, the patter of the dew falling from the trees, and the rustle of the leaves, all joined in the nocturnal anthem, and entered into our souls by the Wakassare with the mysterious lulling influence with which nature affects us, when, in camp, the mind is left open to its whisperings.

The day dawned reluctantly, the morning after our crossing, and so slowly the light broke through the mist that environed the camp, that it was more like moonshine than daylight. Drip, drip, pattered the gathering moisture from the cypress trees into the pools beneath. The osier-grass bent down, heavy with dew, and the ferns were matted to the earth, and the glassy leaves of the magnolia glinted with a double lustre of sheen and water. "Like a sea fog landward bound," the warm fog shut us in, as did a few hours before, the darkness. The voices of the night were hushed with the dawning, and all animal life was motionless, save where, now and then, from the invisible heights of the tree-tops, some moving animal would shake down showers of drops.

One by one the negroes came to life, and yawning and muttering gathered together the remains of the fire. The Doctor raised himself on his elbow, and benignantly surveyed the dull circuit of a dozen yards that the mist left open to his vision. The dogs snuffed the air wistfully, looked into the trees, and sauntered out into the mist, looming as large as the ponies as soon as they gained a little distance. In a moment a sharp yelp was heard from one of the smaller dogs. Again, after a pause, another, then a prolonged "yeough" from an old hound.

"Whas dat air!" said Scipio, raising his curly pate from the coals that he was vigorously trying to blow into a blaze.

"Nebber you attendsiate to de dogs, you lazy nigger; you cook," retorted his comrade, and Scipio renewed his puffing.

"Geow-ou-ou-ou!" roared out all the dogs in chorus, with a burst of clamour that awakened the sleepers, and before anyone could get to his feet a huge black bear, that appeared as big as a bull, dashed out of the fog, followed by all the dogs in full cry, right through the camp, scattering the fire, overthrowing Scipio in the ashes, scaring the ponies from their tethers, and leaving the Doctor sprawling on his back.

"Bress de Lord!" shouted the negro, scrambling out of the coals; "did de Lord ebber see like o' dat?"

"Tally-ho!" echoed the Doctor, hurriedly snatching an axe.

"After him!" shouted Mike, and with cheer and cry every soul dashed out in pursuit, and the camp that stood so picturesquely still in its first awakening, after the one rude rush of the chase was left deserted, while we followed the trail and cry of the hounds.

The game, immediately after crossing the camp, turned toward the river, and entered the dense canebrake that fringed the shore for some miles, and hunters and negroes followed helter-skelter, now over grassy holes, now over slippery trunks of fallen trees that had been floated by the water, and left to moulder green in the damp. One moment held back by a vine, at another so crowded by the reeds as to be obliged to lean down and run like a rail. One moment the crashing of reeds and baying of the hounds were close to us; then again they would gain on us; but far or near, we went plunging and rushing forward with a sense of intentness that gave no thought to anything but the chase. Soon we became separated; one man, plunged into a slough to his waist, was left to extricate himself; another was turned here, another there, by intervening obstacles, and presently I was left alone, following always the sound before me, that wound hither and thither among the reeds, now pausing as if at bay, and then rushing on to the right or the left, as the hunted animal was assailed by the dogs coming up from either side.

25

Shortly there was a pause, and the prolonged "Oo-oo-o!" of the hounds told the bear was at bay, and hastening in the direction, I came into a close thicket of canes that had sprung up as thick as wheat from the rich bottom land.

I could hear the bear, before I came to him, snorting and champing with rage, and as I entered his covert, I saw him on his haunches, with his back against a bank, his eyes red, his mouth open, shedding foam as he surveyed the dogs that were ranged in a semicircle around him, panting with rage, and bearing marks of his claws that had evidently taught them discretion.

But the greatest mark of respect was presented in the person of the Doctor. He sat directly in front of the bear, and scarcely six steps off; his feet were half buried in the mud, and he was seated on the same easy cushion. His coat and vest were wide open, his hat was gone, his curly hair hung matted with sweat and dew, and his axe was held in both hands directly in front of him, the handle sticking in the ground, and the blade pointing directly to the bear. If the bear's tongue was lolling, so was the Doctor's; if Bruin disliked his position, the Doctor appeared more than uncomfortable in his. In his hurry he had tumbled down over the bank directly in front of the quarry, and what with the chase, and the fright of this fearful juxtaposition, the bear was in the better position of the two. The Doctor with his axe presented, and the bear rampant, with his fore-paws just touching the toes of his hind ones as they projected up in front of him, resembled much some old coat of arms.

"Hurrah!" I called; "have at him!"

"Eh—eh," said the Doctor, all out of breath; "shoot him—eh —eh—quick—eh!"

I levelled my gun, and pulled the trigger, and a dull snap followed; the bear shook his head. Another snap, and another—my gun was wet with the dew.

The bear thus insulted gave a low growl, and a quick toss to his sharp nose. The dogs, construing this a challenge, and emboldened by our presence, rushed forward, and the huge brute, with a skill that was incomprehensible, would box them off with his fore-paws. One would be sent with a slap a dozen paces in the air; another would get a long cut from the bear's sharp claws, as he sat up like a boxer knocking over children with a mischievous playfulness that seemed more like fun than malice. Wag was there, as pert as the best hound in the brake, yelping, running, biting, and making much noise, and yet keeping out of danger. At length his turn came; a well-directed blow of that big black paw sent him curled up like a kitten, and as senseless as a rag, into his master's arms.

Poor Doctor! this seemed to awaken him, and springing to his feet he aimed a blow at the bear's head, that, had it taken effect, would have cloven him in two, but a scarcely perceptible motion of the same black paw sent the axe flying away among the canes, while the Doctor, from the parrying of the blow, came over on his face, and the bear, with a growl and crash, rushed off again followed by the yelling pack.

The Doctor, gathering himself together, picked up his axe, and listened with me to the lessening crash of the chase as it turned down the river, cry of dog, and crackle of brush, and now and then the whoop of the negroes, who had apparently come up with the chase. At length another pause, and then the peculiar notes of the hounds, and the calls of the negroes, told us the bear was again at bay, and, having recovered our breath, we started to overtake it.

As we came in view of the spot selected by Bruin for his fight, we saw all the dogs gathered about the base of a tree, the elder ones squatted on their haunches, and the younger ones jumping up and snapping their teeth at the bear, who was comfortably seated on a huge limb, balancing himself with the skill of a dancer and the burlesque gravity of a comedian. The most urbane simplicity marked his countenance; he seemed of a character that would not have harmed a child, and if I had not seen him a few minutes before boxing the dogs with such vindictive vigour, I would have been willing to have climbed the tree and put my arms around his neck. He looked

A Bear in the Camp

down at us condescendingly, now and then winking his eye blandly, and then with a dexterous use of his paw, he scratched his side, or rubbed his nose, when the flies tickled him.

Presently Mike came up, with his rifle on his arm. A glance up in the tree, and he quietly took his seat on a log, remarking, as he did so, "He bear."

"Oh! what a murderous animal!" said the Doctor. "Look at my dog there; how he has treated him."

A rifle shot, and Bruin fell inert to the ground, while all the pack rushed in to insult him.

CHAPTER 4

The Dangers of Fire-Hunting

"The pass was steep and rugged,
  The wolves they howled and whined;
But he ran like a whirlwind up the pass
  And left the wolves behind."

—*Macaulay*

WE HAD MOVED OUR CAMP to the neighbourhood of a settler's plantation, one of the few in this part of the world.

"Mike, what kind of night would this be for fire-shooting?" said the Doctor to that meditative Nimrod, who was busy sewing up a moccasin by the light of the camp-fire, after a week of travel.

"So, so," replied Mike, without looking up.

"I am going, I think."

No answer. Mike put on the mended moccasin, and drew off the other.

"Do you think we can kill anything?"

"S'pose," replied Mike.

"Come, Charlie, let us try it for a little while."

This was all a ruse on the part of Poke, in order to make Mike think our great hunt was an unpremeditated affair, and thereby increase the glory of killing so much game. It had been arranged between us during the day, that we should try fire-hunting that night. It promised to be a cloudy night, which was of great advantage, as it prevented the game from seeing anything of the hunters, and at the same time rendered their eyes more reflective when exposed to the torch-light. We had even gone so far as to make our pitch-pine torches, and the whole preparation was complete. It was a party of two—the Doctor and myself. There would be rather more interest in getting the game alone; and beside that, Mike's opinion on fire-shooting was well known, and we knew he would not go with us—so constant a hunter scorned so primitive a snare as the one we proposed. The

30

negroes we did not want, for the fewer in a party the better. So, one of us taking a gun, and the other carrying a torch, we left the camp.

The boys were chuckling together as they watched us go, the dogs howled because they could not go with us, and Mike gave one of his expressive coughs, that said as plainly as words, "Now for it."

We were soon outside the glare of the camp-fire, the little creek was crossed, and our torch flashed brightly on the taper trunks of the pine-trees, the climbing vines, and the broad-leafed plants that grew by the pools of water. There was no wind, and walking in the pine woods, there was no sound. Once in a long while, a crane, disturbed in his wanderings, would be seen stalking away, with his red head high in air, like a sentry on duty; or the sudden motion of the underbrush would tell us that some one of the many little harlequins of the wood, that gambol most when men do sleep, had fled from this unusual spectacle of a moving light. But no deer rewarded our search; no bear showed us his heavy coat.

"Faith," said the Doctor, "this romantic promenade is getting somewhat long."

"Think of the deer, one buck will well pay us."

"Fudge! if there was no one to laugh at us, I would have turned back long ago. Give me the gun, and you take the light."

Accordingly we changed positions—I going ahead, carrying the torch before me, in such a manner that it would throw the light ahead as much as possible, and none on our persons, and the Doctor received the gun, and took my place directly behind and shaded by my person. The night had become still darker, and a misty rain commenced falling. We had left the pine woods, after walking a couple of miles, and had come into a grove of lower timber. The long moss drooped in curtains, the odour of magnolias burdened the air, and every minute a denser copse would force us to turn aside from our route.

"Hush!" whispered the Doctor suddenly, with a spasmodic pull at my coat tail, "there's a deer."

I was just wondering at this absence of deer, and could not account for it, as it was a rare thing to go a mile in Florida without seeing one.

"Where?" I whispered; "I don't see it."

"Hush! it has gone now; but we will see it in a moment again."

We advanced on tiptoe, both in body and expectation.

"There! there!" said the Doctor, pointing with his finger a little distance to the left; but the luminous spot was gone before I hardly got my eye on it.

We were in the very place for deer. A heavy windfall lay ahead of us, and the mingled trunks and twisted branches looked like the *chevaux de frise* to some great encampment. The flickering light made the shadows move back and forth with a spectral effect, as though dancing, and the hush of the forest was unbroken by any sound. Every moment, I expected to see again the two phosphorescent stars that indicate the deer's eyes, and then the true shot would bring us the prize for our labour. It seemed a long time in coming again.

"That deer must be very shy," whispered the Doctor, just above his breath.

The next time, I saw it first. It was some distance ahead, and there were two; but before I could point them out to my comrade, they had disappeared. Presently, we saw it on one side of us.

"Charlie, that's a will-o'-the-wisp," said Poke, in rather a subdued tone, "or the devil; who ever heard of a deer going around so?"

"He is examining you to see what manner of man you are."

"Perchance it is some spirit of a departed buck, leading us a wild chase to destroy us."

"There it is, right behind me, as I live!" ejaculated the Doctor, in evident trepidation.

Sure enough, as I turned my head, I saw the two blue lights that indicate the reflecting lenses of the eye. The Doctor was taking aim, but I noticed it was not very steady. He pulled the trigger—a dull snap announced a miss-fire. He pulled the other trigger—it snapped in the same way. The gun was wet with rain.

"Was anything ever so provoking!" said Poke, as the eyes vanished in the darkness.

"If it is the devil, he will have you now."

"How *can* you talk so?" said the Doctor, with a strong accent on the "can."

"There is your deer, Poke, in the windfall," said I, as I caught sight of the eyes moving rapidly along near the mass of timber that lay heaped and knotted together.

"That's no deer," said Poke; "no cloven-foot could ever go over that windfall that way. I would rather see the night huntsman of the Hartz Mountains than see those eyes again." As he was speaking, I saw in the inky darkness ahead of us another pair of eyes, and two or three pairs on the left. The truth flashed on me. The scarcity of the deer, the proximity of the

32

windfall, the restlessness of those baleful eyes, all gave me the clew—the wolves were around us.

A word to Poke, and the affair was explained, and we stood still for consultation. We tried new caps on our gun; but it was of no use, the cones were saturated with water. We turned toward the camp, but in our confusion we forgot the direction. To heighten the misery of the scene, our torch was almost burnt out—let that die, and the rest could be easily divined.

We were standing, at the time, under a grove of small pecan trees, and at that instant a low snort was heard from the shadow near us, like the cough of a dog.

Poke did not say a word, but, dropping the gun, and seizing a limb of one of the trees over his head, with an agility for which I had never given him the least credit, elevated himself to the crotch, about ten feet from the ground.

I did not want to do anything of the kind, of course not; I would rather have placed my back against a tree, and won a glorious death in battle against my numerous foes; but, alack! for a bad example, I dropped the torch, that broke in pieces in falling, and, clasping the nearest tree, which happened to be a medium-sized gum-tree, soon scrambled up to a place of safety. Lucky was it for me that I had that torch in my hand, for when it fell it lay scattered around the base of the tree, still flickering and flashing in the darkness, and the animals that had surrounded us, as they saw their prey escaping, rushed forward with an angry noise; they saw glowing embers, and held back just long enough to permit my escape. As I drew myself up on the first limb, a rush of gratitude passed over my soul, and my feelings were as warm as a child's. Nothing could be seen, for the sombre forest shut out the little light there was in the atmosphere, but I heard the pattering of feet beneath my fortress, like falling rain. Back and forward they came and went, and snorting sounds and champing teeth made the black night alive with imaginary shapes. I wondered how it fared with the Doctor, yet dared not call, for the uncertainty was less fearful than the reality might be. I pictured him fallen, dragged back from his half-attained refuge, and divided among the hungry pack; and the very noises below might be the mumblings of his bones,

> "While their white tusks crunched o'er his whiter skull,
>   As it slipp'd through their jaws when their edge grew dull."

At length I summoned courage, and called "Poke!"

33

"Hulloa!" was the response—more grateful to my ear than any sound in the world.

"How are you, my boy?" I called again.

"Safe, thank the Lord!"

"What a disgraceful situation to be in, and how are we to get out of it?"

"I will be grateful if I can only keep in it; for this tree is so small, that the wolves can almost reach me when they jump; and, as I climbed up, one caught my coat-tail and tore it entirely off."

"Climb up higher, then."

"I can't; the tree is so small that, when I get any higher, it bends over, and lets me down—oh dear!"

"Haven't you your pistol with you? Try and shoot one, and it may frighten them."

"Oh, dear, no; there are hundreds of them. Just look at them below!"

I looked down, and surely I could see a drove of them. They were evidently the grey wolf, for, in spite of the darkness, I could detect their motions from their light coats.

Poke suggested they were phantom wolves, and declared they were all white.

All the fearful stories I had ever read came coursing through my brain. I saw snow-buried huts snuffed out and ravished by these prowlers, and heard the shriek of the child, thrown from the sleigh by its fear-maddened mother, and many an old dream re-shaped in my mind the terrors of nights of fever. Were we to be tired out by their devilish patience? Was one gang to relieve another, until we wearily fell into their hot tainted jaws, to be turned into wolf meat?

I shouted in the hope that some one might hear me; but what good to shout in that midnight forest? I heard a voice—it was Poke saying his prayers. I listened devoutly, but could offer none myself.

When he had finished, I called to him. He answered faintly—

"What is it? speak quickly; I can't hold on much longer."

"Fire your pistol; do try, it may bring some help, even if it does not kill."

"I will try," answered Poke.

There was a momentary pause, and then the sharp crack of a pistol was followed by the singing of a bullet close by my ear. By the flash, I saw Poke, hatless, and almost coatless, hanging on to the topmost branch of a young pecan, that bent with him like an orange-tree under a heavy load of fruit. With the report of the pistol, there was a scramble among the voracious crew at our feet; but they did not go away permanently, and were back in a moment.

"Fire the other barrel, dear Poke, but try and fire it the other way—point it down."

Bang! sounded the pistol, and I heard a thump on the ground, as the poor fellow threw away the now useless weapon.

"Hold on, Poke; take heart, my dear boy."

"Oh, it is easy enough to say take heart, but when the tree bends a little more than usual, I am within a foot of these hell-hounds. Oh, dear!"

At this moment I thought I saw a light flashing through the foliage. A moment more, I was sure of it.

"Poke, Poke, they are coming—some one is coming."

"Where—where! Oh, dear, I can't turn my head, lest I slip off."

"There they come; I see them—three torches, and men and dogs."

"God bless them!" I heard Poke say faintly.

I was afraid he was fainting. "Hold on, Poke," I said, and screaming to the men, I called them to hurry. On they came, at a run. I recognised them as they came up with their torches flashing through the woods; they were Jackson and his men. He had been in our camp only the day previous, and told us he had a sheep farm in this neighbourhood. "Quick, this way," I shouted—"the wolves! the wolves!" He answered me. How blessed a thing was the sound of a human voice in our necessity! They came under the tree we were in.

"Hulloa there! where are you? where are the wolves?" he shouted in his stentorian tones.

"Dare's de sheep I's bin huntin' all dis bressed night," exclaimed a negro who accompanied Jackson on his search.

I looked around, and there was Jackson's flock of sheep, staring blandly at us up in the trees, and at their master, by turn. It had been their eyes we had seen in the darkness.

And there was Jackson see-sawing on a fallen tree—hiccoughing, and laughing and crying by turns—and there were the negroes, and they called in the sheep, "Ho! ho! ho! Oh laws a maussy, did I ever—ho! ho! ho! ho!—wolves, oh laws a maussy!"

Poke slid down the tree he was in, picking up his coat-tail, that had been torn off by a broken limb in his hurried ascent, sighing:

"O that I had the wings of a dove!"

CHAPTER 5

The Plantation House of "Far Away"

"Ofttimes, in travelling through the west,
The stranger finds a Hoosher's nest:
In other words, a Buck-eye cabin
Just big enough to hold Queen Mab in."

JACKSON, THE CATTLE-RAISER, whose timely arrival had driven away the phantom wolves, was a fair example of many a planter. He was tall and slim in figure, sauntering in gait, wearing a black moustache, and hair so long as to be confined behind his ears. His hazel eyes were large and expressive, flashing with excitement, or quizzical with mirth, his face was sallow, his lips thin and stained with tobacco, his dress loose, and extravagant in colour when he was where he could select it. His manners were courtly and a little ornate. He was wealthy, after his kind; that is to say, he had dogs and horses without number, and "men-servants and maid-servants were born in his house," and he owned, by inheritance, acres of land enough to have made him a duke in Rhineland; and yet for ready money he was as poor as Peter the Hermit. Debts he had many, but they did not depress him; friends by hundreds, each ready to be his security for a million, yet could not have loaned him a hundred dollars in a month. He lived in a low, badly-built, wind-cracked, fenceless, vineless, paintless mansion in the Pine Lands, yet the proudest chief of the McGregors could not have equalled the courteous manner with which he welcomed the stranger to his home, and made him his friend. No matter for the rickety table; he scorned to mend it, and no one saw its defects, it was so well presided over. He never alluded to the food he asked you to eat, and you never saw it was only pork, sweet potatoes, and corn bread. He was bountiful with wine, when he had it, and with whisky at all times, lavish of command, and never by any possibility did any labour that could be either deferred or avoided.

Yet, for all that, he was an ardent hunter. Strange to say, lazy people love to fish or hunt, and Andrew Oglethorpe Jackson loved the latter. Nor bush, nor savannah, nor river, nor heat, nor rain deterred him. He would ride where mortal man could ride, just for the fun of the hunt. So we camped by the side of his house, in compliance with an invitation from the proprietor, to spend a few days with him in pursuit of the chase.

Jackson's palace was of one story and two wings, and the whole building was raised from the ground about three feet by means of wooden posts, which left a pleasant abiding-place beneath for broods of young negroes that constantly lay in this novel kennel, looking out like young puppies. The cypress grass grew sparsely in the white sandy soil around the house and its few out-buildings. Fences there were none, but the overshadowing live oaks, with their trailing moss, gave an air of grace to the establishment that man never attempted to improve. Some hundred yards from the house were the negro quarters. Small one-room cabins, with a piazza extending across the whole front, and open underneath. A few fowls lay in the shade with a dozen negro children, and the old negroes filled the porch, looking happy and free, though they were all slaves.

"Hulloa!" cheered the lord of the manor, as we drew up to the house a few days after our misadventure with the sheep; "Glad to see you at Far Away. The door is never shut, and the bottle never corked, and we will make you at home for a year and a day. You Tom! Cuff! You Cuff! Hannibal! here, run call the boys to take the horses and tie up the hounds. Run, all of you! Fine day this for hunting. Bring out some glasses, Melissa! Dogs can nose well to-day. Lively there! Well, bring some tin cups, if there are no glasses, you lazy huzzy! Let me get off my wet boots. Here, George Washington, pull off these boots."

The negro boy turned his back to the master, and spreading his legs apart, prepared to seize the boots between his knees in the usual country fashion.

"Liff up your foot, maussa."

"Lift it up yourself, you lazy nigger," replied the master.

The negroes ran, our dogs howled acquaintance with the dogs of the place, the little nigs looked on from every out-of-the-way corner, and with shout, and laugh, and much confusion, we soon had our tent pitched by the spring, the ponies tethered, and everything well regulated about us. Then came a good dinner, cooked in one of the little disconnected kitchens so favoured by the true darky cook, who, when not engaged in stirring the pepper pot or turning the corn-bread, stands in her red bandana in the

doorway, with her arms akimbo, looming as large as the wonderful fat woman in the Museum. We brought game, and Jackson had cooks, and we all dined well, and then a glass of good old peach brandy from his own still carried our minds to other lands, and sent our tongues travelling all around the world for adventures.

It was dark as we finished the bottle, and Jackson unlocked his closet for another. I believe that wine closet was the only thing that was locked on the place. The negroes had crawled out of their curious retreats, and were lying around in groups. The sheep-drivers had come in from the folds, and the tinkling of tiny bells announced that the sheep and cows were penned for the night. The camp-fire was lit, pipes were smoking, Jackson was sitting against one of the pack-saddles, and his daughter was reclining against his knees. His daughter was a brunette of sixteen, and her mother was dead, it was said, many years ago.

"*He* was a gentleman," said Jackson, pursuing a description he had been giving of some one living on the coast. "He never took an insult, and never gave one, sir; what more could be said of any man?"

"And he guv dis chile a dollar Christmas day—course he's a gememan," struck in Hoppin Lem, the planter's favourite servant, who, squatted on his haunches a few yards behind his master, drank in all the conversation, and joined in the laugh, with the low "yah-e—ah-ah-ee!" of the negro.

"Hold your tongue, you black rascal!" said his master.

"Was it not he who shot young Travers in a duel at the Mobile races?" asked the Doctor.

"Of course it was, sir; and did it as bravely as any man ever did. Yet that duel ruined him; he has been a broken-down man ever since."

"How is that?"

"Why, you see, sir, they had a dispute about the winning horse. He said that Centipede came in first, and Travers replied that if he had not staked so much money on Centipede he would have seen straighter. This was a reflection on his honour, sir, that no one was expected to stand. No, sir, he couldn't stand it. He challenged Travers, and Travers fell at the first fire. It wouldn't have been so bad, but Travers' old mother got wind of the duel from some of those Puritan meddlers, and came riding down to the field with her grey hair all streaming, and when she saw her son dead she cursed him. I wasn't there, but those that were there said it was a tough thing to see. He never got over it, sir. It was a windy afternoon, about sunset, when the duel occurred, and to the present time, when there comes up a hard wind about that time of day, the poor fellow rides off as if the devil was after him, and will not speak to man or beast."

"What a diseased mind a man must have to fight a duel!" said the Doctor.

"How can he help it, sir—is he going to have his honour impugned, his character insulted? He would fall so low that no one would speak to him."

"But he does not mend his character by killing a friend, and haunting his conscience?"

"That is an accident inseparable from society. There are certain wrongs which the pistol alone will redress, and the duel puts the feeble gentleman on an equality with the greatest bully."

"No," said the Doctor, his impassible nature gradually warming, "it lowers the gentleman to a bully. If he gets shot, his honour dies with him; if he kills, he is a broken man—either way the wrong is doubled; and it is, after all, the bully that supports the institution."

"No, sir; it is the gentleman that supports the system, and is supported by it. What else gives the navy and army its character and holds it together, sir—what protects the weak, and cows the labouring poor whose strength would make him over-reaching—what gives a tone to the gallantry of the South, sir, but a power that punishes insult?"

"And murders its own children!" added the Doctor.

"Murder! do you call it murder, sir? My own father was shot in a duel, but he died like a man. Where's the poltroon that don't resent an injury?—as he lives, I'd spit on him. There is not a girl in Florida that would dance with Alexander Pell after he got slapped in the face without killing the man that struck him. Is a man a dog, that he should suffer this?"

Jackson's manner was wild, and he gesticulated with his long arms like a phantom. The Doctor's blue eye was kindling in the fire-light. We looked for a war of words that might even amount to a specimen of the battle they were discussing, when the Doctor, with one of his usual strong transitions, cut off the discussion with a favourite couplet:

"A wink to a blind horse is as good as a nod;
    Your faithful servant, Ollapod."

Jackson turned his flashing eyes on the Doctor, his lids slightly contracted like a man in doubt to another's meaning; it was evident he was reading the Doctor, and the bland face turned toward him was like an open page with blue marginal illumination.

"Where do you reside, Doctor Pollock?" he asked, after a moment's pause, and in the indifferent tone assumed by the Doctor.

"I was born in Virginia, and inherited a plantation of a hundred negroes," replied the Doctor, answering the planter's thoughts, and not his question.

A long pause followed. We watched the light wood crackle, and the big particles of fire climbing up into the canopy of woods on the current of hot air, reflecting brief circles of light on the foliage above, and then going out in blackness. The Doctor resumed his pipe. Mike pondered, cross-legged, puffing at his cigarettes, and the boys talked among themselves in undertones.

"This won't do, gentlemen! Mike, hand me that bottle," called out Jackson, rousing himself. "One drink all around, and now for to-morrow's hunt. What shall it be, deer or turkey?"

"Or sheep?"

"That's a shame, Mike!" laughed Jackson.

"Don't let him quiz you on that mishap, gentlemen; older hunters than you have fared as badly. Did you ever hear of my blunder in fire-hunting?"

Of course we had not.

"Then I'll tell it to you."

*Jackson's Story of a Fire-Hunt**

"It came about this way. I was up country looking around for a good two-year-old to run at Charleston races, when I met my old comrade, Stockton. We had been chums together at Princeton, as thick as two cats in a bag, sometimes studying, sometimes courting, and then we were good friends. When we had nothing else to do we quarrelled; it is a sure sign of a good friend when he loves you enough to quarrel with you. Strangers don't care a picayune, and won't quarrel about you any way. Stockton had settled down to a sober life, owned a pew in the church, and as many little carroty-haired tokens as you could stand up endwise in a ten-acre lot. *I* was—well, about the same sort of fellow as when a boy, only the devil had covered me up with his wicked ways.

"The first thing after seeing Stockton that was proposed was a fire-hunt, and a fire-hunt it was. Dark still night—you could hear a peeper squeak a mile off, and run your nose against a cotton bale without seeing it. 'Just the night,' said Stockton. 'Just the night,' says I. 'Come, Jake,' says he

---

* For this tale I am indebted to the graceful pen of my friend, Guillermo.

to his son, a boy about sixteen, long and lank like his father, and always ready to poke away from home. Accordingly, all things ready, we trailed off into the woods, and took a course along the sea-side, thinking to find more deer.

"I led the way with the frying-pan on my shoulder, keeping the fire in it well up with pitch-pine knots, Stockton right behind with his rifle, and Jake keeping within sight in the rear. We had gone about a mile or so and the pan began to grow heavy, when I suddenly felt Stockton's hand upon my shoulder, compelling me to stop, and then the crack of his rifle from under my arm told me that he had fired at a deer that I had not seen. 'That deer shone up bright anyhow,' he said, in a low self-satisfied tone, as he proceeded to load his gun, 'only to get blown out.'

" 'Hadn't you better secure your game before loading?'

" 'Ha! ha!' said he, 'that fellow will not leave there until there is another set of legs under him. But come, I'm ready.'

"So saying, we started in the direction of our prize; when, to our no little joy and surprise, we beheld another blue light apparently just beyond the spot where lay our fallen deer. Stockton again fired, and out went the light.

" 'I first shot the doe,' he remarked, while deliberately loading his rifle, 'and the buck would not leave her.'

"Again we started, but had not taken a dozen steps, when lo! and behold, another eye appeared.

" 'It's deuced strange,' said Stockton quickly, as he raised his gun to his shoulder, 'that I have seen *but one eye* each time.'

" 'Perhaps they have all accidentally been standing sidewise to you,' I replied.

" 'Side or front,' he answered, 'I'll black that fellow's eye for him.' Crack went the rifle, and down went the eye. We had now arrived at the place where we supposed the first deer to have fallen, and made search for it, but nowhere was the game to be found.

"Turning from the place, imagine our surprise at again beholding that single fiery ball glaring upon us with the same identical motion of the others. Stockton mechanically raised his rifle, but paused as he did so. As for me, nothing prevented my throwing down the fire-pan and giving 'leg-bail' but the disagreeable certainty of not being able to retrace my steps. I ran back in memory to childhood's hours, and recalled the old nursery tales I had heard of bears, lions, and hobgoblins, until I was satisfied beyond a doubt that Stockton had been shooting at the devil! I was, however, aroused from my reverie by his exclaiming, 'Ha! I am a pretty fool. Something is the matter with my rifle, and I've been shooting all this time at the same deer! Here, give me yours.' I did so, but could not help thinking that the deer was a greater fool by far if he had stood to so many shots.

"The eye was now hid behind some bushes, but soon appeared again, when Stockton, after a long and deliberate aim, discharged his piece. The eye immediately disappeared, and he turned toward me, triumphantly nodding his head and exclaiming—

" 'He'll not show that infernal eye of his again, I guess, for I put that ball square into it.'

"I made no reply, but the term *infernal eye* seemed to me to be very appropriate. I had now placed the 'pan' upon the ground, and was arranging the fire, when Stockton uttered a suppressed exclamation of surprise and disappointment, which caused me to look up. Down went the fire, gun, and everything else; my mouth gradually opened until my dinner was perceptible, and I felt satisfied, from the progress my hair was making, that I should soon be relieved of my hat, for there was that little ball of fire moving very slowly with the same singular motions of the others.

" 'Stockton,' whispered I, as soon as my feelings would permit me, 'we are a set of jackasses, for as certain as fate, we have been chasing the devil to-night.'

"He turned toward me with a half comical, half inquisitive look, and finally remarked—

" 'Well, hang me if you're not complimentary, very. No, that is not the devil, but I am very well satisfied that the devil is in me. Here, take this rifle, and when he again shows his eye do *you* let him have it. I'll hold the light.'

"I could not refuse, and so I took the gun, and was slowly and reluctantly raising it to my shoulder, when a noise behind me attracted my attention, and looking around, I perceived Jake conducting in a most discreditable manner, twisting and squirming and holding on to his stomach as if he had the colic, and all the while making a noise like choking.

" 'I wish you would be kind enough to stop that infernal clatter!' said Stockton sharply, and adding immediately, 'There he is—now give it to him—right in the eye.'

"I was again raising my rifle to my shoulder, but was a second time deterred from my purpose by a peal or yell of laughter, from Jake, sufficient to have frightened every deer within ten miles of us. For Stockton and myself, however, there was no such thing as laugh, but, on the contrary, we were both rather inclined to raise a row than be laughed at, and Stockton, grasping his son by the shoulder, in a passion exclaimed—

" 'What the devil is all this tomfoolery about? Say! Tell me this instant, sir, or I'll "boot" you clear home.'

" 'Ha! ha! O Lordy! ha! ha! *Amelia Lighthouse!* O Lordy! Did I ever? Five miles—ough—my poor sides!'

"My curiosity was now excited to the utmost, and I turned to Stockton for an explanation. I shall not attempt to describe the expression of his countenance. Mirth and anger were never so well mingled before.

" 'Jackson,' said he, finally, 'we are a pair of asses, and have been shooting at the *revolving light on the Amelia Lighthouse, five miles off!* '

"Then suddenly dropping the fire-pan, he ran to where his son was kicking and screaming about on the ground. He picked him up by the coat collar, shaking him into silence, and then said, 'Now look here, if you say one word about this at home, as sure as I'm your father, you shall never fire a gun as long as you live.' "

As the laughter and comments on Jackson's story subsided, one of the negro boys said—

"Wish maussa hunt dat air varmint wha's a takin' off de lambs so; 'specs as him hab no lamb 'tall soon."

"Lost any to-day?"

" 'Spec a los' two, and two afore yesterday, and gwine to lose two dis night, kase all sheep come in quick, bein' wild: shore sign dat."

"What is it, do you think?"

"Painter, for true! I'se seen his tracks!"

"Why don't you let your boys sleep by the sheep-pen?" I asked of Jackson.

"I am afraid, sir, I would have to pen them in," he replied; "and then, if it was a panther, he might take the negro, and he is worth more than the sheep."

"Then why don't you shoot the beast?"

"I have hunted her until I am tired, and it only ends in her killing my dogs, and keeping out of shot herself. She will get tired here by and by, and then will go further down the coast. She has raised a young one here this season, for in the summer one of the boys, while coming up the river in a canoe, saw her swimming across with her kitten in her mouth. He could have come up with her then, but she growled so fiercely that he was afraid, and made a fool of himself."

" 'Specs anybody make a fool of hisself, when painter want to climb in de boat!" replied a self-conscious voice in the background.

"We had Mike here last year to hunt the same panther, I think, but I believe he got whipped; at all events, he went out one day, and didn't come back since."

Mike smiled his peculiar smile, which meant, like the Germans' "Yah wohl," anything, according to the speaker's intent, but said not a word.

"Tell us of that hunt, old father of Diana," said the Doctor.

"Where, sir, is my panther skin you promised?" asked Jackson.

"Painter is an oncommon onsartin varmint," was Mike's musing reply, as he put his brawny arms around his knees, and rocked himself backward and forward like a China Mandarin.

"I should think that he was *onkimin sartin,* for he comes here regularly once a year."

"Wall, you see, Colonel, this war the way I was done fur that time, and when yer heern it, you'll say that it was skeery, and no mistake."

"A story—a story!" exclaimed Miss Jackson. I leaned forward to see the speaker, and he began his tale.

CHAPTER 6

The Panther's Cub

Marcus. I have dogs, my lord,
Will rouse the proudest panther in the chase,
And climb the highest promontory top.

"WELL, IT WAS AIRLY MORNIN' when I started out after that air painter. Small sign I had to steer by, only the hearin' tell that there was a painter 'bout. But it had been showering o'ernight, and so trailin' was easy enough, and yer could see every stalk of grass that had been shook, let alone the tracks a varmint the size of a painter would leave. I tuck down to Spring Creek, and followed it e'enmost to the barrens that stretch toward the salt water; then I fetched a turn north, and struck inter the big swamp that comes out of the Suwanee. here I saw an all-fired big bar's track, and slathers of deer, and a show of gobblers, but no painter whatsumever. Got a gobbler and tuck breakfast, and then kept on. Struck the branches of the St. John that afternoon. Good painter ground here, tearin' big swamp, and all-fired high cottonwoods and sycamores. No signs, and my dog was gin out, so we shantied under a grape-vine waitin' for daylight. Heerd a painter holler in the night, but knowed it was a young one by the voice, and it was off the wrong way. Mornin' come, and I got around through little Ammaninac Swamp, and by night time had come purty near whar I fust started from, having made a purty tolerable circle, and nairy a painter. Sez I, 'Those cusses at the sheepfarm have been foolin' me, and tuck wild-cat for painter.'

"So arter soundin' around to see where the buildin's lay, and whar the sheep-pen was, Yowler and I lay down together, and were doin' some tall sleepin', when I heerd a soft kind o' crying down the woods. I knowed it in a minnit; it war the same painter—he hadn't been outside of my circle at all, the dratted cuss! He had just been a layin'-to for another haul on the sheep-pen, and so I hadn't struck his trail. I kept quiet, thinkin' he would come up toward the improvements, and I could tickle him, but he reether seemed to move off. Arter a while I heered him purrin' lik, and then I knew he had something to eat—fawn, like 'nough, or some small animal. This guv me a mean opinion of this painter, for your rael snortin' big fellars don't stoop to small fry, but live on deer, sheep, hogs, or sich like. Wall, mornin' come on, and when it bruck enough to see a meetin'-house, I pushed on, but the painter had moved off. I found a sheepskin all rolled up, and I knew then why he had been purring. The painter had caught a sheep on the range some time in the day, and not eaten it, so he didn't have need for more fodder all night. I found the trail, and then sez I, 'Now, Mr. Painter, we'll see who's best at walkin'.' Yowler tuck the trail, and along we bowled for about an hour, when all of a sudden I heerd Yowler, who was some ways ahead, stop his yelpin', and back he come, with somethin' arter him, tight as he could buckle. As they come up, I let drive at what was arter him kind o' promiscuously, for it wasn't fairly dawn yet. The shot hit, I knew, for the varmint held up, and then ran off.

" 'Now,' says I ter myself, 'isn't a painter a mighty onsartin varmint? Here is one that gets wounded, and yet don't pitch inter a feller. Who'd ha' looked for sich a coward in a painter?' Then, after loadin', I put on Yowler again, and we bowled along, not quite so lively as afore, for Yowler was a leetle kind o' shy, but we still did some pretty loud goin'.

" 'Whar's that air painter?' sez I to myself; 'did any painter ever run so far before?' It come on to be light, and I could see the trail, and it was an all-fired big trail. Presently it got into a cane-brake, and then tuck a turn. Yowler guv tongue. I could hear the canes rattle as he jumped, but the painter broke out on the fur side, and made a bee-line agin right straight for the Ouithlacouchee.

"When we got to the river it was noon. I looked down the bank, and saw the tracks along in the mud where the varmint had been lookin' for a good place to cross. Presently I could see where he had laid down in the mud, and then for the fust time I saw it was a she-painter with sucking young ones. As near as I could make out by the marks in the mud she had two cubs lugging at her, the rest of her tits being of no account. Then the track went in a little further under some alders, and there she had laid down agin, this time on her side, and, Jehosaphat! thar by her side, as clare as daylight, was a dozen little tracks of a cub she had been a-carryin' in her mouth all that way. She had tuck to these bushes to give it some milk, and was goin' with it into the big swamps t'other side of the river. It was all as clare as if a school-master had writ. That war the reason why the she-painter didn't come on to fight when I fired at her; she wanted to git her

47

pups clare from the dog; that's the natur of a painter, and an oncommin considerin' natur it is, too. My 'pinion of that painter rose some. Arter the trail left the alder bushes, it went right into the river.

"I soon found a log big enough for me and Yowler, and, puttin' the dog on one eend on't, so as to save him from the alligators, I slung my rifle on my back, and paddled across. I soon found the trail, and went jogging along pretty slow, for it was a tough kind of swamp, when in a minute or so I heerd Yowler burst out in a clear yell. I knowed he seed the painter, and I hurried on as well as I could, but, Jimminy Peters! that painter, when he made a jump across the fallen logs, went as fur in one minute as I in ten. I soon come to where I heerd the dog break out so, and I seed somethin' kind o' curious. The old tracks went straight on south, but there were a set of new tracks that came right back on top the old ones, and just where the dog had come up they had turned off to the east.

" 'Wall, that's queer!' sez I to myself. 'If that's the same varmint, she's what I'm arter, and if she ain't she's just as good, for I calkelate that one painter is just as good as another, providin' allers she's as big.' So I cheered on Yowler, and we went on the side track. Now over logs, then in a mucky place, and now through the water, that dog and I stuck to that painter like two wood-ticks. Arter going a little to the east the track went back to the river, and went across about a mile above where it had crossed before. 'Wall, that's queer,' sez I to myself. There's somethin' onnateral in that painter. She won't tree, and she goes in a straight line to t'other eend of creation, and now she's going back agin. 'Wall, here goes,' sez I, and I took another log and ferried back agin to the north shore. There was the trail as clare as mud, and big as an alligator's. Up the bank and away inter the woods we went. There's no sucking of cubs now. Yowler is a hurryin' her along a leetle to fast for any sich family doin's. So on we went right north. 'Jerusalem!' sez I to myself, 'keep on this way, old steamboat, much longer, and you'll be back where you started from, and I'll drive you into Colonel Jackson's pen, and shut the door on you!'

" 'Bout by the Black Mud Creek there's a flat of land that had been overflowed and had dried off, and as we come here I seed the painter had jumped through, and every time she had jumped she had come up to her belly in the mud, and once or twice had come so low that her neck and chin had sunk in the mud. Thinks I, that must put the cub under in the mud, yet I don't see the marks of the little rat.

"Jist then we got through the creek, and I seed whare the old painter had lain down on the bank with her side to the river.

"Thar were her tracks as clare as Gospel, but whar was the cub? The cub was gone! Whar had it gwine to? It was clare it hadn't gwine anywhare that Yowler and I had been; it had been left on the fur side of the Ouithlacouchee. It tuck just a minute of thinkin', and it was all clare. The bee-line she had made, the two full tits, the bee-line back agin; what a cursed fool I was not to have seen through it afore I had come so fur!

"The painter had littered two cubs somewhar near whar I had seen her in the mornin'; she had been chased, and knew the parts was onsafe; she had made up her mind to carry her cubs into the Ouithlacouchee swamp, and had started with one when Yowler struck her trail. That was the reason she sent Yowler back; that was the reason she wouldn't tree; and jist keepin' in sound of the dog's yelp, had gone right to the swamp, hid her cub, come back on her back track to ketch the dog and lead him away, till she could go back fur t'other cub, bein' sartin' that the hound and his fool of a master were away from her cub, and were chasin' her about.

"Soon as I had reasoned this out I called Yowler in, and turnin' about, struck for that ere swamp straight. Yowler come on behind, and about two hours afore sunset I struck the river, ferried across, took up the old trail in the swamp, and was busy pickin' it out over logs and under vines whar the moss grew so thick it didn't leave room for a track. The scent was cold, and Yowler could jist ketch it, but what with puttin' our two noses together we fetched up in a big windfall, and jist in the snarl of trees, whar the splinters and branches, and growin' vines was the wickedest, there was a little bed of strips of bark and leaves, and the young painter cub was curled up, dreamin' of supper-time. He was about as big as two tomcats tied together by the tails, and his natur', when I come to prick him up, was not quite so sweet. He meowed, and sneezed, and about chawed up my coat-sleeve afore I could bag him, which I did by takin' off my huntin' coat, jammin' his head into one of the sleeves, and buttonin' and tyin' him in bag like.

"When I got all this done, I thought of the old painter, and what she would say to me when she come home with her t'other young 'un. The more I calkelated, the more it seemed onpleasant, for though the varmint was so perlite when she was outwittin' me, I reckoned that she wouldn't be so much so when the boot got on t'other leg. Fust I thought I would get out of that air windfall, and wait for the old lady on the bank of the river, what we could have a clare field, fur I knew it was sartin she would be arter me, and I'd a leetle reether the fight wouldn't be fit out in that swamp. So I put out for the river, and when I got thar took a clare spot, and puttin' the cub down for stakes, sat down to wait fur the other party.

"The wind was still, and I could hear around a considerable distance. A few big frogs, and once in a while an alligator, let on for music in the river. Now and then an owl hooted in the bottom land, and the cranes goin' out to sea were honkin' away overhead, but I couldn't hear any painter, and accordin' to my calkelations there would be some howlin' when she cum home and found her pappoose bagged. Yowler began to get restless, and watched the swamp as if he knowed what was comin'. The woods begun to get blacker, the sun had gone down, and some black clouds bellowed overhead. It looked like a squall.

" 'Why don't she come?' sez I to myself; 'or maybe she's sich a knowin' varmint she's waitin' for night, to chaw me up completely.' Once I thought I seen her eyes in the edge of the bushes, but it turned out to be some rotten fire-wood. 'Jerusalem!' sez I, 'why don't she cum!' It got to be so dark I couldn't see the sights on my rifle, and I thought it all over to myself. I own up I felt kind a mean like. This stealin' young cubs out of their nests is onnateral, any way. It is good enough for an Injin, but's not Christian-like. I could see that old painter comin' home, with her second cub in her mouth. I could tell jist how she felt. I could see her big nostril open when she smelt my tracks about her nest; and when she saw her cub was gone, Lord! what a cry she would give. I'd given a bearskin to put that cub back, and then have fit it out with a clare conscience. But 'twas no use a-talkin'; it couldn't be done, nohow. All that's left when the deal is made is to stand up to yer hand. 'But,' thinks I to myself, 'ef it's right to shoot the old painter, it is right to ketch her kitten.' That's the natur of man; ef they do anything wrong they reason to themselves to make it right.

" 'Jerusalem!' sez I, as it got blacker and the fire-flies cum about, 'why don't she cum?' Jist then, in lookin' around me, I sees a light shine on the other shore a little way below. I knew right off it was an Injin camp, and reckoned it was part of Tiger Tail's band, that had come up from below. Nasty varmints that band was—worse en painters any day. Howsumever, Injins or no Injins, they will help fight the painter; so I rolled a drift-log onto the water, and once more paddled over the river. I looked behind once or twice to see if the painter wasn't a comin' over, too, and climbin' on the log behind me, but it was only the mullet jumpin' in the river, and so I got over with the cub all right, and put right down the bank for the camp. Yer better believe I didn't let grass grow under me. As I cum up to the fire-light, I saw who the Injins were; they were friendly enough that summer, but mighty mean cusses, and had served me many a dirty trick. Their camp was just in the edge of the timber, and the squaws were cooking supper in a pot, while about a dozen men sat around in a ring, lookin' on and suckin' their thumbs, wrapped up in their blankets, just as if it was cold. As I cum up, I looked back on my track, and whar the sandy bank lay agin the water, whar it war brightened up by the sunset, I see the she-painter cumin' like greased lightnin'.

"I walked composed-like and slow into the Injin camp, and right through the ring, puttin' the painter cub, all rolled up in the coat, down in the middle, and then goin' to the fur side, set down as far off as convenient.

"'Injin Mike is welcome,' said a young man, who I made out by his paint to be Tiger Tail's son, wavin' his hand like to me, and keepin' his eye inquirin' like on my coat, that was a wrigglin' about on the ground.

"'Injin Mike is a hunter, and he brings a hunter's gift,' sez I, slow-like, and speakin' Injin; 'he was afeerd his Injin brother would be in want of some game.'

"I knew this would rile 'em some, for Tiger Tail was allers a big hunter, and he didn't like me, for I could take the feather out of his hair any day. I war goin' on to say more, but I didn't have time, fur jist then I heard a thump in the bushes, and the she-painter cum in as ef she was flyin'; ears back, eyes like candles—she was some. She tuck the young chief before she landed with a sort o' flyin' box with her paw, and he never riz hair arterwards, for she tuck scalp and all.

"The lousy devils rolled over like prairie dogs—the pot upsot, the coals flew around, the squaws yelled, the dogs pitched in, and afore any one could get out his knife, that painter did some tall tearin'. They rolled over and over, yellin', bitin', swearin'; some got hit fur the painter, fur they couldn't see whar to strike, and thar was no room for shootin'. Lord, Colonel, it would hur done you good to have seen that air scrimmage. I got behind a tree and larfed 'till it hurt, and when I see they had well-nigh fit out Yowler and me, thinkin' they might blame us, stepped out and I hain't seen them Injins, nur that painter since, though I've heer'en tell that Tiger Tail ware lookin' for me about the Mecaco this summer."

"And if he catches you, you will not be able to raise hair either," said Jackson.

"*Ef* he does," answered Mike, laughing.

"But what became of the other sucking cub after the Indians had killed its mother and brother?"

"I went back arter it that very same night, and found it jist whar the she-painter had left it when she tuck my trail. It was a-meowin' away in the woods all alone, and I felt kind a sorry for it, and carried it into the Fort at

Tampa Bay and guv it to the Colonel thar, whar it growed up, and got so big and sassy that it licked the hull fort one day and then cleared."

CHAPTER 7

The Deer Hunt

"A hundred dogs bayed deep and strong,
Clattered a hundred steeds along."
—*Scott*

THE LIGHT BROKE EARLY on the planter's shackley house, and the smoulder-ing brands of our camp-fire, the morning after Mike's panther story. It may not have been early, though our late hours of the evening before made it seem so to me, and I silently banned the sleepless hound and "the cock's shrill clarion, and the echoing horn," which ushered in the light, and drew us to our feet, yawning and drinking in the misty sights and sounds. Away up on the top of a live oak-tree a mocking-bird was gushing over in song. Sometimes trilling a few notes, descending an octave it would laugh and cry. Then it would sound the call of the quail twice repeated, and then tinkling, laughing, gurgling, it poured out the very music of mirth. Too happy to sit still it fluttered up in the air a dozen feet or more, trilling its merriest lay, then, descending again to the branch from whence it rose, it syllabled love's deepest tones.

The sheep and cattle were crowding out of the pens, and spreading over the open woods. The horses were whinnying for their food. Our boys were lighting a fire, and preparing meat, singing and laughing. There were calls to negroes with fancy names, and shouted answers; guns were dis-charged and reloaded and saddles examined; a dozen things were wanted that could not be found, or when found were not in a condition to be used. The little nigs were running to the spring for water, or to the shed for corn, or around the grounds, merely for the fun of running and shouting. They were all dressed alike, in long, brown cotton shirts, so one sex could not be distinguished from the other. Aunty Blaze, after seeing the table was spread, and the meat cooked, brought out an immense corn-cake, on a wooden turner, and with a commendable feeling of pride threw it down on the table, right side up, steaming hot, and brown as rosewood. Turning to go, she stumbles against a little black girl coming with the sugar-bowl; a smart slap applied with the cake-turner propels the child forward a yard, and elicits a yell of disapprobation, and the sugar-bowl is dropped to the floor.

The Doctor loads his double-barrelled gun, and explains its new-fashioned lock to Miss Jackson, who comes out arrayed in a tight-fitting cap and bodice, and her eyes lit up with the anticipation of the chase. Mike slowly and methodically wipes out his rifle with dry flax, and every moment is seen eating some hidden remains of last night's meal, which he has stowed away on his person, and which are to form more than half his breakfast. We eat our hurried meal—it might be called a passover, as no one takes time to sit—and then ride off down the woods.

Jackson and Mike are leading the van, Lou and the Doctor still side by side, and there goes a negro on a marsh tackey, the pony of the south, and there a neighbour that has come over for the hunt, mounted on a vicious mare as thin as a crane. The hounds, of a dozen different colours and sizes, go along in couples, led by the negroes on foot, and on ahead to a given rendezvous shuffles Pompey Duffield, the oldest negro on the place, driving a mule laden with two baskets of provisions intended for the dinner of the party, and the mist comes up from the river in golden clouds, for the sun is just rising. Down along the bank we went with call and laughter, and the bittern arose from the sedge with a guttural cry, and the alligator sank into the water with a heavy splash, as our cavalcade moved onward to the lower pine lands that skirted the big swamp. The trees were all white pine; there was no underbrush, and we could see down the long arcades they formed for nearly a mile. Now and then a flaunting flower would rear its crimson cheek to the wind, or a vine could be seen clasping a trunk, and drooping from branch to branch in long festoons, but generally the ground was covered only with the yellow siftings of the pine, and free from all vegetation. The horses trod without a sound, and, save now and then a fox-squirrel, we met no animal life, until we came to the hummocks, and drew together to give general directions for commencing the chase, the manner of which is necessary to explain.

A hummock is a thicket often covering an acre or two of land, and sometimes presenting an extent of several miles. The one now in view covered about thirty acres, and half a mile farther down the woods, we could see another. It lay in a low swale of land, and in it the haw, the alder, and willow, grew into a tangled copse, studded with the red leaves of the pinckneya, while above them all, a hundred feet or more, the ash and gum-trees reared their long arms, and the magnolia opened its blossoms to the upper air. It was an admirable spot for game, with succulent grass and flags, and a dusky shade that was but little penetrated by the sun.

"You stay here, Doctor Pollock," said Jackson, as we rode up; "and mind your eyes, sir."

The Doctor drew himself up with a doubtful air, as if uncertain whether minding his eyes referred to the uses he had just been putting those organs to in watching Miss Jackson's face, or whether it referred to watchfulness in the future; so he answered at random, "All right, sir!"

"And you, sir," he continued, turning to me, "take your place two gunshots off on that side, keeping always within five or six rods of the swamp. And you," turning to the neighbour that had joined us, "go on next; and you, Lou, come with Mike and me."

And away they cantered, with the dogs, around the other side of the swamp, dropping one or two negroes, as they passed, to guard some particular point of the hummock, and in this way we enclosed two sides of the swamp with a cordon of hunters stationed just so far apart that if a deer came out, one or the other of the hunters in waiting was certain of a shot. On the further side, and the only portion of the swamp that we were unable to surround, the drivers were to enter with the hounds, and the deer would not be likely to make his escape in that direction. The deer in Florida and the other southern states are the ordinary Virginia deer, but of small size, the bucks weighing an average of an hundred pounds, while in the northern states they grow to an average of double that weight.

The last I saw of Jackson he was winding around the swamp with Mike, having left his daughter on a little knoll that commanded a fair view of the hummock, and where her bright bay horse and little figure stood out in relief against the dark pines beyond. The Doctor I could not see, but my negro, Scipio, stood between us, and only a short distance from me, and perfect stillness reigned over pine woods and hummocks. Moment after moment slipped away, but we could hear nothing, save the impatient champing of my horse. Away down the woods a fox-squirrel flirted his broad tail as he chased his comrade up a tree, or a painted woodpecker passed by in undulating sweeps as silently as a moth. At length a distant call, so faint it just reached me, but I recognised it as the driver cheering the hounds as he cast them off. Now for it. Another pause. The cry was repeated, and with it the low yelp of a dog, then another, and then a ringing shot away down the woods. My horse pricked his ears, and Scipio mounted a fallen tree the better to survey the scene. No cheering shout announced the death of the deer, though the dogs stopped yelping.

At this moment I heard in the bushes the rapid bound of some animal; it came nearer and nearer. From the higher ground where I stood I could see over the bushes a pair of antlers, and I supposed it to be the same deer that had been fired at down the swamp. I dismounted to take surer aim. How my heart beat in unison with the bounding of his feet, while every sense converged into the coming of his presence! But, alas! he did not come out by me, but between me and the Doctor, and very near to him. Pang! pang! I heard his rifle, and immediately the deer turned in again, just keeping the edge of the bushes, and showing his back at every jump. As he passed me, I took aim, and when his flag showed over the grass, I fired, but the deer only moved with an accelerated speed down past the next stand, and receiving a shot there, and two from Miss Jackson, rushed back into the swamp from whence he came. The dogs, with the firing, broke out into a louder chorus. I heard Jackson's horn nearer and nearer; he was following up the dogs, keeping in the open woods, while Mike was doing the same on the other side. All at once the hounds broke out with a louder yell, and at the same moment a buck broke cover again in front of me, accompanied by two does, one on either side. I had just loaded, and had my foot in the stirrup, when, without changing position, I fired at the stag's shoulder. I missed my mark, but shot one of the does, that tumbled down in the grass. The buck and the other doe once more turned back, and coursed down the edge of the hummock toward Poke, who fired his barrel again, and this time, with some correctness, for the buck dropped his tail for an instant with an uneasy motion, when, raising it again, he turned back, followed by Poke, on horseback, directly past my stand. I fired my second barrel without effect, and then, not being able to resist the contagion of the chase, spurred my horse after the flying animals. Away they went down the little swale that led toward Lou Jackson's stand. One hound after another, as he came out of the rushes, caught sight of the deer, and joined in the chase with a double note. Pang! came a shot from my left, missed clear, and the hunter, not stopping to load, joined the chase. Now for it, Miss Jackson! I saw her raise her gun, her father was close behind, riding hard to get to her, and away down the woods I saw Mike trying to head off the chase, his long hair streaming behind him like a woman's. A puff of smoke and a report—the buck staggered, but still ran, drawing in behind him, in one yelling, shouting, crashing train, every man, horse, and dog in the woods.

"You hit him, Lou. Tally-ho! Hi on! hi! Hurrah! Faster! There's Tip, and there's Slasher! Go it, Music! Golly! maussa, gib him fits!" were the cries that were intelligible in the medley of sound, until the yelling of the dogs and the trampling of the horses drowned all words. The horses, as wild in their ardour as their riders, needed no rein. The buck led the way directly for another hummock about three miles away, and which was now within sight; his flight was straight and well sustained, though now and then a spot of blood on leaves showed he was wounded. The dogs were toiling on behind, not two yards away, and close behind the dogs came all the hunters, the Doctor, riding the fastest horse, taking the lead. As we approached the hummock, the pine trees grew closer together, and while going between two of them the Doctor was caught by his gun, which he held crosswise before him on the saddle, and was swept off his horse to the ground. "There's a ten strike!" called out Jackson, as we rushed by. Closer still we came to the deer, every dog stretched to his utmost length, every rider bending to his horse's mane; Mike was just raising his rifle to his shoulder to shoot, when without a sign the big buck fell head first to the ground, and rolled over and over with the impetus of the chase. His heart had broken in the desperate burst just within reach of his lair, in whose close covert the doe, with one long bound, was lost. Up came the dogs and horses so fast they ran over the game, and crowded and jostled together as they pulled up, as a wave that meets a rock on a sandy beach. Then there was dismounting, and whipping off the dogs, and a search for the wounds in our quarry. Two buckshot, in the thick part of the neck from behind, came from the Doctor's second barrel.

"Where is the Doctor? here is his horse. Oh! there he comes limping along rather sore with his fall." A laugh and a sly joke were all the consolation we had to offer him. Two more buckshot in the right side, close together; that is Lou Jackson's shot. They were the only ones of the party using shot guns. None of the shots were heavy enough to kill the deer, though altogether they had broken him down in the chase. We sound a horn to tell the drivers we left behind our whereabouts, and putting the buck on one of the negroes' horses, and coupling the dogs to keep them from entering the swamp, we turned back the way we came.

"Now for the does we left behind," said Jackson. "How many were there, sir?"

"I saw two bucks and four does," said the Doctor.

"Fudge! those were the same deer we have been chasing, only your people turned them back into the hummock two or three times without killing them."

"I killed one," said I.

"Where is it?"

"It fell in the bushes."

"Reckon you did not hit her."

"You had better believe it; I can show you the place where she fell."

"That isn't what we want. Where is the place that she is now, can you tell that? I fired at a doe, too, but a long way off, and she probably is where yours is."

"Doctor, how's your back?"

"He he! golly mighty! he quit the saddle mighty smart dat time!" remarked Cæsar.

As we rode up to the hummock where we had started the game, I found the place where I had shot the doe, but she was not there, though the negroes said she had fallen.

"Throw off a dog, then," said Jackson.

"Let Music try," said his daughter; and accordingly Music was loosened and sent in the grass. Music was a young hound, spotted white and black, like a coach-dog, and with such silky ears they felt like a satin robe in your hand. She was led to the place where the deer had fallen, and taking its track with a plaintive whimper, commenced unwinding it from among the bushes and reeds. Presently a louder effort warned us to beware, and cantering apart a little, so as to be able to see all around the hummock, Mike's grey eye caught a sight of the doe trying to steal out of the bushes. A clear ringing shot was followed by a quick leap, and she fell dead.

We laid them side by side, the stately buck and his gentle consort. The dew of the morning was still glittering on their hides—their eyes were as bright and as full as in life. I wondered if Miss Jackson felt any pity for them, as she saw the dogs licking the blood that flowed from their throats.

One of the negroes dismounting from his pony, we put the two deer in place, and tying their feet beneath the belly of the struggling horse, had them sent to the place where we were to meet for dinner.

"Now one more hunt before dinner. Where shall we go, boys?"

"Saw de ole white buck for sartin, dis day, maussa!" said the planter's head negro, coming up.

"Where did you see him?"

"Down by de run, ober dere," said the negro, pointing with his finger; "his tracks fresh as dis niggah's."

"You mean you saw his tracks?"

"Yes a maussa."

"How does he know that it is a buck?" I asked.

"How fur to know he's a buck? Haint chased dat air deers' s'often fur nuttin'; 'spect I be'ent a dun gone fool!" replied Jumping Lem, with some asperity.

"Wall, if that ere is the buck that run in this range last winter, I kinder guess ye'll all have to rub your legs with bar's grease to ketch him," added Mike.

"Don't you think we can shoot him, Mike?" asked Lou Jackson.

"No, young woman, I don't; thar are too many here to make certain of any deer. When a man wants a deer bad, he goes alone and keeps his mouth shut."

As we rode over to inspect the tracks, I learned, partly from the exclamations of the negroes, and partly from Jackson's account, that this buck passed the winters in the pine woods, retiring, when the mosquitoes became thick in the spring, to the cool swamps of the Ouithlacouchee. It has been so often hunted, and was so successful in escaping, that it became well known at the Jackson plantation, and was the object of a covert superstition to all the negroes, which mysterious fear rather aided his escape, for when the boys saw it coming they became so frightened, they could not hit forty paces off.

On reaching the run that Lem had mentioned, we readily found the tracks, and all drew up to examine them. The presentation of some unknown bone to a company of *savans*, or the appearance of a new bonnet at a country sewing society, occasions not more curiosity and sage comment than does the discovery of a new track in the woods. One mentions its size, another recognises old peculiarities or marks, another says it was the foot of a male animal, another that it was fat in flesh, and another that it was going on an easy trot, and not disturbed, and what is stranger still, from the small data of four marks in the damp soil, all these facts arrived at are the results of careful observation, and seldom incorrect.

According to the congress now assembled, this buck was the old white buck, so called from an unusually white coat, and had gone at a gentle gait into the Black Jack hummock, which lay two miles further on, and before which we presently arrived. It was about half a mile in length by three quarters broad, and was filled, like the other swamp holes, with long grass, bushes, and vines, from which rose several tall trees of those species that spring in swamps and savannahs, and at its upper end there grew a close thicket of black jack trees. In such spots the does dropped their fawns, and young and old sheltered themselves here for their noon-day rest.

Once more the members of the chase separated to take commanding positions, overlooking the edges of the thicket. We were cautioned against

shooting at anything that might come out, until we were certain that the white buck was not there. Once more Mike and Jackson disappeared, and with them the hounds, already snuffing the air from the swamp, and tugging at their leashes to get away, and the forest was still.

In a short time we could hear the cheers of the negroes, and the thrashing of the bushes as they struggled forward in the tangled underbrush. At this instant a doe, followed closely by a fawn almost grown, came to the edge of the bushes. She looked up and down for an instant, her large ears turning this way and that, when, not seeing any one, she came out on a lope, and passing close by me, ran down the woods, making for the river. I had my gun to my shoulder, but remembering the white buck, withheld my fire, lest the bigger game should follow the course of the doe and find me with an empty gun. Yeow-ow-ow came from the hummock; that was Music's voice—her tone was like a bugle's. Then two or three whimpering notes from other hounds.

"Wha's dat air a bobbin' in yer bushes?" asked Scipio, standing near me and eagerly trying to overlook the grassy valley. "A cat—a cat!" he shouted, "sure as gun," and a handsome specimen of the wild cat or the lesser lynx sprung out of the bushes, and then seeing Scipio, darted back again to cover. "Golly mighty, wouldn't dat cat get shook up—yah—ha, yah—ha—he!"

Now the hounds broke out in chorus, with a multitudinous cry that babbled in the bushes and wailed in the air, as though the echoes caught the sound and mellowed it down to a continuous accord. Scipio felt the contagion, and dancing up and down, relieved himself as follows:—

"Dar dey come! dar dey come! Bress de Lord! don't dey skin 'em—dat beats dis chile; hy ah ha, hy ah ha!—go it, Music!"

The dogs had come half way down the cover, when a buck and doe broke out together. He did not appear to be of unusual size; but I could not wait any longer, and fired. He fell and rose again, running over the brow of a little hill with his tail down; here he drew the fire of my neighbour on the right, and fell to rise no more. The doe halted a moment where her comrade fell, as if waiting for him to rise, when away down the woods a rifle rung its sharp crack and she fell like a clod almost on the body of her mate. I knew Mike's rifle by the effect, even if I did not know its sound.

The hounds came closer; we could see the grass and bushes moving where they were winding about, and now and then their sickle-shaped tails above the weeds. The clamour increased, the dogs were almost through, and yet no white buck to correspond with the negro's description of the big buck they had so often hunted. At this instant I saw rise up from the very edge of the bushes, a buck, that from his stately size I at once recognised to be the big buck. He had evidently been watching the preparations for the hunt, and selecting the time our guns were discharged, he rushed out between me and one of the negroes, and, without regarding either, flew down the open pine woods at a gallop. Hardly had he cleared the valley, when I heard Jackson shouting, and saw him riding hard toward my stand; but the dogs coming out and taking the deer's track with loud clamour, prevented my hearing. I sprang into my saddle, and went flying alongside of the hounds, with the air soughing through my hair, and the deer in view a hundred yards ahead. In a moment or two Lou Jackson and the Doctor were in sight, their horses skimming the open woods like birds. Then came the sorrel mare, and next Scipio on the pony, and then in the distance Jackson and Mike, with all the negroes that were mounted. Faster, still faster, heart and sense fixed on that flying buck, and the trees merged together in a mass as we swept among them. Whoop! why cannot a man cheer louder; why cannot a horse fly faster when a deer is in view? There is a crash and a flash of dirt and sticks; the sorrel has gone down, and her rider rolled over and over, and far ahead of his steed. There is no time to see if he can get up again. Hurrah! there is a hummock! See Tiger and Bess turn to the left! They know the buck will not run through it, and they turn aside to cut the radius of the arc he is about to make. He sees the plan and accelerates his speed. His horns are lying on his back, his nose in air; he is stretching away at his highest speed, and whenever a bush intercepts his flight, he leaps it with a bound that must give him a bird's-eye view of his pursuers.

Far ahead of the deer grew a close swamp, and from the straight line the deer was making we knew he was looking to it for refuge. Behind, I heard Jackson calling to us, but who could stop to listen with such a buck in view? On we went, the dogs still nearer the deer, and Tiger almost within reach of his haunches. Lou Jackson held one rein in each hand, her eyes fixed on the chase, and her hair flying loose behind her. There goes the deer in the bushes; he touches a log here and a bog there, and along he went like a rope-dancer. Tally ho! On went the dogs, when, to my surprise, Tiger disappeared from view, and in a second of time the whole pack were floundering in the morass. "Hold hard!" I heard again from behind. "Hold hard, Miss Jackson!" I screamed, as the truth flashed on me. "The quicksands!" Too late; her horse was wild with the chase, and she could not hold him. He made one or two desperate leaps as he found himself floundering, and in a second of time was half ingulfed in mud. His rider still held the reins and kept her seat on the struggling horse. The Doctor was in equal plight, while his frightened beast pawed the air in its attempts to regain a footing. My horse, more used to such ground, turned short around when he felt it quaking, throwing me in the edge of the mud like a clown in a circus. Up came Mike as fast as he could ride, and Jackson behind him.

Mike threw himself from his horse, and while the others were cutting sticks to throw to the ingulfed riders, ran out by quick jumps to the log over which the deer had run, and then cutting off with his knife a grape-vine that had climbed a neighbouring tree, he wound it around his arm and swung himself out toward Miss Jackson. The first swing did not send him far enough, but putting his foot against the trunk, as his rope oscillated, he swung out to where the young girl lay up to her arm-pits, and rapidly sinking in the sands, and putting his hand under her arm began slowly to draw her from her perilous position. When she was entirely above the surface, he swung the vine sufficiently to carry his charge to the root of the tree, from whence it was easy to reach the shore. I would have given a year of life to get such a look of thanks from a lady I know as the breathless girl gave Mike—the ugly scamp! The Doctor's turn came next, and then the horses, until finally, after two or three hours of hard work, we were all once more in the saddle, and some of us looking more like scavengers than gallant hunters under the greenwood tree.

"S'pose you tink dat white buck's de debbil for true now, hey?" said Scipio, as he was tightening my girths.

"No, I don't; why do you ask?"

"Kase I'se not sartin the niggahs here'bouts knows heaps, and dey sez dey ain't agwine to hunt dat buck nohow, and I spec as how I wouldn't nudder. 'Spec as how sumthin' wuss en what we's seen'll come out o' dat eer chase yit. I'se not scared, but dat is very 'plexing."

The day was wearing away fast, and, sending one of the boys for the two deer last killed, we all turned toward the place appointed for our meeting, where after a few minutes' riding a blue smoke column arose among the trees, and the distant gleam of water announced a dinner and a rest—two pleasant things, whose worth is only known to those who have laboured well. From our dining-place, a bend of the river showed us two vistas down the ancient woods, and the broad sheet of water, half in shadow half in sunshine, was broken by the flocks of ducks that were coasting along its banks. The trees that fringed the shore were covered with immense creeping vines, that clasped the trunks and suspended themselves from the branches. Down by the water's edge, the aster reared its purple head, and the love-vine wove its orange thread like a net over many a rank grove of water-plants. The opposite shore was lower than the bank on which we were standing, and the eye took in miles of cane-brake and forest, unbroken by any sign of human labour.

"Look at those turkey-buzzards, Doctor," said Miss Jackson, pointing to two birds that, with matchless grace, were floating in slow circles high in the air. "I would like to see the view they are taking in at this moment."

"So would I; they are eagles in the air, and crows on the ground," replied the Doctor. "They seem never to move their wings, and yet how powerfully they fly, while they watch every motion that is going on in the woods below them."

"Dinnah's ready, gemens *and* ladies," called out Pompey Duffield, with a marked accent on the *and* while Jackson's horn played the stave of a march that made the dogs howl, and we turned away from the bank to the dinner that was spread out on the grass. There was cold wild turkey, and ham, hot coffee, corn-bread and bacon. It wouldn't have been a Florida dinner without the corn-bread and bacon.

After dinner came the pipes and a long talk, and then as the sun went down, tracking the woods with his sanguine tail, we packed up our game, one deer to each pony, and, with Pompey Duffield taking the lead, filed off through the shadowy woods for the plantation.

CHAPTER 8

The Fireside at "Far Away"

"'Tis home where'er the heart is."

LOU JACKSON WAS NOT a beautiful girl—much less did she deserve the title of pretty. Her eyes and hair were both good, though the coarse and irregular eyebrow gave a masculine cast to her regard. Her nose was short, her mouth almost a line, and her complexion, naturally dark, was further injured by the dry climate that made it colourless. The prevailing *pose* of her features was thoughtful, at times almost stern, yet once in a long while the lines of her mouth would curve, her cheek slightly dimple, and her eye would flash out a look of recognition and sympathy, the more gentle for being rare.

She had received the ordinary course of education as practised among American girls. A little geography, a little history, a little of the natural sciences, a little of two or three modern languages, and a little of two or three dead ones; a little music, painting, polite literature, mathematics, crocheting, moral philosophy, and dancing—all this in homœopathic courses; and then was launched out into that practical world where one lesson learned in life's school outweighs the teachings of years.

From the fashionable school she stepped to the monotony of an interior plantation life. No musical instruments, no foreign friends, no foreign books to read, even could she read them, where everything was simple in action, and the bare bosom of the world, with its vegetation, minerals, and animal abundance, was open all around her, and the springs of domestic life, its great needs and small attainments, its social loves and hates, were before her. Then came the question, "What is my place, and can I fill it? If I claim to be a lady and a wife of rank, I have no beauty, and cannot attain it. If to be a literary woman, I have not sufficient education. If a mere waif floating on the stream of life, the very animals on the banks are better than

66

I." She reached out for anything she could do, and turned for some recourse against that nothingness that swallowed her up.

At length, one day, the first time coming abroad after an illness, her mind drank in that confused blending of sound, colour, motion, and fragrance, that is so pervading in the early spring, and which affects the nerves after illness with so acute a pain. The buds seemed expanding with an inherent instinct, the birds seemed arranging their social affairs with a high intelligence, which had never struck her before. There was a relation of one to another, a connection to herself, and an apparentness of creation by that Higher Relative, that had just raised her from her feeble bed, that seemed never so plain or so beautiful as now. The more she pondered and examined, the greater seemed the field of thought. She was not idle now. Body and mind grew strong together. No one slighted her homely face in the fields, and with what aid from books that could be had, she wandered forth a thinking, happy, labouring, achieving student. At last a field was before her; how strange, it had been under her eyes from childhood!

The fire was kindled in the planter's house, for it was a chilly night; the rain commenced to fall after our return from the hunt, and from the pitchpine branches "the light fell off in hoary flakes," painting bright the heavy furniture of the room, and belching from the chimney above the house, as from a smelting furnace. The room was adorned with implements of the chase, antlers, and rude stores of goods, and yet there were marks of a gentler taste in an engraving primitively framed, stuffed birds, and gracefully-disposed Indian weapons, decorated the walls. The interior of the mansion was more comfortable than its rough and dismantled exterior promised; and from its lonely situation, over sixty miles from any town and more than a dozen from any house, it had been appropriately named "Far Away." The door stood open, the negroes sat on the sill, drinking in the conversation and laughing at every joke, while within, Lou Jackson, her father, and his guests, sat or reclined around the room as best they could find places.

"Golly, Maussa, dat air buck's a grave-digger! Da's de same deer for sartin dat Blossom fired at two year agwine Christmas comin', when his gun bus'. Das de same deer dat ripped up Snorter and Grip, de best dogs in dis county, and now wha's dat air he's gone dun dis day? He run Miss Lou's horse whare we like not see 'im till day o' judgment."

"Lem, you fool," called out Jackson, "hold your tongue; you will get all the boys on the place to be as great cowards as you are."

"I'se no coward, you knows dat's well's anybody, Mars Jackson. Ef de

Lord want a brave man, de Lord gonter call Lem; but I'se seen a buck run o' nights in de range, and he feet struck fire, and when I sees dat I comes in, and so'd you, Mars Jackson."

"What for gwine contrariwise to de Lord?" said an old negress, whose white head was obtruding in at the doorway.

"De Lord send de debil and de debil come. Dare's Mars Wilson's Ebo Jane, a rael little drum-cuss of a nigger woman; no genouwine religion 'bout her, and jist afore she die dere, by de door dat look toward de piney wood, an old buck—oh, golly, Maussa! look in at her! She guv one call and die, and de buck go away on de parf to de woods. I seed dat wid dese yeer eyes, an' it make dis eer hair of mine stan' straight up."

On looking at the crisp, curling locks alluded to, no surer proof of a miracle was required than the fact that they could be made straight, for they were kinked into little cocoons of yellow white over the big, black face and staring eyes. As this inspired fact was related, the negroes, with their credulous susceptibility, edged closer in the open doorway to be fully within the circle of fire-light, and even Lem had pulled in his legs from the outside of the open window, where he was sitting, and turned his body fire-ward.

As I looked at the bank of faces at the door, I noticed a feeling of horror dash over their countenances that was singular to behold; following their dilated eyes, I saw them all fixed on Jumping Lem as he sat in the window, though from my position I could see nothing about him to excite the feeling. Mike kicked my foot, and I saw his eye, with a laugh in the corner of it, turned to where Lem was sitting. I leaned forward, and in the darkness beyond, only partially lighted up by the fire, the head and antlers of a large deer appeared.

Lem had not seen the apparition, but continued: "Down on de Waccassasee dare's a deer-parf made by dat air same buck, and when de dogs cum dere, dey down tail an' take de back track, howlin' all de time as if dey"—

At this instant one of the protruding tines of the deer's horns touched the earnest story-teller on the shoulder. He looked around, and caught sight of the spectre at his side. He gave a shriek, and darted toward the door; the negroes, frightened more by his fears than what they saw, came crowding in and blocked up the door, when Lem jumped into the middle of the circle by the fire, crouching at his master's feet, and crying, "Oh, Golly! Maussa! Lord a massa, dare h'is! dare h'is!"

The spectre head continued to advance into the room, when one of the horns, touching the side of the window, it fell down from the pole on which it was stuck, and lay on the floor. It was the head of the buck we had shot that morning.

"That is my deer's head," said Miss Jackson. "I was having it stuffed."

"That's that are boy Scip's doin's; he's a queer critter," laughed Mike.

"Get up, Lem, and tell us something more about that buck," said Jackson.

Lem sprung to his feet, and, amid the jeers of his comrades—who laughed at him all the harder because they were frightened themselves —rushed out of the cabin, and we heard him running around the house in pursuit of the inventor of the ghost, giving vent, as he ran, to divers threats, which had the effect of rendering Scipio invisible for the rest of the night.

Mike picked up the fallen deer's head and examined it closely.

"Why Lou, child, I never heard of your dressing animals," said Jackson.

"Nor I, father, until to-day."

"What are you going to do with it?"

"Make it as correct as I can, and then hang it over the front door until I can make a better one. The ornament is the Doctor's idea."

"The head is as correctly dressed as it can be," said the Doctor. "Don't you think so, Mike?"

"Wall—no, I don't," answered the literal hunter.

"What is it that is wrong, Mike? It must be in the setting it up, for you cleaned it for me yourself."

"It moit be one, and it moit be t'other; but I guess it's some of both. Yer see the hair ain't over slick—that's *my* fault. Wall, arter that yer've got the eyes a lookin' for'ard, and the head well up, ain't that so?"

"Yes," said Miss Jackson, leaning forward.

"Wall, then," continued her instructor, taking the deer's head on his knee and illustrating his position with his fingers, "he's a makin' out somethin' ahead of him, and he'll have his ears for'ard to help him, one on 'em anyhow."

"That's true," replied the pupil, with a glance of pleasure, taking the deer's head in her hand and pulling out the wires by which the ears were supported.

"That's the natur' of a deer. I one'st went to Charleston and seed more lies than you could shake a stick at, and one was a stuffed deer a-feedin' with his flag straight up. Wall, ef that didn't make me sick. Sez I to the show-man, 'Mister, I'd jist like to tie you to a deer's tail in Floridy to show you how they carry their tails; dod rot me if I wouldn't!' "

"Ha ha! that is not as bad as my friend the Doctor," I said.

"You had better stop before you go any further, I warn you," interrupted the Doctor.

"You must know," I continued, "the Doctor, early one morning in Pensacola, saw two deer feeding in the garrison garden on the old Commodore's pea vines. So he ran down, and imagining that they had come in through the open gate and could not surmount the high picket fence that surrounded the garden, carefully closed the gate. Then, with his gun in hand, he ran in to call the Commodore to inquire whether he preferred them dead or alive; but when he returned the deer were half way to the Perdido River."

"Oh, that is too bad, Doctor!" cried Jackson, as the negroes shouted with fun.

"No, no," said the Doctor, laughing away, "that is not all of the story. My friend here was there, too, peeping through the palisades over his rifle, when I shut the gate. It was his proposition that I should go in for the Commodore, and as I came back, I heard a cap snap, his gun had missed fire while endeavouring to kill one of the deer, while I was gone."

The mirth that followed this apocryphal story was like nothing but the laughter that hails some unusual feat of the Polichinelle, before the gaping circle of children and nurses in the gardens of Paris, and it gradually subsided, lingering longest farthest from the door, where the negro boys could roll over on their backs without restraint, and laugh themselves quiet, and then to return for a fresh draught of fun.

"To come back to your deer's head," I said to Miss Jackson, after the laugh had subsided, "where did you procure the glass eyes?"

"Oh, father supplies them with his broken bottles; the shoulder of the bottle makes an eye, only a little too flat."

"And the birds on the wall are dressed by you?"

"Yes, all of them."

"And they are truer to natur' 'an a picter," added Mike approvingly.

"Where did you get your taste for such matters, Miss Jackson?"

"I think I must have got it from associating with them, to the exclusion of other society. We lead a lonely life here in the pine woods, sometimes, and I believe that when one has many gifts he does not gain from them all as much as he does from one well studied."

"Where did you get you original plan, your first lesson in taxidermy?" said the Doctor; "for I have studied the art, and it seems to me that I have never dressed a bird so well as some you have here."

"I have never had any lessons, save what I have read. Once, when first attempting it, I sent to Savannah and bought a stuffed bird which I pulled in pieces to find the secret. But the true teacher is patience. Try again every time you fail."

"They have kept well for so warm a climate."

"That's a woman's secret," said Jackson. "Lou bakes her birds in the oven."

"I'll tell you a joke," said Miss Jackson, "about baking birds. One day there was a bird pie in the oven, the pride of our new cook, and on looking at it, I found it done, and the fire low enough to dry some birds I had just set up. Accordingly, I stood them in the oven all covered with white strings, in front of the pie. When dinner was ready, Dinah went for the pie, but presently came running back, calling out, 'As sure as I's 'live, missus, dem birds is out ob de pie, or else dere ghosts am standin' dere in dere grave-clo'se. Oh, Lor', help us!'"

"What do you do when you are where you cannot have the use of an oven?"

"Oh, I do the best I can; use pepper-grass, dry them in the sun, and then let them slide."

"How pleasant to have a copy of nature's works by your side, so well prepared that it reminds you of the original bird," remarked the Doctor, laying back on a wooden bench, looking at the hawks over head, and swinging his feet back and forward under his lounge.

"Yes," answered Miss Jackson, "and to study the positions and manners of the birds and quadrupeds, so that you can copy in your subject the true position and figure, and not burlesque them. So, sometimes, what would be thrown from father's game-bag to the cook to be plucked, or, more likely still, cast away as worthless, with a little care and study resumes its old shape, takes again its natural *pose,* flashes its eye, and remains 'a joy for ever.'"

As Miss Jackson talked, her grey eye kindled, and a blush brightened either cheek. The Doctor raised himself gradually to a sitting position, then to his feet, and then he walked across the floor, saying, in his clear hearty tone: "Give me your hand, Lou Jackson! who cares which comes first, the love of nature or the mind, to appreciate her, the one is sure to produce the other."

"Wall, that's so," said Mike.

The evening promised a rainy day for the morrow, and therefore it was

71

arranged that Mike and I should have a still hunt while Jackson would ride down to the coast to see some stores that had been promised to be landed at a given point by a boat from St. Mark's.

"I think I will stay home to-morrow and set up some birds," said the Doctor.

"You had better *let 'em slide,* Poke," I remarked in a low tone.

"Never you mind," answered the Doctor, with a low laugh. "A man's a man for a' that and a' that."

The negroes were turned out of the cabin, the fire was covered, and in three minutes, oblivious of rain or deer, all were in the "land o' dreams."

CHAPTER 9

The Still Hunt

L'Aurore paraissait à peine,
Quand dans la brume à l'horizon
Je l'ai vu rentrant de la plaine
Tout chargé de sa venaison.
Redressant sa larage empaumure
Il s'est arrêté par trois fois
Puis il a longé la bordure
Écoutant l'eau tomber sous bois.

As THE FIRST LIGHT STRUGGLED through the clouds and the tassels of the pines overhead, Mike and I alone, with our breakfasts in our hands, were winding our way through the forest.

We trudged on as best we might over the rolling knolls of sand, laced by the long, tough roots of the palmetto, across hollows choked with grass and vines, and down and up the quaggy sloughs that the waters had made while seeking their level in the Ouithlacouchee. The tough little ponies scampered along on the level land, and where it was muddy Mike would slide to his feet and cheer them on with whoop and hulloa, until they ran up the banks as fast as they jumped down. The rain had ceased, yet it was not clear, and the drops hung on all the bushes, or showered down on us from above as we struck the young timber.

Having reached a point of land in the bend of the river, the ponies were unsaddled, their halters were tied to their knees so that they could not run, though giving them ample liberty to graze, and left behind with an injunction to "Stay thar, yer sarcy critters."

Again the word was forward. Mike led the way on a long stride, his rifle lying in the hollow of his left arm, and his body bending and oscillating to conform to the inequalities of the ground. As he walked he turned hither and thither, taking in with his eye everything in the forest. At times, he

73

would pick up a leaf here and there, giving it a glance, and cast it down again. Where the river bent, and we came where we could see around the elbow, his walk was slow, and his foot came down like a cat's; when he was in the hollow he ran, and almost halted as he rose the succeeding knoll, and could take a view beyond.

As we walked, he pointed to a place in the sod, looking at me with that communicative glance that said, "There is something pleasant." On looking carefully, I could just see a mark where the grass was thin, but a mark it was, and nothing more; it might be a natural discoloration, or the result of one of the thousand motions constantly occurring in a forest.

"What is it?" I asked.

Mike picked up a broad leaf, one of those growing in a dank place, and handed it to me. The leaf was cut almost in the shape of the letter V.

"What does that mean—a deer's track?"

Mike nodded.

"How long ago was that track made?"

"Two minutes—'bout."

My looks must have expressed doubt, for Mike replied: "Look here, now, leaves don't tell lies in the piney woods, though I've heern tell they do in books. D'ye see that juice comin' out of that leaf thar jist whar the deer's huff cut it?"

"Well?"

"D'yer think them air leetle drops has been more 'an a week formin' when they're growin' bigger as ye look, and haint run together yet? Tear another leaf, don't it come jist as fast? Ain't that as plain as a bar up a gum-tree? He's a sockdologer of a buck, too!"

"Now, Mike, look here. I will believe what you say about the time, but don't say what you don't know. You can have everything your own way here, but there is no means in the world of telling this deer to have been a buck, so you need not say so till we see it."

"Wall, now," said Mike, setting down the breech of his heavy rifle on the ground, and leaning his chin on the muzzle, while he looked at me with an expression of pity; "wall, now, ef I had a young 'un, and he couldn't tell that he was a scandalous big buck, walking alone slowly like out to the feedin' grounds, ef I wouldn't claw his back with a wildcat, I would. Now, jist look a here, there's one track by the lance leaf."

"Yes."

"Here's the t'other on the same side, and here's the t'other, and here's the t'other. Wall, that shows he's a walkin', don't it?"

"Ye-e-s."

"Thar he's nibbled off that young tree, hain't he ?"

A small birch sprout, of about a foot in height, was stripped of its leaves and bark.

"Ye-e-s."

"Wall, that shows he was feedin' slowly, and warn't the leastwise anxious, and by the way the tracks pint I calkerlate he's off for the meadows."

"Well, but how do you know it was not a doe?"

" 'Cause he writ it up on that pine-tree on ahead, where the tracks are thick at the bottom. Now look on the bark about six feet up, and tell me what rubbed that bark off ef it warn't that buck's horns—and you better believe it was a whopper; no small buck kin scratch up thar."

I thought a moment, and then the only wonder to me seemed why it needed an explanation at all, it was so clear.

"Whare has he gone? Thare's a meadow across here chock full of sweet grass and lily pads, and I reckon he's thar, and slathers more."

A few minutes' walk, and we came on to the verge of a natural meadow, bounded on every side by the forest, and yet smooth and waving as a field of grain or a level prairie. Here and there a water-oak reared itself from the grass, twisting its great limbs on every side, shading the sward below, and supporting wreaths of mistletoe vines covered with waxen berries. But all else was one free rustling field, grazed by the deer alone, and mowed only by the winter fires or the hurricane. Over the grass could be seen the marsh hawk wheeling along the level in long slanting curves, while in the distance, where a tall tree leaned over the eddies of the river, a solitary cormorant watched his primeval realm, where

> "Unheeded spreads the blossomed bud
> Its milky bosom to the bee,
> Unheeded falls along the flood
> The desolate and aged tree."

This was a great pasture for the deer, and ever since the creation hundreds had spent the nights here, retiring with the heat of the sun to the closer cover of the pines.

"I haint seen that air buck's tracks agin," said Mike; "I rather think he haint got in yet. We'll go a leetle further on to this ridge; he will likely come down that way, I reckon. Come, Yowler;" and taking the long ear of his dog in his hand to prevent him taking to the meadow, we ran on to the ridge. By the side of the ridge we found quite a well-beaten deer path leading through an opening in the fringe of trees that surrounded the meadow, and through this, from time immemorial, doubtless, the great horned herds had wound their way in and out at their pleasure. Here, too, were found tracks of wild hogs, and Mike pointed out to me a broad footprint of the cougar or panther that had been made only the night before.

It was agreed that I should lie here concealed behind some branches with my eye on the path leading from the woods, while Mike should go around in the woods and see what had become of the buck. In a moment he was gone, and I was left lying on my breast, with my rifle ready cocked before me, watching the lonely path that led into the forest.

As soon as Mike was out of sight I began to feel that loneliness and shadowy presence that is often with one when in a great forest, particularly if unaccustomed to its solitude. The stillness, the majesty of the woods, the strange insects crawling about, the flickering light that complexes the eye, the heart counting the time with heavy throbs, the apprehension of making a noise, all press on the senses with a bewildering power. I felt this, and longed for the deer or Mike, I cared but little which. I sighted my rifle, and tried to determine from which way the deer would first come, feeling certain he was mine if he appeared.

As I thus lay putting propositions to myself, I heard a loud snort or whistle directly behind me. I turned hastily, and away bounded a buck that had been standing apparently within ten feet of me. How I apostrophised my carelessness, and watched the waving grass as he wound among the meadow paths far away on the plains!

Again I watched, and this time more successfully, for over the knoll I could see a pair of horns coming slowly forward, though the deer was still out of sight. They advanced like a rower in a boat, with measured but irregular speed, and once in a while stopped altogether. Then my heart beat like a drum, but when the horns advanced again I felt more composed. At length the head appeared above the brow of the hill, then the shoulders, then the full length and height of the animal; there was no more doubt—it was *the sockdologer of a buck* described by Mike. When it reached the hill it seemed to halt for a survey, and viewed the whole extent of the woods and savannah. Trees, and waters, and waving grass, the cool retreats of low hanging bushes, all appeared to his eye like the pleasant meadows to the monarch bull, when, released from his winter's stall, he looks over the farm in the spring. All kinds of nervous apprehensions arose in my mind. I feared lest he might turn back, and almost called out in my anxiety. I dreaded lest he should see me, and crouched to the earth to prevent it. Presently, apparently satisfied with his examination, he marched down the hill to where I lay in ambush. His head high up, his great horns back, his step like the step of a race-horse, he looked like a marching king. I could not see any part of his body but his breast, and did not like to take a front shot, but waited until he should present some other view. But the stag did not intend to turn aside; he saw his feeding ground beyond, green with the succulent herbage of the lowlands, where his mates had awaited him all the night, and he walked right onward. Now he was too near to shoot. What should I do? If he sees me, he will dash off, giving me the worst possible shot. My heart beat so I could not lay on my side, but raising my gun gently on my left elbow, I depressed the breech, and without taking sight, when the deer was almost over me, pulled the trigger. With the report of my gun the frightened animal sprang into the air as though he had been blown up by a mine, and then dashed off into the woods. He flew over the hills, and just as I had given him up for lost I heard the clear ring of a rifle in the direction he had gone. It was Mike's; I knew its voice. What a load fell off my mind—the deer was ours!

On reaching the place from whence the shot came, I found Mike loading his rifle, and the deer with his antlers ploughed into the ground by the force of his running fall, and his throat cut. On looking for my shot I readily found it in the breast, and the ball had gone through the thick part of the neck without doing much damage. Mike's had struck him in the head.

Selecting two small trees that grew from the same root, we lifted our quarry up until his horns caught in the angle, and his body hung down with his back to the tree. Mike then cut the skin in a line from the throat to the tail, and also a transverse line down each foreleg, and drew the entrails. Then loosening the neck from the skin, he cut the neck from the head at the first joint, and pulled the fore shoulders directly out of the skin. Then cutting off the fore shoulders, the loin and the hind-quarters were left hanging by the horns. The shoulders were thrown aside, while the hind-quarters were neatly rolled in the skin with the branching horns, and hung on a sapling to await the time of our return at night.

Our original plan had been to drive the deer from off the meadows with the dog, we standing at the runways, thus getting very fair shots on the open plain, but by reason of the advanced hour of the day it seemed doubtful if this plan would succeed; however, we resolved to try it. Selecting two paths, apparently much frequented by the deer, and in some places worn into channels, we sent Yowler off to hunt. The old dog seemed to know his duty well, for he hied away with a look at his master, and we could occasionally see him, where the grass was thin, making long casts, and occasionally his mellow voice would be borne in faint from the distance.

Mike was stationed not far away, and looking across the grass I could see him leaning against a tree surveying the scene before us. Afar down in the horizon a gang of deer headed by two bucks was going out of the meadow by some other path on a long lope. I pointed them out with my arm, and a nod from Mike showed me he saw the game and understood my gesture. There go two herons, blue and grey, flapping up from the grass, and turning their heads first on one side and then the other; the dog must be in that neighbourhood and have sprung them, though we cannot see him for the grass.

There comes a deer; he is close by before one can see he is started—a young buck with spike horns. How fast he comes! once in a while jumping high above the grass to view his pursuer. Mike has disappeared behind the tree against which he was leaning. I wonder which path the deer will take. I raise my rifle; no, he is running for Mike. He comes now fast, and close behind him is yelping the hound! he is within shot of Mike, running right for his stand. Spang! rings the rifle; the deer jumps, staggers, halts, and falls. Well done, old Red Beard! next to shooting game one's-self, the best thing is to see it well shot by some one else.

Yowler is caught by his master, and sent back on the meadows. Hardly had he gone out of sight before I heard his yelp again, and a great rustle and shaking of some reeds that grew a hundred rods in front of me. There it is! one, two, three deer—and there goes another—and here comes a third party! The firing has alarmed them, and they are off with a snort and a whistle, each his own way. One has turned this way; no, he has gone toward the river. There is another; he is coming this way, surely; yes, here he comes, head up, horns back—a noble fellow. "Dear me!" I ejaculated, "this is like shooting deer in park." As I crouched low in the narrow pass I was occupying, with a dense thorn thicket on either hand, and the grass growing in front of me sufficiently high to conceal me from view, I heard the grass rattle furiously, and out dashed an old boar, seeming in a desperate hurry; he ran close by me, giving a malicious lunge with his snout at me in passing; I sprung aside in time to avoid the compliment, and gazed after his retreating form with feelings of great indignation. The Spaniards of the coast had turned out some hogs in this neighbourhood in previous years, and their offspring, increasing with great prolificness, had become as savage as the boars of the Black Forest.

Before I had recovered my composure, another hog and a sow came rushing past, grunting and tearing along, followed by a whole herd of young, that thrashed down the grass, and jammed past me in their haste; as the last one came, I lost all patience, and fired. The crowd was too thick to miss, and I had the satisfaction of seeing one tumble over on its back. But my satisfaction was short-lived when there swept by me a beautiful deer on a long lope, and running as if playing with its pursuer. He came so near me I could almost have hit him with my gun, and did not see me until directly abreast; he then rushed onward with a terrified leap, and was immediately lost to view. At this instant I heard Mike fire a shot, but could not see what he had killed.

When the dog came in, which he did in a moment, on the trail of the deer that had passed me, he seemed much worried, and laid down close at my feet and refused to go out again. I could not account for his behaviour, but, not seeing any more deer on the meadow, I took him by the ear and walked around to where Mike had taken his stand, and where he was busy taking off the skins of the two deer he had shot.

"What did you shoot at?" he inquired, as I came up.

"A young hog!" and then I told him how the drove had rushed upon me, led by the vicious old boar, until in desperation I had made bacon of one, and so lost my chance at the deer.

"Some takes kindly to pork," replied Mike, "and when hard up I can worry down a leetle roast pig myself—but I don't keer fur 'em for steady fodder. Howsumever, they like 'em at the house."

So taking up the two saddles of venison, we hung them in the woods by the side of the other, and went down to get my porker, but, alas! like the old lady in the nursery rhymes, when I came back my porker was gone.

"I am sure he was dead," I replied to Mike's quizzical smile. "He lay there at that spot, and I had my feet on him while I loaded my rifle. There's blood on the grass now."

"What druv the hogs out so fast—was Yowler arter 'em?"

"No, they seemed to come alone, and Yowler skulked down, trembling, just as he is doing now."

Mike glanced at the dog, and then leaned down until his face almost came against the sod, when, drawing himself partially up, he said, "We'd better make tracks out of this corner; there ain't room enough for a free fight heyar."

"To fight what?"

"Painter," he replied.

I looked at the speaker, but there was not the least bit of joking in his face.

"How do you know that it is a panther?" said I, in a half whisper, the skin on my head contracting in spite of myself at the idea of the animal having been there where I stood only five minutes before in such fancied security.

"Wall, I know it in two ways," said Mike, in his natural hearty tone, but without raising himself from his stooping posture, and slowly bringing his rifle to a level, "and one's 'bout's good as the t'other. In the fust place, thar's the mark of his foot on the grass; and in the next place, thar's the old sarpent himself under them air bushes."

I leaned down and followed the direction of Mike's eye under the bushes, and truly there was the panther crouched under some wild plum-trees not forty yards off from where we stood. He was in a sitting posture, and one arm was stretched out and placed on the body of the hog that laid beside him. There was something handsome in that position of easy grace, with the careless claim of ownership that he extended over his prize. I caught his yellow eye, and could scarcely remove my own from the fascination of its glance. He had the air of a sentinel challenging us strangers, and I, for one, felt like an intruder, and had a mental desire of apologising, taking off my hat, and retiring.

"Jist keep steady-like," said Mike, in his usual slow tone. "Don't move fast, but step a leetle away from me, and ef I miss him he will come out, and then you try."

As he finished speaking, his rifle was at his shoulder, and the clear report of the piece was followed by a rushing bound as the animal came out. Mike drew his knife, but it was useless; the panther spent his life in that prodigious leap, and lay dead on the grass. The rifle ball had gone through his brain.

"Ha!" said Mike, with a prolonged accent and strong out-breathing that showed the force of his feelings. Then, leaning down and laying his hand on the tawny face of his fallen foe, he caressed him as he would have done a child, smoothing his cheek and lifting his paw, and speaking to him in the proud yet tender way he would have spoken to his sweetheart. "And ye be a purty critter; yer eyes has babies in 'em. My beauty, didn't you know me when you squatted thar? I've knowed you, pet, I reckon, when yer were quite a youngster. I've seen you sleepin' on my coat like any cat.

I've watched you almost ever since, and heerd of all yer doin's. Yer forgot me, but I didn't forgit you, no how at all, little yaller back, and now yer dead, poor thing. Wall, wall, we'll all come to that soon, only let's have our traps packed and ready. I wish Lou Jackson could see you where you're layin'."

When this funeral address was ended, we dragged the body out of the bushes into a more open place, to take off the skin. The shooting of a deer was an every-day work, and they were skinned in a minute ; but the death of a panther, and the taking off of his robe, is an incident that calls forth the keenest pleasure in the hunter, and only he can understand the accent of pride with which Mike at length held up in both hands the huge tawny skin, with its pendent claws and cat-like head, saying, "Ain't that a bed for a king?" When he had completed this work, noon had long since passed away, and we looked around for a spot to dine.

Near where we had hung our first deer, on the sloping side of a clay bank, a spring of water rose from the earth, "and a clearer one never was seen," which, filling a natural basin among the roots of the trees that over-hung it, poured down the hill in a trickling rivulet, and joined by other smaller springs, sought its level on the great savannah, where its course could be traced by the eye for a mile or more by the line of joint grass and flags that took root in its waters. By the spring we carried our three saddles of venison, our hog, and our panther skin, and sat ourselves down to dinner. Not a grand dinner of cold fowl and claret, sandwiches and cakes, with which upon the Scottish moors the sportsmen regale their inner man, but a dinner that consisted simply of a large square of corn-bread, and an equally large square of venison steak, but so hungry were we that no rich repast, even though spread at Verey's, at Paris, would have been more highly honoured, and surely no table, even on the Santa Lucia, with the broad bay of Naples, and the flaming spire of Vesuvius before the door, could have been spread in a more graceful place, or with a more characteristic view. The deep well-spring with its seething sands at the bottom churned into a constant motion, the trees that for ages had guarded that source, the rippling murmur of the brook, the soughing of the pine leaves, the broad perspective of the meadow, with the distant belt of river beyond, so far away that its gleam was like the horizon, the nearer scamper of the squirrel, or the flap of the heron's wing as disturbed by our presence he rose from the flags, all gave a landscape to the eye, or a sense of solitude to the mind, and occupied us in contemplation for an hour or more after the dinner was ended.

"Do you think you ever saw that panther before to-day?" I asked of Mike, as I tossed him over the tobacco-pouch.

"I'm not over sartin, but I reether spect. Yer see thar ain't many on 'em heyar bout, and it was jist two years ago when that ere painter cub I guv Colonel Brown, at Tampa, vamosed, and then he was two years old. This one, you see, would be nigh on to four, and that would jist make it." A long puff or two followed from his short pipe, when he said in a musing manner, "That air cub left bekase of a fight he got in with a soldier at the fort. Yer see he guv the soldier a slap, when the soldier struck him with his bay'nit, and then the painter just chawed him up and sloped. Wall, now look a heyar, do you see that mark on his cheek?" There was a triangular scar on the animal's cheek, just under the eye. "That, I calkelate, is that ere bay'nit dig. This is the last o' that settlement. Grey Wolf's band got the old painter, and the cub I left thar in my coat, so I've heern; the t'other cub, the one I toted to Tampa Bay, is this heyar, and that's all the painters thar is round these diggins."

Without precisely understanding the reasoning by which Mike arrived at this last affirmation concerning a wood that apparently might contain a thousand such animals without any one being aware of it, I could not help smiling at the particularity of his genealogy.

"Thar's somewhar here about another varmint, and a purtier one yet, though tain't of much account as a fighter. I've seen his tracks and have promised his skin to Lou Jackson, and ef he ain't a ghost I'll git him some day, though I've been a month tryin' to find him."

"What is the animal?"

"Tiger cat; a rael likely little critter; yaller with black dabs. I reckon he's 'bout the size of a small hound."

"You were in a hurry to make your promises. How do you know you can get it?"

"Because Lou Jackson wants it," replied Mike, with the assurance of a man that had never failed in any thing he desired with his whole mind.

"How long have you known Lou Jackson?"

"Goin' on to three years."

"Where did they come from?"

"Oh, Jackson had a big plantation on the upper coast somewhere nor'east; but I've heern say he lost his crops and got in debt, and fit a duel, and then cum heyar, and built this house, and called it 'Far Awa'.'"

"I thought you had known his family longer, you seem such a friend of Miss Lou."

"I have known them only three years; and some folks you know soon, and Lou Jackson is one of them kind."

"She is a pleasant girl."

"Yes, I can say that. Thar's nobody in Floridy that can say so much, and be so sparin' of words. She's always the same; she makes it light all about the Ouithlacouchee when it's black dark everywhere else, she's so happy like. Even the Injins, when they come there, draw in their claws and act genteel, and that's oncommin for an Injin."

"They are very much exposed, living here so far from protection, and bands of these Indians roving about, and sometimes Jackson himself away."

"No, he don't leave often unless she goes with him; but many a night I've kept round that house when nobody knowed it, jist to know that she was sleepin', when these cusses has been about."

"What did she say to you when she heard of your watchfulness?"

"How would she know? Do you think *I* would tell her sich like stuff? It's natural enough that I should watch fur her. Wall—wall—thar are piles o' painters in this State purty as this one, but there ain't no woman that is as handsome as Lou Jackson. That's so?"

"Do you know anything about the duel that Colonel Jackson fought?"

"I've heern tell that it was a hard go; they fired one at the t'other till the Colonel bored his man, and then he larnt it was all a mistake, and they needn't have fit at all; but who the man was, or what they fit about, I don't know. Whar's the terbacker?"

I passed the pouch of squirrel-skin over to the hunter, and filling his pipe again, he relapsed into a musing silence, while I watched the lengthening shadows, and thought over the strange life at Far Away, the moody, reckless, proud planter, and the gentle though strange tastes of the daughter. What a wasting, sensitive, weary heart he seemed to carry, joyous only by turns, and then boisterously gay! What a cheering controlling presence, hers, so earnest and frank, yet all the while so lively and self-willed! And the house itself was a perfect mixture of roughness and grace, the life within contrasting with its appearance, as did the fancy of its name with the rudeness of its exterior. No news of the world, no society, no lover, no music, the literature of the most meagre kind, and yet the whole family instinct was graceful and thoughtful, and like to no western farm that ever yet was seen.

As I thus ran on, I noticed the sun was low in the west.

"It will be dark soon."

"I reckon," said Mike in his usual manner.

"But we can't stay out here all night."

"I've lain by this spring right often, but I s'pose we may as well go now; you go ketch the ponies, and I'll get their pelter ready."

I accordingly went after the ponies, which were found near where we had hoppled them. As I rode back I saw a single buck feeding in the open woods, but stopping to attempt a shot, he ran off in the direction that we had come in the morning. On returning to the spring, Mike had the game already bound, and balanced so as to hang over the ponies. The hog balanced two saddles of venison, and the panther's skin another saddle. After loading the ponies we started toward home, Mike promising to get the buck I had seen when I went for the ponies. I showed him the place where the deer had been feeding when I first saw him, and the direction he had taken.

"Wall, that'll do," he said; "he's so much nigher home."

In a few minutes after, as we mounted a hill, we saw the deer in the distance again, and as we came in view he looked at us for a moment, and then gently trotted on, and some small galls or swamp holes intervening, was soon lost to sight.

"Thar, he'll do now. Take your pony by the bridle, and follow fast right for that gall."

We came within a hundred yard of the brake, and then hoppling the ponies, ran on to the edge of the bushes, that afforded a good cover. Having reached this, we passed carefully through, looking out toward the open land beyond in hopes to see the buck within shot, but, alas! he was too wise for that, and had only stopped when fully beyond the reach of harm from the thicket close behind. Near by, a turkey-hen was leading a large brood of young ones, nearly full grown, clucking and hopping along, and running hither and thither in the pursuit of spiders and lizards, that showed she was utterly unconscious of her dangerous neighbours.

"Now we'll have to crawl for it," said Mike.

"The sooner we begin, the sooner we get within shot," said I, moving forward.

"Stop," whispered Mike; "wait till those turkeys get away. If the deer sees them run away in a hurry he'll make tracks too, for he knows thar is something wrong hereabout, and having seen us once, he'll know it's us."

So we waited patiently until the turkey brood had sauntered down the woods, and then emerged from our place of concealment. Mike ran ahead in a stooping posture, and I followed close behind, running when he ran, and halting when he stopped. The first run we made was comparatively

easy, for an immense pine-tree, made doubly large by a large grape-vine that wound around it and hung in clusters by its trunk, fully concealed our approach. Here we took another survey of the ground and the game, and then, when a tree intervened between us and the head of the deer, which stood with his side toward us, we ran forward again until the deer wagged his tail, when we halted, in whatever position we might be.

It may be necessary to explain, for the benefit of those who have never learned the fact from deer-stalking, that a deer feeds and watches at irregular intervals, and that always a second before raising his head, either to walk forward, or to cast a glance of watchfulness around him, he gives his white tail a quick whisk or two. The knowledge of this simple and peculiar habit is of immense use to the still-hunter, who is thus forewarned when to advance, and when to lie still.

Thus by quick and short advances we approached to within a very long shot of our deer. My heart was beating thick and fast, and the sweat of great mental excitement stood in drops on my face, and rolled in my eyes, causing me to wipe them with my sleeve every minute.

"Now," whispered Mike, "ef yer want to try him, yer must crawl alone while I wait; we can't get any nearer together, but mind his tail."

So Mike laid still behind the weeds that were sheltering us, while I went on alone. Horatius advancing before the Roman army to defend the bridge, could not have felt more keenly the prominence of his position under the eyes of all Rome, than I did as I stalked forward, under the keen eye of Mike the Spook, to shoot that deer. First I had a little shrub between me and the buck, and about twenty feet ahead; to this I advanced safely. As I arrived, the deer whisked his tail and looked round. Waiting a moment, to my great discomfiture he turned his face toward me, and then commenced eating again. This was a state of affairs that I had not anticipated, for it shut me out from a view of that barometer tail. However, I calculated the time during which he would probably feed, and made a short advance. The deer now turned quarteringly toward me, and taking advantage of this change, with my eye fixed upon him, I was hastily advancing, when something disturbed the animal before his usual time. I laid down flat on the grass, with my rifle before me, as the buck, now within shot, raised his crowned head, and took a long and deliberate survey of the ground. There seemed to be some latent suspicion in his mind, for, though not seeing me, he yet looked all around him several times, and then over me, and finally commenced walking directly toward me. I slowly elevated my rifle on my left hand, my elbow all the while on the ground. The piece reached its level—my heart

beat as though it was tugging with the blood that flowed through it—the
deer was at a close shot, and all the time coming nearer, yet I could not aim
correctly. Still on he came toward me, his ears turned back and forth, his
head stretching forward, his nose dilating as he snuffed the air, and his eyes
seeming to look me through. I summoned my courage, and held my breath;
every sense seemed to pause while I sighted for the white breast not forty
yards off. Dear me! the gun was not cocked. A pause was required for this,
and I became more nervous than ever. I aimed again. A brief instant—it
seemed an age between my pulling the trigger and the discharge of the piece
—when the clear crack of the rifle sounded, and the deer, wheeling around,
flew away "as if the wolves of the Apennines were all upon his track."

I looked around for Mike; there he lay in the weeds, and on the end of
his ramrod he had been waving a little red rag that had attracted the attention of the buck, and lured him on to his dangerous position. I saw the deer
for a mile down the open woods flitting past the trees, and I knew I had
made a clear miss. On coming up to Mike his dry smile glowed in the
corners of his eye as he asked me, "Did yer hit him?"

Without answering the question, I asked him why *he* did not shoot, as
the buck was clearly within shot for him as well as myself.

"We've got our pile of deer's meat, and 'nuff is 'nuff, and what's the
use a wastin'?"

So we went back for our ponies, and again started for home, where we
arrived late in the evening, to find the big fires blazing, and a supper waiting
our coming. How pleasant the cabin looked, from the damp darkness
without!

> "And sweet the music of the step
> That meets you at the door."

CHAPTER 10

The Florida Pocahontas

"Their memory liveth on your hills,
Their baptism on your shore,
Your everlasting rivers speak
Their dialect of yore."
—*Sigourney*

THE EVENING MEAL WAS ENDED; the planter's family and the hunters were circled around the fire, weary with the day's fatigues and enjoying rest as none but the weary may. Pipes and home-made cigars were lit, and the negroes crowded the doorway, while, as in many a hunting-lodge before,

"The stag-hounds, weary with the chase,
Lay stretched upon the rushy floor,
And urged in dreams the forest race
From Teviot Stone to Eskdale Moor."

"Now for a story, Mike," said Miss Jackson.

"No, 'taint my turn. Doctor, slide along with a yarn."

"No, no; stories are dealt like cards, always to the left. It is your turn, Jackson."

"Well, sir, what shall it be?—anything from a fight to a foot-race."

"Let my lady name the subject," I suggested.

"Tell us a tale of woman; we have the chase in reality every day."

"As you will—woman for ever. Throw on another log, boys."

The fire belched up a million sparks to the dark sky. The flames started out afresh, and Jackson, putting his pipe in its buckskin cover, and drawing himself up by his elbows to the convenient support of a log, where he could face the whole of his auditors, in a deep voice, and with occasional gesture, as he warmed with his theme, spoke in the following most romantic and poetical style:—

"Three times, since the Spaniard came to this country, has a century rolled over the Floridas, each time burying a generation of oaks, that mature and fall once in a hundred years, each time obliterating three generations of man—more transient than the trees of the hummocks.

"*Now,* the land is a common everyday reality. The planter eats his corn-bread in his cabin; the negro toils at his daily task; the Indian hunts in the pine-land, at peace with the settler; and if there is anything of the romance of life in the land, it is to be found in the tropical vegetation, and the life of the everglade, and not in the noble daring of man.

"*Then,* in the Floridas, there was romance in thought and action —romance in history and in fiction, in dress, in races, and the love of man and woman, and all the world was tame when compared with this El Dorado. Here was the warrior's field; here the adventurer's goal, and hither came the poet to sing of Eden. Here landed the courtly cavaliers of the most chivalrous nation of the earth. In an age of discovery, when all the world was intoxicated by those vistas of wealth and novelty that the Genoese opened to the ardent, no one Arcadian land loomed from the waters of the Occident, so clad in purple, so vocal with music, so voluptuous with beauty, as this so-called 'Island of Florida.'

"Its discovery was wrought by, and illustrates the romance of the age. Ponce de Leon was a hidalgo of Spain—noble, accomplished, and renowned. With grey hairs had come honours and high command in the Indian Islands, when the tales of his mistress, a Carib girl, told him of a spring whose waters would bring back the fire of youth, and renew his wasted years. This fountain was situated on the coast of the great Mexican Gulf, where the oak, when dropping into the sea, is transformed into coral groves, its pendent moss waves beneath the waters changed into sea-fans, while, mirrored in the sea, the scarlet flamingoes reflect the colours of Paradise.

"The old knight sailed with his cavaliers in search of this fountain, and landed among the mangroves of the western coast, on Easter-day or day of flowers of the year 1512, and thence baptized the newly discovered land by the name of Florida. Not finding the fabled waters, the Quixotic knight and his followers succumbed to those years they sought to reverse, leaving a heritage of poetry and fiction to the coast they discovered, as rich as the tales of the Genii to Araby the Blest. They died by shipwreck and wars; or, if the legends of those seas may be believed, they still live among the coral reefs and keys that girdle the coast, and there, having at last found that fountain of perpetual youth, wander where the coral bowers make forests of beauty—where the sands are strewed with gems, and the summer never wanes. It is said to be a comely sight to the diver there, when the waters are clear, to see the Castilian knights, in their armour and their trailing plumes, loitering with the Indian girls of long ago under the pink shadow of the coral."

"What a ripper!" ejaculated Mike.

"An untimely remark, sir," replied Jackson, turning to the hunter, with a solemn wave of the hand, "and it savours of unbelief."

"Wall! the Gulf is a mighty safe place to yarn about—for nobody knows enough to know nothin' about it—that's sartin. Pile on."

Thus enjoined, Jackson, after a glance at his daughter Louisa's wondering eyes, continued as follows:—

"Following fast in the wake of the explorer, came noble and vassal, for fame, or greed, or heroic quest. Velasquez, De Guerray, Narvaez, succeeded each other as conquerors or visitors to the newly discovered land.

"Pamphilo de Narvaez was no mere adventurer. To family honours and name he added the higher title of fame won on the battle-field, and wealth and love added their charms to bind him to ease. But he also had heard of that fabled spring, and from the esplanade of his home in Cuba had seen the evening sky refulgent with what was said to be the reflection of the gold of the Floridas; and so, when the wind came fresh from the eastward, the morning-star saw his black-eyed lady watching from her balcony the lessening galleys that were bearing away her chief and four hundred men.

"After seven days of favouring winds, Narvaez landed on the western shore of the peninsula, near where the Mecaco River empties into Charlotte Bay, and forthwith the bands of armed men, with their standards and their horses, landed on the beach, and took possession of the land in the name of Spain. A curious spectacle did the adventurers present. There were the chiefs, with their haughty mien, and Moorish war-horses, the soldier with his pike and lance—the blue-steel cuirass, the chain shirt, and Toledo blade—all contrasted with that tropical country of birds and flowers, and the gentle mien of the Indians that welcomed them. Around their leader were gathered chiefs of noble name: Cobecca de Vacca, the treasurer; Quesada, from his stately house in Cordova; and La Manca, the most gallant gentleman of Castile. There came, also, priests to cure the souls of the benighted—hooded priests, whose convent stood high on the hills of Sierra de Diego, and boys to swing the incense at the altars; and hounds in couples nosing the scented air with their tawny muzzles. All the paraphernalia of war, and the emblems of religion, or wild sports, swept by Gaspiralla Island, and with the sound of the trumpet and the horn landed on the main land.

"But a short history remains to be told. Treachery to the natives aroused revenge. The arrow soughed on every wind, hostile bands disputed every stream. One battle followed another. The troops were divided in different bodies, under different leaders, and fought their way northward, until all but fifteen of that hopeful army found a grave, either on the field of battle or the quicksand swamps. Fifteen, under the command of De Vacca, coasted the Gulf, and gained a shelter in the Mexican colonies. But one man, a common soldier named Ortez, escaped the others' doom. Being left wounded on a battle-field, he watched his opportunity, and, as night covered the shattered dead and trodden field, he crept down to the water's edge, guided by the splash of the sea. Here, finding a canoe of the natives, he hastily gathered some fruit to support him on his voyage, and setting a sail, was soon beyond pursuit. He coasted down the shore, only landing at night to gather the turtles' and birds' eggs that were abundant on all the islands, until he reached Cuba, and saw once more the towers of a Spanish town.

"A sad day it was in St. Jago de Cuba, when Ortez came back with that Indian boat, and the grim tale of disaster. Solemn-moving men, cloaked to the chin, in spite of the tropical air, clustered together in the Plaza. Lustrous eyes were dim with tears, and duennas hurried hither and yonder to gather some scrap of hope for mistresses whose young love was buried in the buzzard's maw.

"Ortez was summoned to the presence of Narvaez's widow. In a few moments he had entered the quadrangular stone court, and stood in a room where the light came in through latticed windows, and the air was cool with the splash of waters, whose music brought back to his memories the houses of Seville. The stately dame of the lost knight sat on a cushion by a window. Her eyes were hollow with watching and grief, and her voice was deep and low. Behind her sat her daughter with a black veil shrouding her face. The soldier, leaning on his sword, at her word of command, told the story of their cruise, of their landing and bitter war. He narrated how, one by one, the leaders found inglorious deaths by disease, by heat, by arrows, or flood or quicksand, and how presently they had none to command but De Vacca.

" 'But your chief—your chief, man! Where did he fall—how did he die—did you kill the foeman that struck him, and honour his corpse as a king's?' demanded the woman.

" 'De Narvaez did not die by my side, or I would have revenged him; nor was his body buried by our band.'

" 'Where did he die—how—when? Speak faster, man.'

" 'I don't know how he died. They say he died like a hero; and when attacking a fort at Apalachi, with his good sword cleared a road so far into the stockade, that his men could not get to him, and there he remained and fell.'

" 'And where were you, did you leave your chief, heathen Moor?'

" 'No; would I come back to Cuba had I done that? I was not with Narvaez's band; they had separated before into five parties.'

" 'Who was with my husband?'

" 'They are all dead that saw him fall, or prisoners among the Indians.'

" 'There were Spanish prisoners among the Indians, then?'

" 'Yes, they seized three or four; but we counted them dead, for they never kept Spanish prisoners.'

" 'What, then, did they do with them?'

"The soldier replied not in words, but taking his unkempt locks in one hand, with the edge of the other he made a circle around his head, and then with the first hand gave a twist, and a wave that was horribly significant of the scalping process, that had then but just come to the ears of the Spaniard, and possessed, to his mind, the double terror of mystery.

"A groan and a long pause followed this pantomime.

" 'Soldier,' said the lady, 'he was your chief, you left him in a hostile country; you do not know his fate—will not honour, a soldier's name, tempt you to return, and seek to bring some tidings of his death?'

" 'Ha! where is the honour to all my comrades who are buried in those woods? There is no honour there.'

" 'Where is your religion, man? You swore on the cross in our Holy Mother Church to defend your liege and propagate your faith.'

" 'By my Lady, I kept my oath; but where there is no standard, and even the priest is slaughtered by savages, there is no piety in staying.'

" 'Have you ever loved since you left the Tagus?'

"The soldier's eye glanced quick at the lady's, but he did not answer, and the young girl peered from her veil beside her mother, on the comely form of the soldier.

" 'Ortez, I will give you the fairest girl in all the colonies if you will do this one thing for me.'

" 'I can't. What is love worth if you cannot enjoy it? I have been a true soldier in many a war; but this is no war. We have lost our ship, our lives, our horses, our chief, everything is gone of that array, and never a real have we won to repay us all. What, then, could *I* do alone?'

" 'Soldier, you are a poor man now, are you not?'

" 'As poor as a muleteer.'

" 'Do this for me, and I will make you rich.'

"The lady's eye was on the adventurer, and noted his look.

" 'Do this for me. I will send you with a pinnace, I will name you a lieutenant before you go, and when you return, I will pay you here in this chamber two hundred ounces of gold. Stay here now as you are, and you remain the bankrupt soldier, pointed out as the man who left Narvaez in Florida.'

"Steadily Ortez weighed in his mind his chances of life, and the golden sum that was as sure to him on the promise of that woman as though belted at his waist. His eye looked at the soft light that came in at the window, and the spattering fountain in the court below, vacantly, while one could count a score; and then, turning to the widow, he said—

" 'I will go,' adding, with Spanish grace, 'and may our Lady Mother keep you well till my return.'

"In a few days the adventurer was again in the Mexican Gulf, steering for the battle-fields where he had left his chief. He sailed among islands covered with mangroves, and pillared on coral, touching at every prominent point, and threading the broad lagoons where the sea-ferns spread their palms to the light of the upper air. Where opportunities offered, he landed on the shore, and tried, by presents and gentle words, to gain from the natives the information he desired, but they remembered the fierce forays of Velasquez and Narvaez, and only treated to betray. He was induced one day by the Apalaches to visit the shore, and was at once seized; and being recognised as one of Narvaez's band, was condemned to death. His frightened comrades, having lost their guide, made haste to weigh anchor, and sailed away to Cuba, glad to escape from the terrors of that Stygian shore.

"Ortez was a true Spaniard. His haughty mien, dark hair and eye, his active strength and bronzed face, all spoke the soldier of fortune, and impressed the feebler natives with a respect in spite of their hatred. His dress, in the fashion of the day, of embroidered velvet and lace, gave him the appearance, to their eyes, of a chief of rank, and they rejoiced that they could punish their Spanish foes by the sacrifice of one of their great men, and led him, bound, to the village of the Apalachean Cacique. This town was situated, as near as the old histories of those days can inform us, on one of the many islands that crowd the mouth of the Apalachicola river. It is the more difficult to designate the spot, because, from the currents of the river, new islands are formed and the old ones are buried in the lapse of time, and the whole character of the timber has been changed. Where now groves of stunted pine surmount the sandy ridges, and the swamp poplar and the rank titi cover the piles of driftwood that lodge on the upper end of the islands, there formerly stood the life-oak, the gum, the maple, and the pawpaw, while the deer grass beneath was purple with its fragile flowers, and the blossoms of the running gourds that the natives loved to cultivate.

"Ortez was rowed in a canoe among many an island covered with this rich vegetation, and dotted by the rush-thatched cottages of the people. He saw stockade forts built of reeds frowning down in mimic pomp on the waters that had never bristled with more dangerous arms than the tomahawk and the arrow. He heard the shrill sounds of clarionets and horns, and saw waving standards of gaudy feathers. The women that rowed the boat in which he was bound were dressed in the simple robe that befitted the summer land. Their linen, or sea-grass kilts, were trimmed with feathers or furs, and sea-shells ornamented their hair and ankles. Their olive-coloured limbs, unshackled by dress, were as graceful in form as the children that played on the sand; and the men in the stern of the barge, though warriors, all had that gentle manner and expression that belongs to the natives of southern climes.

"On arriving at the village, the prisoner was led to the Indian chief and his council, before the public lodge of the village. There was a short discussion as to the punishment, and no remarks were made by the prisoner at the bar why sentence should not be passed, for, in sooth, he could not say a word in any tongue they could understand. An Indian communicated to him, by a symbolic motion of shooting with an arrow, that his death was appointed; and then, pointing to the setting sun, and describing a semi-circle with his hand, assigned the time for the morrow morning at sunrise. The prisoner was led away, little noting the laugh of the Indian child that pointed him out to his comrade at play, little heeding the wondering eyes of the Indian girls that followed his steps, for his thoughts were where the Alcanadre river was leaping his native hills of Arragon, and the castanets clacked to the dancer's tread under the walls of his home in Huesca.

"But there were others in the village who did not join in the verdicts of the chiefs. Those simple hearts, whose love and faith in the forest, or the

town, all the wide world over, makes the sunshine to man's gloom, the hope
to passion's rigour, had seen the stranger, had sorrowed for him, and had
longed to save him. First among them all was the daughter of the chief.
Availing herself of her rank, she had stood without the ring when Ortez was
under examination. She had seen his melancholy attitude, and met the fiery
glance of his Spanish eye. She had marked his slashed doublet, and the
graceful embroideries of his vest. His heavy moustache was different from
the smooth-faced warriors of her tribe, and his form, by their lithe figures,
towered like King Richard's at Askelon. Her uncovered bosom throbbed
beneath the necklace of coral, her deep eyes were vacant with thought.
Yahchilane was in love; and the object of her love was the Spanish soldier
that was to die at sunrise."

"That's not nateral at all; an Injin woman is a leetle wuss nor an Injin
man, and is allers down on a prisoner."

"You, Mike!" said Louisa Jackson, with a hushing gesture of her hand;
and the hunter relapsed into silence, and sat as before, listening to the story,
and rolling backward and forward, with his arms clasped around his knee.

"It was the old story of Pocahontas anticipated among a gentler
people, and Yahchilane did not need to throw herself under the war-club to
gain the prisoner's pardon. She came, when the moon was up, to her
father's house, and with her came one of the young girls of the tribe, the
friend of the chieftain's daughter. They brought a roll of cloth, finely woven
from the inner bark of trees; they brought tatooed gourds, filled with the
precious stones that Indians prize so well, and wampum belts of amber-
coloured shells, they brought their gayest kirtles of the skins of the merganser and wood-duck; and the moccasin, deftly sewed with the porcupine's
quills; and when the old man, the chief of the Apalaches, sat at his door-sill,
and the next eldest chief beside him, Yahchilane and her maiden threw all
these things at his feet. Then stripping from her head the long white
feathers of the egret that shaded her neck, and unwinding from her waist
the cocoa-fibred skirt, she tossed them on the pile and sat down in the sand,
saying—

" 'Yahchilane is sick, and will need these things no more—she is ready
to go with the dead that go to-morrow morning.'

"The old chief sat silently looking at his daughter; but he understood
her not.

" 'Where will the Young Swan go to-morrow morn; and why is she ill?'

" 'She sees a great man, with eyes like an eagle's, and hair like a
bear's—with a mantle of moleskin and gold, and a silent tongue—he is

alone and a stranger—and to-morrow he dies; and Yahchilane would rather hunt with him in the Happy Land than stay here alone.'

"When the old chief heard this, he knew what the offering meant; for it was all of his daughter's goods, and all that she and her maidens had woven through the year. He knew how fast love comes under a tropical sky, where the blood is hot, and how far the wild feeling would carry an Indian girl. He remembered the days when Yahchilane's mother was a maiden; and he turned away to his brother chieftains, and left his daughter still bent on the sands.

"At a summons hastily sent, the warriors came again together, and sat as before around the door of their chief. They kindled a fire, and the flames flashed red over many a reed-covered house—over the pickets and lagoons, and the still bowed figure of the girl. None looked at the chief's daughter, though all saw her sitting, and wist why she remained; and then they talked long and slowly, and from mouth to mouth passed the pipe, fringed with eagle feathers and the long beard of the turkey-cock. Hardly would it have fared with the Spaniard if they had confined themselves to his deserts—for the cruel wars of Narvaez were fresh in their minds, and they remembered Anta, and how their kinsmen had fallen there under the arquebus and the long Spanish blade; but when they frowned and looked down, they still saw the young girl in her beseeching posture, divested of her robes, with her face in her hands; and their hearts failed them, and they consented. The council again broke up, and the old chief, raising his daughter there under the palm-trees, gave her the life of her captive.

"When the morrow's sun glinted athwart the persimmons and sycamores, Ortez was again brought before the council. But how different the scene! His eye was bright and hopeful—his step as proud as a Don; and in every corner and on every face, fell his glance in pleasure and in love. How had he learned this change in his fate? Who could tell him that he had been pardoned, when none in all the land spoke a word of his tongue? When he was led before the council, Yahchilane stood beside her father arrayed in her brightest dress. Ortez walked to her, and raising her hand to his lips with the dignity of a cavalier, kissed it and drew her to his side—she was already his wife. All the chiefs, the women and children, understood that mute ceremony; and they clapped their hands and shouted unintelligible words, and Ortez and his young bride were the fairest and bravest for many years of all the Apalacheans."

"Pooty poor kind o' marryin', that," quoth Mike.

"Better than yours, for you don't marry at all," retorted Poke.

CHAPTER 11

The Florida Pocahontas—*continued*

"Entre le ciel qui brûle, et la mer qui moutonne
Au somnolent soleil d'un midi monotone,
Tu songes, O guerrière aux vieux conquistadors."
—*De Hereda*

"AMONG RACES BUT LITTLE ADVANCED from a state of nature, no human quality excites greater reverence than personal bravery, and Ortez inheriting this power as a natural birthright, soon sat in the first ranks among his adopted people. He had to throw aside his arquebus for lack of powder; but acquired the art of shooting the bow, and flinging the metal ball, with as much accuracy as his instructors. He still retained his basket-hilted sword and his shirt of link mail; and in the different wars of the tribe there was none who could strike a surer blow, or stand longer in the breach, or was greater feared for his prowess than the adopted Spaniard, who rose to the position of second chief of the nation, passing those who were immeasurably above him when he began his race. Some were proud of his young renown; but others, as in every land, imputed their own subordinate position to the honours showered on his head, and were proportionately jealous. But honour or jealousy made no difference in the love of his wife—the same passionate kiss greeted the soldier if he came back honoured or suspected. It was a woman's love, and it flickered not; and when angry voices told of Spanish aggressions and coming wars, and pointed to him, she merely said, 'He is not a Spaniard, he is my love.'

"There had been a fierce battle fought between the Yupaha tribes and the Apalaches, in which the latter had returned with not their usual success, bringing home with them the bodies of many of their warriors. They came to the village with all the insignia of woe, beating of drums, formed of the sections of hollow trees covered with deer skins, and the mournful blast of their conch-shell trumpets.

"Wealuste, the great black water chief, had been killed, and they placed him on the shore, with his arrows and his quiver, his knife and his eagles' plumes, and a goodly store of chinquapin nuts and maize, to support him on that long journey to the Happy Hunting-ground that he was to make in darkness and alone. His body was sewed in deerskins, pictured with the scenes of his life, and then placed in a wooden canoe formed from a cypress log. This canoe was fixed on upright posts, and the warrior was left to float away, as a chief should go, to the silent realm. But for forty days and forty nights, or for one whole moon, the corpse was to be watched by comrades of equal rank with the deceased, so that neither beast nor bird disturbed the dead. This is a part of the simple faith of the tribe; and they affirm that after decay has taken the body, the departed chief is safe beyond earthly harm.

"Ortez was the first in order that had assigned to him this honourable duty, and in the early part of a summer eve he took his post by the dead man. The sun laid down in his golden bed in the western waters, and the stars one by one stepped to their places in the sky, as the watcher paced to and fro by the side of the scaffolding where the dead chief slept. He heard the distant wailing of music from the village, and the nearer hooting of the owls, and the honking of the herons from the wood. He saw the pawpaw wave its purple bells between him and the sky, and the green balls of the buttonwood looked like the olives on the hills of his native land. But it was not of the storied peaks of Spain the soldier was then thinking—nor was he listening to the twittering of the birds in the reeds. He was watching the path that led toward the village, and his heart was beating thick with the anticipation of meeting some one that was fairer than the pawpaw bell, and dearer than the towers of his native town. He listens on his beat with one foot raised—he turns his ear aside, and his thin nostril quivers like that of a horse. He hears a splash in the water—it was not the grey duck. A canoe touches the shore, and a girl steps out on the strand. Her luminous eye is half veiled by its lashes—her limbs are trembling with delight. She falls into the arms of Ortez, and after an instant of fainting embrace, they turn aside into the ilex groves that fringe the bank of the lagoon.

" 'Ortez, does not honour call thee to the dead man's side? Ortez, does not thy wife's low voice, that saved thee once, beseech thee now?'

"Ha! who hears voices pleading in the mad tumultuous hours of night—thought comes with the bare-faced morn. The glare of the torrid day is for rest, and penance, and prayers; and the tropical night is passion's own holiday, when love and hate roll like the sea."

"Hold there, and turn down a leaf," called out the Doctor. "That's pure error. It is the day that is made for action, ambition and hope—pride and quick deeds come with the sunshine. Then man does his works for good or evil; but when the day is gone, the grey of twilight, the hush of voice, and emblematic sleep, bring thought and repentance. Man's good spirit comes to him then, and whispers of errors done, and cools his ambition; and, if he is a true man, he says his prayers, and"—

"Goes to bed," laughed Jackson. "That's all very nice for a man who lives in a land where water freezes after dark, and nobody but a bear can keep out at nights without the ague. That is not the way the hot blood rolls in the Creole veins; nor was it the way that the Spanish soldier reasoned with the Indian girl. Where was I?"

"Ortez had just met the Indian girl."

"Ah! yes; Jumper-boy, give me a light."

Taking the stick from the hand of his negro, he lit his pipe, and resumed the story.

"That young Indian girl had left the village, as quietly as the dew, her moccasin had made no foot-fall on the path, and her paddle scarce splashed the lagoon. When she met her lover, their voices were as low as the eddy of the wave in the river; and when she parted, and took her course back to the village, though her speed was slow, and her stroke was languid and uneven, yet still, her boat passed like a shadow beneath the low, arching titi boughs, and the hanging folds of the Spanish moss. But, for all this, an eye was on her in the darkness, and an ear heard her very breathings, and when she landed, and her bark canoe was hidden in the joint-grass, she passed so near Yahchilane that the tails of fox-squirrels, that fringed her kirtle, touched the shoulder of the young wife.

"The girl, once in the path toward the village, walked swifter still, now and then pausing to listen, when in the deeper shadows. On her route, she crossed a dense grove of wild plum-trees, where the scarlet fruit dotted the ground, and the low-reaching branches made a shadow as dark as a stormy night. When in the centre of the grove she started, uttering a quick, aspirated sound, for a hand was laid on her shoulder, from behind. She turned, but could not see who it was, the grove was so obscure.

" 'Who is it?' she demanded, in a low voice.

" 'An eagle who had a mate,' said Yahchilane, in a voice so quick and fierce that the young girl could not recognise it, though she cowered from the threatening shadow and rasping voice that continued. 'And who are you? The wild cat that killed him.'

"Nothing more was said, though the ground doves that roosted in the grove flew frightened away. If any more there was, the lamentations from the town, and the beating drum, prevented it from being heard. And then, down among the mourners, with her proud head at its uttermost height, and her black eye flashing fire, strode the chieftain's daughter. Old chiefs lay there with their lips in the dust, but hers were as proud as a conqueror's; the women of the tribe were there, with distorted faces, beating with hollow canes the war-drums of the Apalaches; the conch shells uttered their loudest wail, and maidens sat, in their shame, uncovered in the sand; but with no semblance of sorrow on her sovereign face, Yahchilane walked among the bonfires that lighted all the town, and across the council-lawn, and went into her father's house.

"The next morning, when the young girls of the village, in laughing troops, with palmetto baskets, wound down the path to gather fruit for their simple meal, they found one of their number dead in the grove. A knife of fish-bone, with a carved handle, was driven in her breast, so deep that the point came out behind, between her shoulders.

"Hardly had the news been told, before a young warrior came rushing into town with a tale, whose horror exceeded even the crime of murder.

"It appeared that the relief-guard that went out early in the morning to take the place of Ortez, at the tomb of the dead chieftain, found the Spaniard absent from his post. On coming to the scaffolding they discovered the canoe overturned, and the body of Wealuste dragged out and mutilated by some wild beast. Depth of all disgrace! the face that had fronted a hundred battles had been mutilated by a carrion wolf. Where was now the soul of the chieftain in the shadowy land? What great doom was hovering over his people for this neglect?

"As the warriors wondered and mourned, and hastily gathered up the body of their dead, Ortez was seen coming back from the woods, dragging the body of a huge black wolf. The animal, while making off with its prey, had been pursued by the soldier, wounded with an arrow, and killed with a dagger, after severely tearing the arm of his antagonist. Ortez could give no explanation of how the animal had succeeded in mounting the scaffold, unobserved, or what he himself was doing during the scene of sacrilege. The fault was fearful, and the Spaniard was bound and dragged back to the village. Again he was the outcast criminal, chained and reviled. Now, all the suspicious spirits that mistrusted his prosperity gloated over his fall, and reviled him. They called up every misdeed that had come to their knowledge. They cited his Spanish origin; and reasoned, that because he was one of their natural enemies, the comrade of Narvaez, and the countryman of Velasquez, therefore he had committed this unpardonable sin, and brought down the anger of the Great Spirit on the tribe.

"Justice is not slow of foot among simple people, and that evening, while the young mistress of the soldier was wrapped in fawn skins and sewed in palmetto leaves for her long sleep, her lover was brought to trial before the chiefs of the village.

"The fire of loblolly pine climbed up in the air, and lit the scene with the whiteness of noon. The bamboo and grass cottages; the overshadowing palms, with their colossal trunks and spike-leafed crowns; the solemn circle of chiefs, and the background of women and young boys, formed a picture glowing with the colours of Rubens.

"Ortez stood in the centre, bound to a stake. He appeared the same man as three years before, when he stood in the self-same place. He wore the same steel shirt, the same fierce look of pride; and from his ragged arm, the blood, unnoticed, dropped slowly on the ground.

"The warriors smoked long and silently; and when they had done, and the pipe had been laid down before the cacique, they spoke their views with the gravity of Roman Fathers.

"When all had finished, Ortez replied. His words—in the Apalachean tongue—were broken, though his voice was deep and clear. He recounted his deeds, and alluded to his offence in comparison; but the oldest men shook their heads, for the soldier never gave any reason for his neglect, or told whether he was absent or asleep, or how that shameful fate came to pass.

"He alluded to his wife, calling her by name, when a step without the ring drew all eyes in that direction. Yahchilane stood in front of her husband, as beautiful as a panther. She tore off from her soldier an embroidered sash, which is worn by the married women of the tribe to support their infants at their back, and which is the distinguishing badge of the matron among the Apalacheans, and tossing it in the circle, it fell at the feet of her husband. She never said a word, but her steady eye was on the Spaniard, and it did not fail in its effect, for a tremor passed over his frame, so that the links in his mail rattled together; and all the chiefs and all the tribe knew that Yahchilane renounced her husband.

"There was no more doubt in the council. Ortez was condemned to death at daylight, and was led away to confinement.

"The council fire had burned low in the village, and the few smouldering brands gleamed among the ashes, or sputtered brief jets of flame and smoke, like the smouldering passions that tossed the sleepers strewn around in the open cabins, still dreaming of the stirring events of the day. The sentinels by the fort walked backward and forward, or leaned on their lances tipped with the spikes of deer's horn, tasting in anticipation the savage pleasures of the execution of the coming morn. The young moon had set, and millions of frogs and peepers in the marsh filled the air with their shrill calls, and forewarned the rain that was coming up with the easterly wind. Masses of damp fog rolled in from the sea, and left the palisades of the fort, and the zizania grass that grew from the water at its side, wet with their soggy breath. It was drawing toward morning.

"Within the adobe cell of the fort the condemned man sat on the ground; and if a man's mind is ever occupied with his coming destiny, he must have pictured the approaching execution, of which he was to be the victim. The stake and the fagot, the red-hot brand, the pricking reed, the scalping-knife, the gauntlet, the jeer and the death-song, had all been familiar to him in his short episode of Indian life. If the southern savage was of gentler mien and comelier appearance; if his women were fairer in face, and more lustrous in eye, than their more northern tribes, they were in no wise inferior in their ferocity of punishment to their prisoners. Even the Spanish Inquisition was not more refined in cruelty. Well might Ortez ponder his death, and mumble long-forgotten fragments of Latin prayers.

"There was another in the Indian town who kept vigil that night.

"Yahchilane, the daughter of the cacique, who had been loved by many in her tribe before the hated name of Spain was heard—she who had saved the prisoner's life—who had taken him from death to be her lord and chief in the land—who had cradled his head on her bosom—who had borne him sons—who had been deceived and slighted—who had risen in her wrongs, and condemned to death the mistress and the husband—she, the fierce, proud, vindictive heart, and woman withal, through the moonlight and the fog, roamed and wrestled with her inner self. There was no prouder blood from Natchez to Honda Keys; and for four-and-twenty hours it had coursed through her veins like rivers of fire. Had she met her husband and the native girl together, she would have slain them both. When she saw his blood flowing from his wounded arm in the council ring, she sorrowed only that she had not made the wound from which it flowed. Had the council acquitted the prisoner she would have tracked him like a hound; and now her wild delight made her fevered step carry her to and fro, like the panther that sweeps his tail while watching to leap. Down by the fort she went, and away on the point, wading into the watergrass, until she seemed like the Naiad that lives under the sea. Then she walked back again with a long, elastic step, eyeing the palisades and the sentinels, her kirtle draggled by the dew, the long plumes in her hair broken on her shoulders, and her symmetrical limbs cut by the sword grass. Another turn would take her to the lagoon, where she had watched her husband's trysting, and then again she flitted through the plum-trees, where still a dark stain lay on the grass. So back and forth stalks a tiger-cat, when the spring water intrudes on the island where she has dropped her young.

"The night gradually passed away. The big wave that the Southern tribe declares comes landward when the god of night turns to go back in the sea, had broken along the shore with a hollow roar, and the marsh rosemary had turned its petals to the east to await the rising sun.

"Yahchilane noted these tokens of the hours. She had taught them all to Ortez, and they had heeded them many a night when fishing in the lagoons. He had narrated for her the legends of Spain, and the wild Moorish pranks that haunted the old towers of his native town, when the chimes told midnight. She had plumed for him his arrows, and softened his tongue to the liquid accents of her language; and he in exchange had sung her fairy tales, and drawn on the sand the outlines of great houses and sailing ships. He was a handsome man. How his moustache curled over his chain mail! How he took the arrows and gave the blows in battle! How proud she had been at village galas! How sad at distant forays! How her heart had yearned to him in that second love, when his child had tugged at her breast, and they three had laughed together!

"Sad thoughts these to the bitter woman, and she stopped in her walk, and leaned against the palm-trees.

"Yell, and curse, and seething iron probed in the quivering muscles, while the naked wretch feels the licking flame.

"Ha! had he not slept in her arms many a night and day? And up and on dashes the tortured wife, balancing her hate, that was of her race, with her heart, that was of her common motherhood. And the hours waned, and sick and hot the wind came in, and the odour of the honeysuckle and the water-lily were oppressive to the senses.

"Chatte Echo, the Red Deer, was a young chief of the Apalaches, of a noble name, and tried courage. In Chatte Echo's cabin hung the skins of ten panthers, and behind his house stretched a field of maize and melons that was smaller in size than none but the cacique's. This warrior had loved Yahchilane; but when Ortez came to Apalache, his suit was discarded; and ever since then he had remained unmated. He had always been an enemy to Ortez, and was now one of the sentinels that watched over him in prison.

Posted on the side toward the sea, from the low rampart where he stood he could look out on the water and down into the inner fort where Ortez sat. A proud man was he that night, and none in all the band would guard the prisoner surer. As he was leaning on his spear and thinking of his revenge, a canoe floated up from the water, and among the bending reeds. It came so whist the sentinel did not hear it, and the fog was so heavy that he did not see it until it touched the wall, and an Indian woman stepped on to the parapet. Chatte Echo would have struck at her with his spear, but she seized his arm, and, bringing her face close to his, he recognised Yahchilane.

"A moment's pause followed this strange interview. She seemed to be studying him; and he was wondering at her. Had she attempted force, he would have called; but her pleading look kept him silent. A little of the old love seemed softening his eye, and the touch of her hand thrilled his arm.

" 'Chatte Echo, you have my husband here, let him go.' Her voice was low and inquiring.

" 'Sooner a wild cat when I had my arrow drawn to shoot,' replied the warrior in a bitter tone.

" 'He shall flee us, and will trouble you no more.'

" 'He can trouble me no more than a few hours if he stays.'

" 'You refuse me this, and you will be my enemy.'

" 'I am your enemy now,' said the warrior gloomily.

" 'No, Chatte Echo; you are my friend,' whispered the Indian woman, in her lowest tone, laying her arm on his shoulder.

"The chief's voice trembled, as he replied: 'Where will be your friendship when you get your lover back?'

" 'Ha! he is no lover to me!' said the woman, in her quick, fierce mood. 'Listen, boy; that brave is a wolf—yet he must not die—I do not love him—he is no more of mine—let him go, and he will flee, and—Chatte Echo, I will love you. Refuse me this, and I will hate you. No one will know it—he will take that canoe, and go without a trace, and the dawn will find him leagues away. Say it quickly, chief; for the air is grey, and the gulls are going seaward.'

"There was a hesitation in the warrior's eye, and doubt and hope, love and hate, chased each other over his tawny face like the fog-clouds that were scudding by.

" 'How will I know your face will be the same to-morrow?' he inquired doubtingly; 'the doe may flee with the buck.'

" 'Keep me here—take me now—I am yours, Chatte Echo!'

"The wild light lit up the coal-black eyes of the brave, and the prisoner was free. Ortez silently hurried out of his cell, and stepped on the low rampart, saved once more. He saw his wife, and recognised her as the means of his deliverance, and, with the quick perception of a reckless adventurer, accepted the chance without a word. He stood in the canoe, with the paddle in his hand, and awaited, for his wife to enter with him, while the young chief stood by her side at the water's edge. She leaned down to speak with her husband, and her voice, necessarily low, was so distinct that not a word was lost.

" 'Sail south to Macaco's land in the Great Bay—stop not for your life, and tell Macaco who sent you.' Then, in a lower and a harsher tone, she continued: 'The canoe you are in carried your mistress to see you at the grave last night. She is dead now—stabbed while her lips were yet wet with your kisses. Go, hound of a Spaniard, or I may stab you too.' The last words were fairly hissed by the woman, the old tide of hate welling high and fast as she saw the Spaniard safe again. Ortez's countenance blanched under the swarth of years. Chatte Echo gave the light canoe an impetus with his foot, and shoved it out into the lagoon. Her eyes followed the spot where it disappeared, her outstretched arm trembled, she staggered and fell into the arms of the young chief, who carried her into the fort. He had won her."

"I don't like that story, father; it gives a low ideal of woman."

"But, child, remember it is savage woman that I tell of; you can't paint a crow green."

"How much is true?" asked the literal Doctor.

"Is it not all written," answered the narrator, "in the faithful annals of Garcilasso de la Vega?"

The Battue on Bonda Key

"The stout Earl of Northumberland
A vow to God did make,
His pleasure in the Scottish woods
Three summer days to take."
—*Chevy Chase*

AS THE OUITHLACOUCHEE RIVER EMERGES from the bayous, lakes, swamps, and drowned lands, which it has drained for many a square league, and reaches the salt water, it widens its bed, and harassed by the heavy beat of the sea, deposits its accumulation of vegetable matter with the sands of the ocean in little islands, that are presently covered with the rankest vegetation. There grows the cane like a gigantic grass, and the cabbage palmetto there rears its huge, twisting, bayonet-bristling trunk like the fanciful verdure of Utopian land. Sometimes these islands are based on the conglomerate shells, and are as stable as the main land, but again they are the mere accumulations of floating vegetable matter, rank weeds, and decaying rafts of trees, lashed together by sea-weeds and clamping vines, and resembling those floating gardens that the ingenious Celestials moor in the rivers of China. The aquatic plants and nameless vines cover them with festoons, and a large shoot striking down in the water anchors the raft, which will float hither and thither by the wind, closing or opening some water passage, to the great discomfiture of the bewildered explorer.

Beyond these ranker islets, and acting as outer piers or breakwaters to the still inner bays, lie other islands in long coral reefs, covered by sea grass and a smaller growth of trees, and washed on their outer sides by the surf of the Gulf. All of them abound in game of every kind, the fame of which led our party of hunters with our hosts for a few days' hunting and sporting, bringing tents, dogs, and servants enough to beat up all the woods on the Gulf Coast. These species of hunts are frequent in the Southern States,

110

where time is not regarded with the monetary eye to value with which it is measured in Doctor Franklin's proverbs, and where an ample range of unclaimed ground is open to all that choose to come and enjoy it. Such hunts are called marooning, and we were marooners as soon as we had reached the low sandy shore of Bonda Key, and pitched the two white tents that formed our travelling homes.

One hut was occupied by Poke, Jackson, and myself, the other by Lou Jackson and her girl Rosa, a bright negress of the same age as her mistress, and around the big fire a large row of screens of blankets or evergreen branches sheltered the dozen negroes that constituted our party. As to Mike, he always preferred to carry up his canoe, and elevating the side next to the fire on a stick, would crawl under it and sleep like an alligator.

In many respects our camp was more orderly than the plantation house we had left. There were no sheep to tinkle and bleat away the hours of the night, reminding you of your bed in the Tyrolean châlet, with all the herds stabled beneath you. There were no young negroes constantly disputing or tumbling under your feet; there was no Aunty Blase tyrannising over your culinary department, and ordering around all the boys within reach. But we still had one nuisance, in the shape of dogs—

> "Both mongrel puppy, whelp and hound,
> And curs of low degree"—

melodious hounds that bayed at the moon; sullen dogs that snapped at your heels; insinuating dogs that crept under your tent and into your arms when you are half asleep; spiteful dogs, with their voices attuned to the sharpest chords, "fit for treason, stratagems, and spoils." All this mongrel herd had been kept in peace at home; some were quartered away from the house, some were chained, and others meditative and sleepy. But here, as sure as pleasant harmonies came over the soul, and the hush of sleep fell on the camp, and the loudest sound abroad was the squeaking bat and droning sea, some canine tyrant would infringe the etiquette of the brotherhood, and immediately there would break out a fiendish turmoil of snarls, yells, bays, howls, growls, and yelps, intermingled with the babble of the negroes' voices and the whacking of sticks, and when fully awake, and you had seized your gun, or a paddle, determined on deeds of revenge, peace would be declared in a loud voice; in some such phrase as—

"Ketch you yowlin' again. Tink I'se got a stick here for nuttin', eh?"

Bonda Key was perchance half a mile in width at its widest part, and three miles in length, where we were encamped. The thickest growth of trees and shrubbery stood at our end, and near the outer side was a long pool of water, formed by the sea throwing up a bank of sand and leaving this isolated pond. The nearest land adjoining this island was at the two ends, the sides being bounded without by the open ocean, and within by the sheltered bay, which, dotted with islands of different sizes, extended to the broad mouth of the river and to the mainland.

Thus much for the geography of our temporary home; as to its geology, it might be said to be, in the words of Mike, "sand-some;" its botany was represented by sword-grass, palmetto, sea-wrack, some wild plums, and a few water-oaks and pines; by the pond the reeds and joint-grass grew very closely, and in the centre we could see a close tangle of vegetation, that would defy the best hunter in the land to crawl through. As to its conchology, I can only say that it produced excellent clams, and a kind of conch shell, that Scipio manufactured into a species of annoyance called a dinner-horn, and which, when blown, made all the dogs on the island howl. As to its zoology, man seemed absent, and every other created thing had its representative, particularly those classes that preyed on man, which seemed the more voracious from being so seldom gratified by visitors.

I am thus particular as to the peculiarities of this place, that the battue we adopted the morning after our arrival may be understood. On our arrival in the evening, the hounds had all been tied to prevent them coursing over the island, and the negroes had been restricted to a narrow range in the collection of firewood and fish so that nothing should be done to disturb the game that might be on the island.

The next morning, as we came out from our tents with the first grey light, the wind was still coming in from the land, laden with the flavour of marsh and magnolia; the negroes were poking together the half-burned brands, and preparing the breakfast in haste, or rather all the haste a negro ever assumes, and I plunged into the sea with the happy anticipation of a grand hunt, and all aglow to hear the first cry and ringing shot of the battue.

"Good-morning to you, Miss Jackson; you look like Diana this morning, in your canvas jacket and gown."

"And you look like a shipwrecked mariner, with your dripping locks, and jacket on your arm."

"Where's Mike?"

"Mars Mike's agwone off he shell on he back, like a gopher," said Scipio.

"There he comes; he has been around the head."

"How are you, Poke?"

"O—ho—hum—oh—ho—heo-o—hum!" yawned the Doctor, rubbing his eyes, as he staggered out of the tent.

"How are you?" I reiterated.

"Oh, ho!—there's one of those dogs named Music, I believe. I'd have his name changed after to-night. I didn't get a wink o' sleep."

"Hulloa, gentlemen, a pleasant day to you!" said Jackson, just protruding his head from the canvas. "You boys, hurry there with breakfast!" and with this general order, the head disappeared.

"Oh, oh! dear me! Break—breakfast—on thy cold, grey stones, oh! oh! sea—and I would that my tongue could utter"—

"Pete, you boy! pour some water on the Doctor to wake him; he's dreaming yet."

"You, Sam! tie up that Black Bess; she will be clean gone presently. Where is Sumpter?"

"Mars Jackson, Pomp say you's agwine to leff him shoot a gun to-day?"

"Go along with you!"

"Yah! yah! yah! I knowed de niggah lie!"

As the noise and hurry progressed, breakfast began to smoke on the fire, the boats were launched, and in a few minutes everything was ready for the chase, while a hearty breakfast of venison and fish was spread before us, and the sun arose in the woods on the shore, and his level beams trailed the smoking water, and painted the tops of the taller island trees with golden tassels.

The hunt was arranged by the dogs being led to the end of the island, not far from where we were camped, and thrown off, and all the party were to follow, as they came up, either on foot or in boats. One boat was to keep on each side of the island, close enough in-shore to shoot any game that might take to the beach; the rest of the hunters, with all the negroes, were to follow the dogs, and, keeping at equal distances apart, and to beat down the island, and thus drive before them everything that would run. As the chase progressed, it would come to the narrower portion of the island, and thus the men would come closer together just at the time when the game would be most anxious to turn back, so that they could form a barrier through which nothing could return.

After all had reached the point agreed upon, and taken their stations, Mike harangued them, telling them what should be done. Lou Jackson was in one boat, with Rosa to paddle; the Doctor in another, to guard the other side, and all the rest were to follow the hounds. Scipio had been sent at starting to the other end of the island, in a canoe, to lie close to the nearest shore, to head off anything that should attempt to cross to the main.

"Now remember!" said Poke to Jackson, just as the hounds were being loosened.

"What?"

"Thirty centuries look down upon you from those gum-trees."

"Shough! Go ahead all!" shouted Jackson, "and don't you boys bother the rabbits!"

The hounds were cast off, and with their noses high in the air coursed into the underbrush, and with yelp and cry the boisterous crew of coon-dogs and half-breeds rushed in their wake, while the negroes, each armed with a big cudgel and a heavy knife, with which to clear the vines, dashed off, yelping very much after the manner of their dogs, cheering on their particular favourites with endearing cries, and all were soon scattered out of sight in the dense undergrowth that succeeded the sandy ridges and level grass of the coast. From time to time, we could hear their shouting, and the crashing that was caused by their progress, and when within sound, many a rough joke and laugh came down the line.

I was nearest the inner channel, and close to the beach. Jackson was next to me, then Mike and the negroes all beyond, and toward the open sea. At first we could not see each other except at intervals where the woods opened, but as we advanced we came into a less tangled ground, and we could maintain a connected vision entirely across from one to another.

"Thar's deer," said Jackson, as we crossed the fresh tracks of one. "And thar's Beauty," continued he; "do you hear her?"

"No, I cannot tell one from another; they are all yelping, each on a different track."

A loud burst of voices from the negroes proclaimed something started.

"What's that, Mike?"

"Coon," answered Mike.

"No—thunder! it's a cat; see it come."

Grimalkin, however, did not like such a multitude of foes, and turning to the right, shot in under the underbush ahead of us, while two of the younger dogs came full cry on her heels.

"There's a coon—two of them!" I shouted.

"Out of the frying-pan into the fire, I think," said Jackson, as they ran into the same thicket the cat had taken to.

114

Here the bushes became so thick that I had to take my hunting-knife to cut my way and free my legs from the close binding of tenacious green vines that seemed stronger than packthread. We could hear the dogs on either side yelping and scudding hither and yon, and I at once saw the advantage of the mongrel pack we were using. They wound in and out of every corner, and under every fallen leaf where a hare could lie, yelping as poor puss started from her form, and only following her a few steps to pursue their researches in another cover.

Slowly we progressed, and after about two hours of labour had come down one half of the island, and had drawn so near together we could see each other. On calling down the line we had reported two deer as having been seen, and "some coon" with such a strong accent on *some,* that we were inclined to think that this particular game was very plentiful. Indeed, Scipio was seen with two hanging to his girdle. I could see, from time to time, Miss Lou's boat paddled by Rosa, and the young lady seated in the bow.

"What's that ahead?" shouted Jackson.

"Can't say, though it looks black," I replied, as some indistinct body rushed out from under some grape-vines, shaking down the fruit in showers.

"Yeow! yeow!—oohow!" chimed in two or three dogs in chorus, on some new and fresh scent, and Wag, who had been keeping very near me, dashed off to see.

"There's a buck,—look out!" said Jackson, firing.

"Never riz a hair!" called Mike, as the deer crashed on.

"Big buck! big buck!" called out the negroes beyond.

"Spang!"

"There goes Lou's gun," said Jackson. "What is she shooting? can you see?"

"Yes, a young buck."

"It's getting lively, Jackson."

"Wait a little, there's game here! Hear the boys sing."

The lively chant of the negroes sounded in the clear air, accompanied by the crashing of their sticks:

> "Wake 'em up dare!
> Waugh and a waugh da!
> Git out possum!
> Waugh da dey!"

"Da she goes," called a negro, as something bounded out of the bushes.

"What's that?"

"Big buck, sah, got horns like a dead tree."

"There's that cat again!"

Sure enough, the cat came spitting along, and dashed up a tree, sending down the bark in showers on the dogs that were close after her.

"Drap, you hussy!" said Mike, following her zig-zag course up the pine-tree with his rifle; and as she paused he sent a ball through her head, whizzing her down with a whirling motion as though she had been swung down by her tail.

"Git out, you dogs! Clare away, that's my cat!" he shouted, cuffing the dog aside, and taking possession of his prize.

"Kehunck! Kehunck!" There goes a blue heron, fanning the air with measured stroke. See him sail. He got up so slowly that one of the dogs jumped up at his long dangling legs.

"There go three deer altogether."

"Don't shoot the does, thar's no use," called out Mike.

There was only one buck, and three shots rang so close together we could not tell the report, but the buck fell over among his wives, who leaped ahead, sadly frightened. Mike cut his throat, and left his cat beside him to keep him company.

"There's that varmint again," shouted Jackson; "it's a panther!"

"Whar's a painter?" asked Mike.

"On ahead; we've seen him twice."

I heard the Doctor's voice from the other side of the island, and the quick repeated report of his double-barrel. Then a shot on our left.

"That's Lou again; push down to the beach there, will you?"

I came through the young willows that shut out the view, when I saw Lou gesticulating and pointing ahead, at the same time she was loading. I tried to see what it was, but could not, on account of the intervening bushes. She hurriedly rammed down the wad of shot with which she was provided, sewed up in muslin, and taking aim, fired again.

"A wolf!—look out—he is turning in the bushes."

I ran back just in time to see the animal attempting to sneak back, when, seeing me, he turned ahead, and ran on so quickly I could not shoot, though I saw by his track he was wounded.

At the place we had now reached, the island was not more than a quarter of a mile in width. The trees had ceased to grow, and only a few

116

copses of willow were found in the hollow between the ridges, and the tall grass that lined the pond. We could see the negroes away hither and thither, chasing the swamp raccoons that seemed to overrun the island, and striking at the hares that dodged hither and thither, and, escaping the men, were sure to run directly in the mouths of the dogs.

Ahead of us we could see the deer coursing over the knolls, hard pushed by the dogs, that had separated, and were each hunting on his own hook.

"There's Yowler and Music. Here they come—they are after the wolf. Hi, dogs! hi, dogs!" shouted Jackson, running to a knoll where he could overlook the chase.

The negroes yelled as they caught sight of the game and the wolf, availing himself of every copse and hollow, ran on, hard pushed by the dogs, and dodging on every side to avoid his numerous foes. Whenever he entered a thicket he remained there until the dogs were about entering the other side; then he dashed away with an angry snap of his jaws that sounded like the ring of metal. As he approached the farther shore, the Doctor saluted him with a double shot that stung him badly. He passed down the line of negroes, but there shouting and dancing deterred him from attempting to break their array.

"Now, Mike!"

"No, no; it is your turn; I've had a cat."

"Take him, Charlie!"

I levelled my rifle, and as he ran I fired. At the report he rolled over and over like a ball.

"Well done!" shouted Lou Jackson.

I thought him quite dead, but when the dogs came up where he fell, he turned around on his haunches and snapped at his pursuers with such effect that the foremost lost a piece from his shoulder as broad as my palm, leaving a ghastly wound. The dog turned away, yelling with pain. Wag, who was always in every scrape, received another nip, sufficient to put him on the sick list for the rest of the day, and doubtless some of the other dogs would have been hurt, had not Mike fired, and killed the wounded animal as the hounds came crowding up.

"Cat! cat!" "Yow! yow!" "Hit um a dip!" "Ough! ough!" were the sounds that came on the right, as a big cat broke away down the beach. The Doctor was just landing from his boat, and had a fair chance, as the animal was close by. The shot wounded the furious beast, so that it became completely confused, and, being hard pressed by the dogs, it took refuge in the only *trunk* it could see, which happened to be the high curve of the Doctor's cypress canoe, just landing end-on to the beach. In rushed the dogs after the animal, crowding the boat, knocking about the paddles, and forcing the Doctor up on the thwarts. The fierce animal fought with desperation against the crowd of pursuers, thrashing about the Doctor's legs, and tilting the boat from one side to the other, till it finally upset, and dogs, and oars, cat, and hunter were all thrown into the water together. It only needed a moment of open field, and the dogs, smarting with their scratches, tore the cat almost in pieces, and left the cat-skin, as one of the boys remarked who had run down to help the Doctor, "'bout chawed up."

Jackson and I did not like to leave our places to help in the fray, though we assisted all we could by laughing, and Miss Jackson called out, after vainly trying to peer over the land, to know what the matter was.

I explained how the Doctor had presided over the fight.

"The Colossus of Rhodes!" she answered back.

"I won't stand for a Colossus again," he replied, shoving off his boat, and resuming his paddle; "that miserable cat has scratched my legs bare!"

As our line advanced, we could see the end of the island that ran out in a long narrow bar. Hundreds of gulls and black-headed terns, with snow-white breasts, disturbed from the sands, were screaming over us, and cur-lews and plover wheeled in circles, uttering their plaintive cries. Crowds of merganser ducks that were sitting on the shingle, basking in the sun, rushed out to sea, piling up the water in front of them, and small birds took flight to the neighbouring islands, or flew high in the air to regain their accus-tomed haunts in the thickets. As some great seine that has enclosed a broad bay, at last contracts its semicircle toward the beach, exposing to the light the flashing fishes that in vain attempt to leap its cords, while the gulls and fish-hawks wait above, so our line closed up, the prey rushed hither and thither, the black heads of the negroes above the grass, like the floats on the net, bobbed up and down, and with shout and cry, the terrified animals made their last leaps and tricks for their lives.

The first thing that broke our line was a doe, with a fawn nearly grown. The doe was let past, but one of the negroes caught the fawn as it attempted to run by, and with a blow of his knife across the back of its neck felled it to the ground, before a voice could be raised to stop him. Then a doe was pulled down by the hounds, and a dozen dogs piled up over it, very brave when its resistance was overcome.

"There go two deer to the water; see the boats pull after them—the Doctor, and Lou, and Scipio in his canoe."

"Whoop! see the turkeys—I'll have a gobbler!" I said, firing at their leader, who spread out his wings and settled down into the grass, while the hens scattered in every direction, some taking wing and flying off to the mainland.

"Thar's a bear!"

"Where?"

"In those thorn-bushes."

"I don't see him."

At this moment, Scipio, who had been paddling after the deer, turned his canoe landward, shouting, "A bear! A bear!" and the dogs, that had been scattered about in the underbrush, made a fresh clamour, and rushed into the thorn-trees, from whence they came howling back, some of them with blood running from their shoulders.

"Who saw it?"

"I saw it," said the Doctor, hurrying in from his canoe at the first intimation of a bear, as did both of the other boats, letting the deer escape; "I know it was a bear."

"Fire your gun at him."

Lem was lying down flat on his face, trying to peep under the bushes, when the Doctor, at the suggestion, fired into the thicket. At the report of his gun, out rushed the animal, stung, probably, by the shot. So quick was his charge, that Lem did not have time to get out of the way, and was run over by the brute, as, dashing right through the midst of us, he hied away for the woods from which we had just come. There were too many crowded around, when he first came forth, to make it at all safe to shoot, and the moment he gained a little distance, his round stern presented a target as little vulnerable as the rump of a rhinoceros, as he ran with a lumbering gait, but with great speed, for his old haunts. But the hounds were soon after him, and as they came up they ran alongside, snapping at him without stopping him; then the smaller dogs came to their assistance, and seizing him behind, forced him to bay, which he did by standing on his hind legs, and making sweeps with his front paws at his pursuers. It was an amusing sight to see the dogs run, but still more so to see the negroes madly excited about the danger of their favourite curs, and yet cheering them on with cries, and grotesque denunciations and warnings.

"Now for it! Whose shot is it?"

"Let the Doctor try."

"I ain't loaded; wait a minute."

"Ho! ho! that's a good one! Jackson, shoot."

Without a word of parley, Jackson fired, and struck the mark, as we could see, for the animal flinched, and attempted to run, but there were too many dogs, and they brought him to bay again after running a dozen yards. I fired, and so did Mike, both together. The huge brute turned the way we stood, his eye gleamed a fierce glance of revenge, his jaw fell open, showing his long rows of white teeth, and then he sunk down a lifeless lump amid the ring of dogs.

"That air is rael murder!" said Mike.

As the heat of the chase subsided in my veins, I felt as if Mike's remark was true.

"Four hunters, twelve men, and forty dogs, against one bear!" called out Lou Jackson, who had been a spectator of the chase from her boat.

"I plead guilty to tyrannical oppression," said the Doctor; "deal gently with me."

"I fine you all one bear's skin, to be paid into the Court," she replied.

Bruin was dragged down to the beach, under the shade of a tree, and the men were sent back for the rest of the game that lay scattered about the route of our chase wherever they had fallen. On putting them together in a row, it was counted: one bear, one wolf, two wildcats, four deer, one wild turkey, one sand-hill crane, seven raccoons, and hares without number.

"Not a bad day's sport!" ejaculated the Doctor, standing with his feet wide apart, and his hands in the side-pockets of his shooting-jacket.

"How many did you shoot, Poke?"

"I think I shot all of them, for I fired at everything, only may be I did not kill; but I contend the sport is as good if you get the shots."

"What did you kill at your first shot, Lou?" inquired Jackson.

"That young buck. Don't you see my buck-shot? they are scattered over a hand's-breadth of distance."

"I fired at some ducks, getting up out of the pond," said the Doctor.

"What kind of ducks?"

"There's one of them," he replied, tugging at a mallard drake he had stowed in his pocket.

"Ha! I am glad to see that; he is one of the first of the winter migration. Wait for the big flights, and we will see sport. Come, boys, off with that wolf's skin, we don't want his carcass at the camp, and so with the bear, too, I reckon."

But the negroes pleaded for the bear's meat, and it was concluded to carry him to camp. So the boats were pulled up opposite the place where the game was lying; and while a couple of the negroes were skinning the gaunt-looking brutes the rest loaded the two canoes with the game, and when the wolf was disrobed, two negroes taking their places in the stern of the boat, gaily started on their return. We all followed the canoes, taking the line of the beach, laughing at the different accounts of the day's adventures, and the droll remarks of the men, who were in the greatest glee at the success of the hunt. The shore birds were running before us, or wheeling over our heads, and Lou Jackson was telling their names, and how their coming marked the progress of the year. The sands were hard and level, just rippled by the sea. The day was waning in that clearness of atmosphere and stillness of decay that marks the early fall, ere a leaf has dried enough to rustle. Mike's ugly faced seemed to draw a reflection from the season; Poke's laugh was as musical as the waters, and, wearied with the day's exertion, I scarcely knew how pleasantly the moments were falling, until now, when looking them over through the telescope of years.

CHAPTER 13

The History of an Old Friend

"The poor make no new friends,
But, oh they love the better
The few our Father sends."
                    —*Lady Dufferin*

THE NIGHT HAD DRAWN ITS CURTAINS when we reached our bivouac, but the fire made it day between the two white tents, where our supper was spread, and where, when supper was done, we stretched ourselves in dreamy mood, watching the embers glow and listening to the tale go round. It was my turn to tell a story, but being of a philosophical frame of mind I narrated a history, and was about to preface it with a few deprecatory remarks, when one of my auditors rudely cut me short by saying—

"Bang away; never mind the priming."

The following was the tale I told—It is THE HISTORY OF AN OLD FRIEND:—

There are some persons in this world of ours that are incorrectly estimated. They are not the talking people that boast themselves into our notice, nor the silent people that, with an air of profundity, impress us with their powers, while they repress all of ours. They are not the showy people, whose dress and equipage, house, wife, and watering-place dazzle us, nor the men in great places in the nation, nor the very pious men. They, perchance, are very plain folk, and don't obtrude. They are composed in manner, and simple in their words. You will not hear anything very bad of them, unless some fashionable person says it in her manner rather than her words, when alluding to them. If you know them, and you can't know them in a day, you will like them for ever.

Such characters are sometimes found in society, in the full sweep of restless, flattering, envious fashion, just endured, half forgotten, sometimes in literary life, sometimes toiling in some hard handicraft, where the gains they make are applied to those they love, sometimes in the wood, or by the sea-side village.

The friend of whom I am about to speak, and who belongs to this class, is oftenest seen by lakes, or the slow-moving streams of the woods. I deem it my duty, for many a lesson taught by him, and hours of quiet companionship, to speak in his behalf a kindly word, and save him and his family, as far as in me lies, from that unmerited neglect which seems to be the fate of the humble and the unobtrusive.

The friend to whom I allude is the Muskrat. Let no one smile at the name, or mock

"The short and simple annals of the poor."

His coat may not be of as many colours as a courtier's, but it covers a kindlier heart; his house may not be of as stately proportions as a banker's, but it shelters a more tranquil soul. Writers may have slighted him, school-boys may have pelted him, poets left his name unsung, and the boor may have sought to deride him by naming him Musquash and other opprobrious titles; but this is not the first time in the annals of the world a similar fate has overtaken modest worth. Pass by their crude opinions, and let us visit my friend.

Down by many a softly-purling brook, whose sinuosities have un-earthed the gnarled roots of oaks and hickories, and where the school-boy hastes from tasks to find a shady nooning, the Muskrat builds his nest. His selection of a home shows his cultivated taste, and gives a lesson to the more unobservant rustic. By the cloudy water that lies in the canals, that lead beneath the oaks, you may know his retreat. There he rests, while the day is warm, in the quiet enjoyment of his domestic pleasures, safe from pursuit in the winding galleries of his earthen fortress, but,

"When the sheep are in the fauld, and the kye at hame,
    And a' the world to sleep are gane,"

when the moonshine falls on bridge and reeds, and twinkling stars are floating on the water, then this gentle friend comes forth to view. You see him, with his keen eye and grave countenance, draw himself upon a root, and with careful fingers arrange his dress, wash his face, and smooth his whiskers. By his side sits a little picture of his sire—a tiny counterpart, that is destined one day to take his place among the reeds and by the bridge, and

124

rear the mimic dome upon the lake. After the parent has completed his toilet he gives one or two caressing touches to that of his young heir. A moment more they sit, eyeing the bubbles or floating nuts descending the stream, or watching, their faces reflected in the moonlight waters. Who can say that they do not appreciate the beauty of the night, or the soft murmuring music of the woods, or the fragrance of the air, laden with the odour of calamus buds and the breath of the birch and sassafras? Presently, diving down together, they disappear under the water, from whence, after a moment, they reappear, each with several muscles clasped to his breast by his fore paws, and, resuming their seats on the roots, they eat their food with the readiness of squirrels, casting the shells down at their feet, which fall on the pile of pearly bivalves that adorn the entrance to their home. Another pause follows, while they look up and down the brook.

Are they not comely in their dark-brown coat and black feet? Does not their soft hair, that sheds the water, and the strong flat tail that steers their course, befit well their pursuits? Do not their manners well become their place? Is it not true they are free from cares and inordinate greed—that they know their simple duties and enjoy them?

You say they are idle? Wait till you have seen their whole life.

Presently the father swims off on the water and across the brook. We may not see him go, for only his head is above the surface, and his tail floats like a rudder. By the wake in the water we may tell his course long after his round head is lost to view, and his child is following him close behind. They are bound for the low reeds on the other shore. There the calamus lifts its waving wands and spicy buds, while beyond the water-pad's broad leaf floats on the surface, and their white and yellow lilies stud the waters, and from the sandy edge of the channel the osier's round tapering wand, the bayonet flags and the sedge grass appear above the tide and point the way the current flows. This is the playground of our friend. You may see him here when the moon is full, pulling the roots of the lilies, or the long eel-grass that is growing beneath. You can hear his quick splash and dive, and, by the rattle of the cat-tails and the shaking out of their floss, you know he is off chasing the wild duck's brood that intrude on his gardens. On the shore his paths are running hither and thither, wherever a better grass can be found, or the seeds of grain that have come down with the freshets have taken root, and on these grounds which he is often compelled to cross, a deep hole is dug down to the water, and connects with the brook, through which he will take refuge if disturbed. At length, when the morning star shines dead, and the cock's loud clarion comes from the farm, the provident botanist bears away for his home, with his arms full of grass and roots to lay up for a day of need.

It often occurs that my friend has selected for his residence, being allured by the wild beauty of the scene, some lake whose shores do not present suitable accommodations for shelter. Either they are so rocky as not to be pierced, or they are so low as to be liable to be submerged with the spring rains. No more discriminating judge of the security of such shores can be found than my friend. No scenery fitness will tempt him. If there is any liability of danger on shore he goes out to the centre of the lake, or to a point in the lake from which he can readily obtain good grass, and there he builds himself a house. Sometimes he takes the end of a half-submerged log as a proper foundation. At other times the bottom of the pond, and yet again he will take a mass of weeds as an anchor, and construct on this slight support a house that is to last for years. His bricks are eel-grass and twigs; his mortar is mud and clay; he is his own architect, labourer, builder, contractor, and upholsterer. Gradually the house progresses, without shaped like a dome, and within divided into many chambers. The door is beneath the waters, and so nothing but a diver can enter it, and being built on the open water, and at a distance from shore, nothing will attack it from above. It is formed and fashioned with a precision that no science can excel. In and out is the strong eel-grass woven, and the clay that covers the walls is patted down with many a thwack from his paw until it is as smooth as a plaster wall. At length winter comes and bridges the lake, and makes an easy access to the house for the wolf and the bear. How is the Muskrat to save himself from their snuffing nose and strong claws? The careful student of nature swims the first freezing night by the side of his house, and ever and anon with his tail spatters the water over the dome, until finally the house is massed in ice so thick that none but the summer can break it. Within, in his goodly chamber, lined with the river grass, the plumage of ducks, and the soft floss of the silkweed, my friend lies with his wife, safe from enemies, from want, and from cold, and reads me a lesson of skill and providence I have not yet followed.

In some lakes a hundred of these little domes appear rising about three feet from the water, and resembling an Indian village. When the nights are still in autumn, the inhabitants of this modern Venice will be found floating about on the lake, chasing each other around the houses, or playing tag on the open water. They lie on the surface, with their tails slightly arched, which is a sign of watchfulness, and by a quick motion will disappear so suddenly that even the hunter's shot is ineffectual to stop them. One old beadle will now and then be seen mounting one of the houses, and with an august dignity survey the surrounding shores and when well satisfied, will dive down so softly as not to leave a ripple; but if, perchance, he should see some cause of alarm, he leaps back with an angry splash, and the whole tribe disappear in an instant. Should you be tempted to fire a gun at some impudent member of the colony, before the bright flash has faded along the shore, every one will have disappeared from view. You may wait hours for another shot, and though the pond is full of them, you will never see one. Once in a while an old sentinel will float to the surface, and the point of his nose, about the size of a chestnut, will be exposed, while he breathes and takes a view, and after a moment of watchfulness, it will be so quietly withdrawn that even if you see it you will not suspect it to be one of your prey.

A long time ago—I remember the woods and the waters were very bright in colour then, for I was a boy—there lived a bachelor Muskrat in a small pond not far from my home. After watching him some evenings, I set a trap to catch him, baited with a rosy Spitzenberg. Early in the morning I was at the pond; the trap was sprung, and peering into it through a small hole bored in the end, I saw crouched in the corner an animal with long whiskers and bright eyes, that appeared to my happy vision as big as a polar bear, but by the musky smell I knew it was my friend the Muskrat. If the woods and waters were bright the night before, they glowed with fire now, and the sun rose in the east. I carried my prize home in the trap, and tying a string to his leg, after getting somewhat bitten in the operation, secured him in the shed, and tried to tame him, but quite unsuccessfully. He refused to eat apples or cake, though always ready for a piece of my finger. When I could watch my captive no longer, I went to bed to dream of him, while he, cutting the string with his sharp incisors, gnawed a hole in the door of the shed, and made his escape. I followed his track the next day in the light snow that lay on the ground, and it led in a straight line to the pond from whence he came. I set my trap again, but though I tempted him with the rosiest of apples, he was never induced to enter. At this time the pond in which he resided froze over, and gave me an opportunity of getting out to the centre, where he had built for himself a dome as classically correct as the Pantheon. I confided my secret to a comrade, and we consulted an old work on the Northwest Fur Trade, and there learned the Indian manner of catching these animals. We accordingly provided ourselves with a small net, and going down to the pond with a pickaxe, when school was out, we commenced a regular siege. First we cut four holes in the ice, at opposite sides of, and close by the house; then with bent sticks pushed the corners of the net through the holes, and my comrade fastened them at the four corners, thus stretching the net beneath the house in such a manner as to prevent the animal diving down in the water. By the time this advance had been effected it began to grow dark, so I hastily with my pickaxe cut a hole in the top of the house and looked in. There was nothing there but the materials for a warm bed, that had been occupied not long since. I pulled away the partition that divided the interior, but could see nothing. I put my hand in to feel, and was rewarded with a gripe from an admirable set of incisors that have left their impress on my hand to this day, and pulling out my arm, I pulled out my captive of the night before, who immediately, amid the laughter of my unsympathising friend, scampered to the shore, where the ice had left an open margin of water, and dived beyond pursuit.

This bold burglary on our part evidently caused alarm and uncertainty in the mind of the proprietor of the house. For the next morning, when I returned with an eel-spear, intent on warlike deeds, I found that, after putting a few armfuls of mud on the broken dome, his ratship had changed his mind, and, leaving the house altogether, had made his exodus to a safer land, under the waters of a neighbouring stream, to which I followed his trail, and where I trust he still lives, undisturbed by marauding boys.

The Muskrat is no noisy roisterer. His ways are gentleness, and he only frequents the most placid scenes. He abhors the noisy rapids of the river, the clank of the wheel, or the fashionable highway, but where the stream has the softest tone, where the birch droops lowest, where the leaves in autumn lay in yellow and crimson wreaths upon the eddy, and the fish-hawk from his eminence can scarcely see the perch that turns his golden bars to the sunlight, so hid in foliage moves the water, there my friend finds a favourite bank, and may be seen, even in the day-time, plying his busy feet, or mounting some stone or slanting root to view the disrobing year.

To this unfrequented place, when troubled by cares that oppress, or those greater cares that may oppress, I often come to hold counsel with my friend. I hear the waters croon, the leaves whisper, the wood-thrush warble his low chant, and I forget to listen to that inner voice complaining. I see the bold plunge of the kingfisher diving for his prey; bright eyes are peering at me from bush and hole, cautiously at first, familiarly afterward; the leafy vault above me dazzles the eye with a confused motion of waning, glimmering brightness, and catches of sunshine come and go athwart the foam and on the flowers, and I do not see the cold hard faces that were staring at me but now. I drink the water, smell the odour of the moss, I lean my face against the cool beech trunk; every sense is drinking in the religion of nature, and the soul, forgetting itself, goes up in the million-coloured, million-formed works of creation, through their instincts, their changes, and their birth, to that pervading Essence that made them all and guides them all, and placed me among them all—a very little thing in this wonderful place. And then comes forth the Muskrat; he swims out to an apple tossed in the stream, and, smelling it in an instant, takes it in his mouth, and bears it away to yonder stone. He sees you now; a moment's pause; he is watching you; perchance he sees that softening heart that has come over you with the teachings of the hour, and does not fear you. He goes on munching his apple, while his whiskers move up and down with every movement of his grave cheek. His keen eyes wink with satisfaction. When he has finished his meal he passes his hand over his face, and dresses his robe a moment. He looks up the stream and down, but there is nothing there save a flock of wood-duck, halting for a day on their southern migration. He looks at you; do you see his contentment, his happy face, his honest ways—enough of labour to provide him a home—enough of leisure to learn the world his God has made? He moves into the water, and, bowing low his head to his now cheerful friend, he bids the day and you good-night.

When I had finished my history, I looked around upon my auditors, and found they were all asleep.

CHAPTER 14

The Drowned Lands

"Seekest thou the plashy brink
    Of weedy lake, or marge of river wide,
Or where the rocking billows rise and sink
    On the chafed ocean's side?

      *   *   *   *   *

"And soon thy toil shall end,
    Soon shalt thou find a summer home and rest,
And scream among thy fellows—reeds shall bend
    Soon o'er thy sheltered nest."

—*Bryant*

FOR SOME TIME PAST, on the mainland, we had been noticing the signs of the departing year, and at Bonda Key these indications became more marked and numerous. The air had not lost its balsam or the leaf its colour, yet there were other shadows on nature's dial slighter in appearance, but as true in reality. The ear missed the whir in the evening air of those summer insects, whose short lives had already terminated. The eye saw a clearness in the atmosphere that brought objects several miles distant apparently near at hand, and sometimes elevated them above the horizon. Some birds that wore in summer the livery of a rainbow had apparelled themselves in plainer garments, and from day to day new arrivals among migratory tribes of the air would recall the mind to those northern hills where the jagged pine and lichened rock were already grey with the first flurry of snow. We were all standing one morning at the "creak o' day," on the island, watching the first effects of the sun before its rising, and noting the little indications of the progress nature had made during the night. Thus travellers at sea will come forth early in the morning, and for a few minutes scan the ocean and

130

ship, and note the bearings and the winds before they turn to the regular thoughts and occupations of the day.

"See those ducks coming?" said Jackson.

"Where?"

"Close by the mainland, sir, low down."

"Yes! they are coming this way, too."

"Teal," said Mike.

"How do you know that, Mike? have you seen that flock before?" asked the Doctor.

"By their flyin'; you couldn't throw a picayune edgeways through the flock."

The compact body of birds that seemed when first in view a fleck on the red sky, gradually extended in size until they swept high over our heads, with a sound like a strong wind in a pine wood, keeping well toward the outer side of the island.

"Jist think of them air critters bein' hatched among the icebergs!"

"But think of their all going back again next spring to the very spot they were born," replied Miss Jackson.

"I trust they all won't get the chance," said the Doctor, looking the way they went with covetous eyes.

"Wall, that's easy enough done with the chance they've got stuck up higher en a meetin' house, a-prospectin' over the country; they'd be booby birds to forgit their own trail. The rub was to 'eve done it the fust time, when it was all strange like."

"They are always piloted by some old bird that has been here before, I think," said Miss Jackson.

"How do you know that, Miss Wiseacre?"

"By seeing the flock come straight to some favourite feeding-ground, where they will always alight at nearly the same time every year. Now, had there been no old bird piloting them, they would have alit in open water, and found the feeding ground subsequently."

"I shot in a flock ones't in the spring-time and winged a young mallard duck," said Mike, pushing up his cap from his face, and spreading his arms out on the muzzle of his rifle. "I tuck the thing hum and penned it up with the tame ducks, and so I kept it all summer. When fall cum the diver ducks kim fust, and then a purty considerable show of teal, but he didn't scrape his foot to them or say a word. But airly one mornin' I heerd that duck settin' down by the bayou, quackin' away as ef he had the pip in his gizzard (there comes a row o' widgeon now). Wall, I couldn't see what 'twas that bothered him. I looked all around; et was comin' on mornin' like, and things out was quiet, and every minit or so he'd set up on end, and stickin' his bill up like a musket, would quack three or four times. As I looked I seen a tearin' big flock of mallards cum from the north, high up; they bore around when they got over the cabin, and presently landed down by the side of the wounded duck, and sich a goin' on and duckin' of heads and gabblin' you never heered in all your born days. It was all as plain as a bear's track. The wounded duck was waitin' for its friends; it knowed jist when it was time fur 'em to come to the very minit, and sot out there to stop them."

"And I presume the noises they made were mutual inquiries after friends and the compliments of the season," said the Doctor.

"Asking if there had been much ice in Baffin's Bay the past year," suggested Lou Jackson.

"There comes another flock," said Jackson, pointing to the horizon.

"Blue bills, there's a grist of 'em," said Mike.

"See how they swerve one way or another! Look how fast they grow in size! There must be ten thousand in that flock! All night they have been travelling and yet not weary!" exclaimed Miss Jackson as the flock came pressing on in a huge irregular shadow, soughing like the wind, and keeping straight south.

"Oh, you beauties!" ejaculated the Doctor, looking up at the passing mass of intelligent life overhead, with his mouth wide open and his body gradually leaning back to permit him to see as they passed, until his round little figure nearly lost its balance.

"Thou shalt not covet, Doctor."

"Mike, can we get some of them?"

"Reckon."

"I think there are a good many on the Drowned Lands," said Jackson; "they have been coming on pretty thick, lately."

"Let's try them. I don't think the Doctor will look earthward again, unless it is to shoot ducks."

A laugh followed, and the party being of one accord, it was arranged that we should spend the rest of the day in the marshes taking a supply of food to last till night. So we walked back to camp, Miss Jackson and the Doctor chatting away about some theory of the Doctor's upon the cause of the variation of the plumage of birds, which, like most theories, was all wrong. The moment our intentions for the day were announced the camp was in a hurry; the idlers bestirred themselves; guns were examined; boats

made ready; ammunition bags, that had not been used in a year, were over-
hauled and filled; and at length, when the sun arose, our breakfast was
ended, and four boats were all equipped and manned with two negroes
each, ready for the sportsmen. The boats were dug-out canoes, made by the
negroes from cypress logs, but their graceful shape and high sharp bow and
stern made them resemble the Indian bark canoe, or the Canadian pirogue.
Mike had his neatly arranged, and a soft tanned deer-skin was spread in the
stern. The negoes, with their sinewy arms and breasts bare, sat at the oars;
they were the handsomest negroes on the Jackson place, but would
generally run away to the woods when their master was off; so to obtain
some use out of them they were always taken along on the marooning
excursions. The boats lay with their sterns on the beach, waiting for Miss
Jackson. Her father took his seat and pushed off, calling out as he went—
"Come, Lou, hurry up! Who will you ride with?"
She stepped down to the water's edge and into the Doctor's boat. Push
off! Away they go, moving on the water like shadows, so little ripple do
they leave behind. The shore recedes, the camp-fire smoke lessens; Rose can
just be seen by the beach with her hands on her hips, watching the lessening
fleet; the hounds' complainings come fainter and fainter; islands are passed;
new vistas open to the eye with semi-tropical vegetation; gaudy birds on the
sandy points; low swathing mist in patches on the water, and no wind to
drift it away. How luxuriantly calm! The land seems all afloat!
Jackson was in the lead, and we all followed in a line after him.
Presently Mike's boat shoots ahead, a feather of spray at its prow, and the
sweat guttering on the foreheads of the oarsmen. Yowler's head was lying
over the edge of the canoe. Mike had a paddle in his hand, steering, and I
saw the deer-skin that had decorated the seat had been left behind.
"Where away?" called out Jackson, resting on his oars, as we rounded
a point where numerous openings and bays came to view, and the boats
glided together.
"Any way is beautiful enough," answered the Doctor, in the highest
tone of enjoyment, chanting away snatches of songs, and Lou Jackson join-
ing in the chorus.
"Hyah, you Scip, you pull a baby oar."
"Git out a de way dat air clam-boat!"

> "Row, brothers row,
> The stream runs fast."

"That song isn't true in fact or music either, Doctor."

"There goes Mike; he will show us the way."

"The old rat, he has stolen the march! Give way, boys! All together!" and the boats filing off followed in the wake of Mike, who was making for a level shore about two miles ahead, where the bushes grew so dense you could scarcely see the land. As we approached, we could see no passage beyond, and even Mike seemed uncertain, for he steered along the beach a hundred yards distant, examining carefully the bushes that grew close to the water, coloured with red hawberries, and spiked with cactus. Presently the prow of the hunter's canoe was turned shoreward; ours followed the leader. The boatmen bent to their work and the boats flew.

"Trail yer oars!" called out Mike.

The negroes threw their oars from the rowlocks, letting them float by the side of the boat. Mike's canoe dashed into the bushes and disappeared. Ours followed one after the other, and when we lifted our heads from the crouching position we were compelled to assume, the boats all lay floating together on a large lake completely land-locked, and cluttered up with reedy islands and bogs of coarse grass, with here and there an osier nodding among lily pads or floating scum.

With the first exclamation of delight there was a rush in the water at our side, and a couple of wood-ducks, that had been under the edge of the bushes, took wing so near us we could see their scarlet eyes and hear their piping cry; at the same instant came the pleasant and long remembered quack! quack! quack! of the black duck, as a dozen of these clergy of the marshes beat upward from the grass at our unexpected coming.

Two guns fired at the wood-ducks; but as usual when in a hurry, there was not a bird killed, though a dozen or more arose from neighbouring shelters at the cannonade, and after one or two circuits settled down in the grass beyond.

"O Doctor, how could you miss that beautiful drake! I will shoot the next one myself," said Miss Jackson.

"You see," replied the Doctor, rather humbly, "they were too near when I first fired."

"And when you next fired, they were too far away," said Miss Jackson.

"*You* need not say anything," said the Doctor. "Why didn't you kill some of those black ducks?"

"Gun hung fire."

"Pooh! what nonsense!"

"Come, no recriminations, load up!"

"How shall we shoot?"

"Each boat is to paddle its own way through the reeds, and shoot what rises, and so we will get a good many passing shots overhead. That's so, isn't it, Mike?"

"I reckon."

"How will we come together again?"

"Thar's an island clare up to the eend of this water, and it's got one cabbage-tree on it, I reether think the biggest cabbage-tree north of Tampa Bay. We might come together thar."

"Amen!" said the Doctor. "Now let's start. I am on warlike deeds intent."

"Quack! quack! quack!" sounded close by us, and one of those wayward ducks that sometimes, against all rules, skulks behind his comrades, got up near us. The Doctor was standing up at the time, and fired, but from the rocking of the unsteady canoe he missed, as before.

"What a shame, Doctor! I shall not ride with you."

"Try him, some one."

"He's too far away!" said Jackson, with his gun half way to his shoulder.

"Shoot him, Mike?" said Miss Jackson, turning to where the hunter sat in his canoe.

Mike passed the back of his hand across his forehead, as he was wont sometimes to do when in earnest, and raised his rifle to his shoulder. A second of pause, and the crack of the piece sounded. The duck had arisen perpendicularly until it had reached a height that gave it free passage over the reeds, and then taking its direction, was bearing away in a straight line, gradually decreasing in size as its velocity increased. At the report of Mike's rifle it fell over and over, striking the water with a splash, while in the air where it was flying one or two feathers floated away on the wind.

"Well done, that!" cried Jackson.

Lou said nothing, but her kindling eye rested on the marksman, while a smile lit her whole face, and the party separated for the hunt.

The Drowned Lands were formed by the sea banking up with a sandbar the outlet of a stream that ran through a low country. This natural dam flooded the lowlands on either side for several miles, and the soil being sandy, with a slight deposit of alluvial matter from the descending fresh waters, many varieties of grass and aquatic plants sprang up, and formed attractive food for the myriads of water-fowl that here passed the winters. Patches of cane grew on the marshy land not yet covered with water. Osiers and rushes sprung from the shallow water, and a long grass, with a tassel like the onion, opened its crown and scattered its oily seeds over the water. Now and then a floating log, or some still living bulb that had come down the stream had taken root in the shallows, and formed an island, on which rose one or two trees, and a rank vegetation of vines and grass. On the dead upper limbs of these trees the ahnega and other species of cormorants could be seen all the day patiently watching for their prey in the shallows. Fancy could not picture a more suitable home for the water-fowl, whose food was abundant in the matted grass and succulent weeds, and who hid in bending rushes for better shelter from the northerly winds.

Up this extended marsh our boats gently floated, each one following the openings that seemed best, and diverging so as to form an extended front. The negroes shipped their long oars, and used only the paddle, in order to move with greater stillness, and to pass through the narrow openings. As we advanced, I soon lost sight of the other boats, but from time to time could tell their position from the report of their guns and the rising of the ducks they disturbed. I had changed positions with the men, taking the bow of the boat, and letting them paddle in the stern.

"Dar, Maussa, black duck!" whispered Scipio, after we had paddled a short distance, changing with a wave of his paddle the direction of the canoe, and pointing it toward a mass of reeds that lay twisted and broken together, as though some wind had twisted them off half way up.

I pointed my hand inquiringly to the reeds. Scipio nodded, and the boat floated noiselessly as a fish. We were close by them and no sign of the game, save a feather or two on the water. The neighbouring tufts of grass shut out the wind, and it was warm and still, like summer in the grassy bower, while bright little fish darted aside on either bow of the boat. Then came a flopping sound, a rattle of the reeds, and a brazen cry that so many thousand times, in a thousand hearts, has sent the blood leaping with its memory-haunted tone, "Qua-ack! qua-ack! quack!" Some notes in this world are clearer, and some more rhythmic, but there are few that when repeated will so picture to the mind, in the twinkling of an eye, the extended reach of sedge, the downy reeds, glassy water, and young hopes, with which it is so associated.

With the alarm-cry two ducks broke forth, scattering the floss of the cat-tails in clouds about them, their long necks stretching out as though straining to be away. I aimed at the drake as he poised himself to bear away, and with the report of the piece he fell, head and wings pendent, with a splash on the water—a dead shot, I knew by the way he came down.

The duck had gained some distance by this time, going straight away. No fear of her escape; the success of my first shot gave me confidence, and I knew the power of the little Mullen gun I held at my shoulder. Canny John Mullen, in his grim little smithy in Ann Street, working away with his brogue and cunning hand—how often I have thanked him when he never knew it! "Quack! quack!" The sound was faint from the distance when I fired, but the duck rolled over and over, with its wings spinning, till it was lost to sight.

"Yah! ha! ya! Maussa; good shot. Did you ebber? Well, now, I gives up—dat beats dis child!"

We paddled on, and found the first duck dead, and the second with both wings broken, and easily secured. While loading, four ducks came flying over from the direction of the other boats. I hastily poured in some loose shot, and crouching down in the canoe, capped my gun, while I watched the birds approach, and when they were so near I could see the mottling on their breasts, arose suddenly to my feet. Scared by my sudden appearance, they breasted the air, swerving off to the right and left. Ho! what fair shots! I could have killed them with a pistol. The first barrel brought two, the second, one, and the other bird departed sadly frightened.

Thus we passed on, getting fair shots every fifty yards at small bunches of ducks that arose from the little lagoons, and an occasional long shot at some passing bird that had been frightened from his proper feeding-ground by the incursion of the hunters. The difficult shot was the one where the bird came directly toward you, and twenty yards or so overhead. The sportsman must then take his aim on the duck, and when it is within distance, jerk the gun forward and fire blindly. At the instant of firing the bird is not seen; no matter, practice makes perfect, and this is the killing shot. Another plan is to let the bird pass, and then shoot. This plan enables the marksman to see the bird at the instant of firing, as his aim is then under the bird. Either plan is good if it gets the bird.

At the same time that the game was abundant, the scenery through which its pursuit was leading us was strikingly peculiar. The level waste of sedge extended beyond the vision, waving in the wind. The constant opening and closing of watery passages, the little reed-locked lakes, the tortuous course we were obliged to follow, the sameness of the grouping of the reeds and little islets, repeated over and over again till the mind was all afloat as to locality and distance; the weird trees with their dead and naked arms, and the occasional mass of broken reeds and matted driftwood that in the summer had formed the alligator's lair, all contributed to impress the mind

with a feeling of strangeness and solitude. The wild birds, too, were un-
wontedly familiar in their demeanour. Marsh hens ran over the drifts before
the boat, and gulls came screaming around us.

About three miles from where we had entered the Drowned Lands, we
came to the edge of open water, and found a large lake. Before entering it, a
glance ahead showed the farther end of the pond literally covered with
ducks. It was impossible, being on the same level, to tell how many there
were, but there seemed acres of them. A hurried council was called to
decide how they were best approached, and after two or three plans had
been proposed, it was settled that we should try and paddle around on the
farther side of the pond so as to be near the flock, and then take our
chances of their coming over us, as they probably might when alarmed by
the firing in the other boats. So with much care as to the noise we might
make, and some self-control in not firing at single ducks that would rise
close by us, we ultimately got around the flock, so as to place them between
us and the other boats. We pulled our canoe into the thickest of the grass
that completely sheltered us, and from where I sat I could see the ducks
lying on the open water, moving hither and thither, and diving down for the
eel-grass below the surface. We recognised them as the same flock of teal
that came over at the early dawn. It was a beautiful thing to see so much
graceful life so bountifully supplied and protected by its own instincts in the
solitude.

Away down the marsh came the frequent boom! boom! of my comrades' guns, but it did not seem to interfere with the comfort of the ducks,
who still fed on, though keeping out of shot from where I sat. Soon the
report of the guns coming nearer caused the ducks to crowd together with
all their heads up. There was a long pause, and then a negro's voice
sounded close by: "Mars Jackson, mark!" followed by the clear ringing of a
double shot, and at the sound up went my flock of ducks. Three or four
arose first, and then the whole mass cleared the water; and the beating of
their wings on the surface was like a long-continued roll of thunder. I had
no conception, before they rose, of their multitude. It seemed as if they
could be counted by tens of thousands. When they had attained a sufficient
height to overlook the meadow, they wheeled like the line of an army, and
apparently catching sight of the other boats, came with the bright linings of
their wings turned to the sunlight, and their countless pinions, hurtling
through the air directly over the place where we were concealed. I had given
Scipio, as a reward of merit, the musket I had brought with me, directing
him to take his own time, and fire as he chose. He, however, could not wait

for the best shot, but fired as one wing of the army wheeled over us. The aim was not a bad one, for a dozen ducks fell at the shot, and several more at intervals came slanting down from the flock. The effect of this unexpected attack drove the wing of the flock into the main body, clustering them together in a compact mass, when I fired both barrels. My stronger shooting gun bored a hole through the black mass, and twenty-seven ducks fell on the open water, and two or three went down aslant into the reeds. Three and a half dozen ducks was the contribution that one flock made to our booty. I still looked longingly after them as they went floating around the horizon, like banks of minute flies that wave at midsummer from prominent points on the shores of great lakes, undulating with the wind. But they passed away in the dim horizon, probably being unwilling to make another trial of the Drowned Lands.

"Hulloah!"

"Hulloah!"

"How many birds?"

"Ah! plenty. Talk of hunting!" said the Doctor, "this is my hunter's paradise. A good boat to row you, and boys to pick up the game; no running yourself out of breath, or heavy pack on your back!" And the speaker took off his slouched hat, and rubbed his curly hair and shiny face with his handkerchief till it was all a-glow.

"How many ducks, Miss Jackson?"

"Oh! ten for me, I believe; but they are all beauties. Paddle up closer, boys, and let us see."

"Hulloah! where did you get all those? Great is Diana, but that is a pretty sight!" exclaimed the Doctor, leaning over to look at our ducks, that were neatly piled up on one of the seats, with their breasts up, and their heads hanging one way.

"These are out of the flock we saw come over to-day."

"I thought so; they just got up here, didn't they? It was a noble flock, blue-wings, all of them, not a green-wing among them."

"Oh! there are your ducks. Why, you only have ten altogether. Where are those you shot, Doctor?"

"Oh! I didn't care to shoot. Miss Lou, here, is a pupil of mine, and I like to let her try."

A suppressed nasal explosion from one of the boys in the Doctor's canoe informed me, if I had needed the information, that the Doctor was not a very true hand with the ducks, and that the lady was doing all the work.

"Well, there is Palm Tree Island, I presume, not a great way ahead. Is it time for lunch?"

"Yes, I think so," said Miss Jackson, "if appetite is any test."

"Try some cold tea," said I, extending the bottle of that refreshing hunter's beverage.

"Ah!" said she, after a long drink, "that is a spring in the desert."

"Let me try a little of that spring in the desert," said the Doctor.

"Not till you tell me one thing," said I, getting possession of my bottle. "How many shots have you missed?"

"Will you give me the tea, then?"

"Yes."

"Ten! Give us the tea."

"Ha! ha! you are looking at Miss Jackson when you should be at the ducks."

The boys took the direction of the palm-tree, and we paddled on together, getting up two or three birds. It was a pretty thing to see Lou Jackson shoot. She had a light double-barrelled gun, the same one she had used on the deer-hunt, and when the duck beat up to the level of the tall grass and poised for his flight, she fired with such accuracy that the bird generally fell in a shower of feathers, amid the Doctor's laughter and merry jokes. He did not pretend to shoot unless there were three or four ducks rising together, and then he generally followed their flight, with his gun to his shoulder, until, when a long way off, he would finally say, "Too far," and taking his gun down again, give a sigh of relief, and look around for some more game. On reaching the little island we found Mike was there before us, and the negroes had landed the provisions and prepared our simple meal. Yowler sat on the narrow beach, evidently more melancholy than usual at the unaccustomed nature of the sport, and seemed reflecting upon the worthlessness of birds as compared with deer and panthers. Wag ran around the limited extent of our land several times without anything but a solitary snipe that went "eskapeing" away, and then returned, to worry Yowler. Jackson soon came in with a couple of score of ducks, and we learned from him that the great body of the winter ducks had not yet come on. There were no geese or brant, and no red head, and he said, what was easily credible, that late in the year a good sportsman could kill four hundred ducks a day.

"But I will tell you what it is, I have seen English snipe flying over, and as we go home we will try some of those low islands outside, and get a dozen."

"Much walking?" suggested the Doctor.

"No; you can shoot from the boat."

"I believe I am somewhat of a shot on English snipe," said the Doctor. "I remember once killing a dozen."

"You didn't have Lou Jackson in the boat with you?" I replied.

"No; something a great deal worse—you were with me."

"No, never—not when you killed a dozen English snipe."

"Yes, I shot them all at one shot on the beach."

"Fudge! those were yellow-leg snipe."

"Maybe they were, but they were just as good."

"Doctor, try a piece of hot venison steak, or some cold bar?"

"No bear for me; I would be thinking all the time about his ugly teeth when he was shot."

"It is not *his* teeth, but my own, I am afraid of," said Miss Jackson, laughing; "give me some corn-bread, if you please, Mike."

"What are we to do with all these ducks?" said the Doctor; "we can never eat them."

"Yourn?" asked Mike.

A laugh.

"No, ours; those defunct, and those that are to be."

"Never fear, a camp of fourteen people requires something more than Indian corn."

"What are you toasting there before the fire, Mike?"

"Breast of crane."

"Let me try a piece?" asked Lou.

"Sartin; it's better en deer's meat," he replied, handing over a strip on the end of his toasting-stick.

"See de ducks!" exclaimed the negroes, less busy than we with their dinner, as a long train of ducks came floating over, pencilling the clear sky.

"Those are widgeon," said Jackson.

"How can you tell so far off, father?"

"By the shape of the flock, I think; I can hardly tell how. They would be black duck, if they were not lighter in complexion. Am I not right, Mike?"

"Reckon," replied Mike, following the passing cloud with his eye till they faded away, and then continued musingly: "Some takes kindly to that kind o' larnin'. Some kin tell what kind o' duck is comin' by the sound he makes beatin' the air. Thar was Picardo, Picardo Duck Legs he was called, because he had bow legs. Wall, that man lived in his canoe, and he could tell what a duck was a-goin' to do jist by the waggin' of his tail. He had lived on duck-meat so long he could smell a duck like a pinter dog. Thar's the natur' o' man; when God gives him a callin' he's bound to go it, or be a lazy cuss ever arterwards. Duck Legs was no a'count on shore, but it larnt a man somethin' to paddle a canoe with him."

"Come, boys," said Jackson, lighting his cigar, "it's high noon now, and there are seven miles from here to the open water, and seven more to Bonda Key, and two dozen snipe to kill on the way."

"And some more duck before we leave here," said the Doctor.

"Mind your bearings now, or we will get lost here. There is no palm-tree to row back to."

"Take the range of this palm-tree, and sunset; purty good marks, both on 'em," said Mike.

"All aboard!" cries the Doctor. "Push off!" and away the three boats went, leaving Mike watching our departure, smoking away at his cigarette, seemingly as unconscious as his hound that sat beside him.

There were some good shots made, as we returned, at the various bunches of ducks that were hid away in the close coverts of the reeds, Lou Jackson, in particular, firing well, although her gun was so light that the game though hit sometimes refused to come down. We were a good deal together, as we were paddling more to return than to get game, and only shot those birds we saw on our way. Once, while paddling fast, a wood-duck drake arose from an open pool, uttering his wheezing cry of "Oh hee! Oh hee!" as he stretched away. Lou fired, and at the shot he staggered and sunk for a moment, while a dozen feathers floated away, and then he rose again.

"Stop! stop!" she cried, as I raised my gun to shoot, "I hit him! I hit him!"

But the duck didn't fall, and continued his flight until lost in the distance.

"Oh, what a fool I was! I forgot all about I had another barrel! And why didn't I let you shoot? But I thought, to be sure, he would fall."

"Why didn't you shoot, Doctor?" I asked.

"Oh, I thought he would fall, too."

To kill ducks well, a twelve-bore gun should be loaded with four and a half drachms of powder to one ounce of shot. The general mistake is too much shot for the powder.

Sometimes we would come across a floating log surrounded by

feathers, and worn smooth by the tread of the wood-ducks that would sit here half the day pluming themselves by the mirror of the water. The hazel-breasted drakes here displayed their Tyrian plumage and elegant shapes to their dove-eyed consorts, and scolded away the little bitterns that alone could compare in beauty to themselves, and who alike with them inhabited these great morasses. We sometimes would float on one of those happy families, dozing away the sunny hours, and they would arise, when we were close upon them, in the greatest disorder. The ringing of a half dozen shots, the fall of the game, the shout and laugh, would end the scene, and break upon the stillness of the solitude with a burst of fun and activity all the wilder for being so rarely heard in the marshes.

We had almost reached the confine of the open water, when Jackson fired at a black duck flying overhead, and it fell in the water, wing-broken, and immediately dived. He commenced, with the assistance of the Doctor's boat, to look for the game, probing with his paddle the bunches of floating sedge near by, while I, lying a little farther off, was watching their search. While thus engaged, I happened to notice under the water a duck swimming toward the surface; it was the wounded duck trying to escape. Then his bill protruded from the water, the duck in the meantime keeping his head and body completely hidden. I leaned over my boat and caught the nose of the cunning fellow, bringing him above water amid the shouts of the negroes who witnessed the duck's ingenious trick.

Being joined by Mike, who had turned aside to get some roots with which to colour deer-skins, we all passed through the narrow outlet of the marsh, and turned toward the low islands, where it was said we could find snipe.

"Round that grape-vine point!" called out Jackson, as the headlands we had passed in the morning again opened to our view.

The paddles had been exchanged for oars, and with long, measured strokes, keeping time to the song of the oarsmen, the lithe boats skimmed the water toward the low islands Jackson had indicated to us. On reaching the shore we found the land was marshy and wet, and about half the area overgrown with flags, now blown down by the fall winds.

"Not a bad place, is it?" said Jackson, looking around the island.

"By no means; see these little red-scummed puddles, and bare spots of mud; they'd make a snipe's bill water."

"Escape! Escape!" shrieked a snipe, as he sprung into the air a few yards in front of us, tacking from side to side, and settling again on the further side of a little pond."

144

"There! I told you so! Hold on now till I draw my duck-shot. Lou, are you ready?"

"Ready as I will be. I am going to rely on the Doctor."

"I will take a little fine shot, then, number ten. I follow your lead, Jackson."

"Mike, are you ready?"

"Yes, I reckon, 'bout, though I don't see nothin' to shoot here."

"You just keep even, and we will see plenty to shoot. Send out your dog, Doctor."

"Hi on, Wag! Hi on!" but Wag seemed to suspect some trick under such unaccustomed attention, and skulked behind his master. The first step ahead sprung another snipe, and, being intent on the game, I shot it as it balanced.

"Hulloah! give a fellow time," said the Doctor.

"That bird flew right in the way of the shot!" said Mike, his eye kindling, and his mouth expressing doubt and curiosity.

"Have you ever killed a snipe, Lou?" said I, the formality of the family name having been gradually dropped on all sides as the freedom of our hunting excursions brought us into closer intimacy.

"Yes, two; I never had much opportunity for such game, and never learned to shoot them on the wing."

"Now is your chance, then; there goes a shot!"

Two barrels were discharged, one by Jackson, and one by the Doctor, but the birds went off.

"There, I know I can do as well as that," remarked Miss Jackson, looking at the bird skimming over the ground.

"I'm sure you kin," said Mike.

"Escape!" "Escape!" "Escape!" croaked out three birds, as they launched away from before us. Miss Jackson fired a double shot, and one bird fell.

"Well done, that!"

"Escape!" croaked another bird, as it rose on our left among some flags. Mike, who had been watching the hunt with great interest, ejaculated, "Wall, I'll take a turn now!" and, aiming with his rifle, fired. The bird fell as if knocked by a ball-bat, and Mike going on up to it said, as he lifted it up by its wings, "Knocked into a grease-spot!"

There was a universal laugh at the quaint figure of the hunter, in his buckskin suit, and the air of derision with which he picked up his fragment of a bird, and held it at arm's length.

"Wall, ef any body had told me that I would have ever gone a-birdin' with this ere old rifle, I would hev told that body he was a fool!"

Wag seemed to have got somewhat in the mood of hunting around, inspired by our shouts and firing, and ran about hither and yon, springing the birds up before us like a cocking spaniel.

"There!" called out the Doctor, as the dog got up another bird, "I told you that dog had a great deal of intelligence; this is the very first time, would you believe it, he has ever been hunted over snipe."

"I can certainly credit it, sir," answered Jackson drily, as he capped his gun.

Away went another snipe, right before the Doctor, who banged away with both barrels, and brought down the bird.

"Escape!" "Escape!" said two more snipe, flushing right by the Doctor. Bang! bang! sounded Jackson's gun and they both fell at the shot.

"Hold hard there, don't shoot over me that way; just think, I can't dodge!" cried the Doctor, waving his hand energetically toward us, as he sunk in a quagmire.

"That proves your valour in the face of danger. There's Scipio with a log. Now, altogether—that's it! Why, Doctor, you look as though you had high top-boots on!"

"Never mind, it is clean mud," he replied good-humouredly.

"Now we are all ready, let us form in a line, and beat down the island regularly," said Jackson, the ardour of the hunt awakening him from much of his listlessness. "Fall in, boys; one of you walk between each of the hunters."

The long, irregular line being formed, it stretched nearly across the island, and we advanced, sinking in the soft mud occasionally, but oftener finding a sandy bottom, with pools of water. The snipe were abundant; we could see them sometimes on the ground in couples, on which occasions the Doctor would always fire with pretty certain success. Most frequently they arose singly, uttering their peculiar harsh cry, and were tumbled over by one or other of the party before they had gone five yards, amid the shouts and guffaws of the negroes.

Lou shot well, after a little practice, and she trod over the flags, with her eye fixed ahead of her, with that earnestness of look that a person attains never so greatly as when watching for upspringing game that he feels confident he can hit.

"Mark!" called Scipio, as a snipe launched in the air from our feet, the brown and hazel paintings on his back glittering like soldiers' bayonets at

147

the charge. The first spring he makes seems to toss him twenty feet in the air, and then a pause, as he collects his wings to strike out on that erratic swinging motion that is his safety and beauty. He eyes the array of pursuers behind him, and hears their strange talking; he sees before him his accustomed haunts and oozy swales, and hears the rustling of the reeds that shelter his mates. In the pride of swiftness, rings out his exulting cry, the same that had made vocal the great morasses of the Coppermine River, where he was nested, and the same by which, through the ghostly night, in the upper air, from front to rear, had kept in rank the long flight of his kindred in their semi-annual migration—"Escape!"

Pang! rings the clear shot, and over falls the wild bird among the sedge.

"Golly! Missa Lou, yah! ha! he dead!" shouted one of the negroes. "Makes dis child picaninny agin fur to see young missus wake 'em up so!" said Big Sam.

"Mark! Mark!" "Escape!" "Escape!" Two more snipe sprung up, followed by two shots, and they fell ahead of us in the grass, and then there arose three or four together. The island seemed to be full of them, and when raised, they would dodge about in long irregular circles, calling up others from the grass, until they collected in whisps above us, and bore away to some adjoining islands.

It was difficult to keep the line regular, for the negroes were full of excitement in picking up wounded birds, and seeing others spring beside them. We needed no dogs, for every bird on the island was raised, and there was so little heavy grass we lost few dead ones. Occasionally we would start one of those heavy grey herons that frequent such marshes, flapping up heavily from the grass, and casting his keen eye back over his shoulder at the intruders; and twice we sprung that tiny prince of the heron tribe, the smallest and most beautiful of all the genus *Ardea,* called the Least Bittern in the books, but which the people sometimes name the Tiger Bittern, from his brindled coat and wild eye. We shot them both, and Lou, wrapping them carefully in her handkerchief for preserving, stowed them away in one of the pockets of her hunting-coat.

At last the point of the island was reached, and while the men were sent back for the boats we sat down on the beach and counted out thirty-six snipe. Taking some willow switches, we ran them through their bills, carefully smoothing down their ruffled plumage and washing off the occasional mud, and made as beautiful six bunches of game as ever delighted a fowler's eye. Even Mike consented to praise, with the reserving clause that we had wasted too much powder and shot on them. How graceful they looked beside the green-headed mallards and the dusky ducks that were piled knee-deep in the boats.

"A glorious day well spent," said Jackson, as the island on which we had been shooting dwindled in the water, red with the reflection of the sunset, and Bonda Key opened its headland of stately verdure.

"Ay, it is!" responded one and all; and the boats slid along the glassy waters side by side, the shadows fading and brightening with the glow of the sky, or the twilight of the shore, as one and then the other opened in the west. The hunters stretched their weary limbs in listless attitudes, and their heads swayed to the springing motion of the oar. Miss Jackson sat in the bottom, trailing her hands in the water on either side of the boat, while the oarsmen sang, with deep voices and perfect time, the old negro boat-song:

> "Gen'ral Jackson mighty man,
> Waugh my kingdom, fire away!
> Fought on sea, and fought on land,
> Waugh my kingdom, fire away!"

CHAPTER 15

The Skin of the Tiger-Cat

"A dragon's tail was flayed to warm
A headless maiden's heart."

A NUMBER OF DAYS FLEW BY at our island home in the simple pleasures narrated in our last chapters. The cheering cry of the hounds as they scoured the islands, the ringing shots in the marshes, now a long exploration in the canoes through the winding channels of the archipelago, and again some expedition to the uttermost keys, where the pelicans dressed themselves on the sandy points in lines like soldiers; and strange sea-birds excited our wonder and admiration, were the daily amusements of the party. Once in a while the members of the hunt would branch off, and while one party pursued the chase, another would make an excursion to the mainland, or fish in the rivers. The weather had been constantly clear. One cloudless day would follow another with an exhilarating yet motionless air, that seemed as if nature had exhausted her prodigality of production, and then, breathless, had paused to dream.

Once in a while Mike would disappear, and be gone for a day or a night, but as he never made any remark on what he saw or did, no one seemed to take any note of his incomings or outgoings. One evening, after he had returned from one of these lonely excursions, I was sitting by the willow copse on the shore, casting with my line into the channel after some large fish I had noticed were breaking the water near the shore. The negroes were getting supper ready, and Lou Jackson came walking down to the beach, where Mike joined her, and they came toward the boats on the other side of the willows, and so near I could hear their conversation.

"Miss Lou, I've been a-wantin' to see you."

A pause followed.

"That is, you don't see me every day."

"Yes, oh! yes; but then it aren't every time that a man wants to see—I

150

mean it aren't—I mean sometimes a man wants mighty bad to see some 'un, and talk to 'em, an' sometimes I want to see you more 'an others."

"Well!" said Miss Jackson, moving on slowly toward the boat-landing.

"End ef I was the Doctor, I could say anything, and talk right through a board fence; he's oncommon nice at talkin', he is," said Mike, looking earnestly at his partner's face, who looked seaward, but did not reply to this expression of opinion. "Thar's somethin' I want to say, Miss Lou," continued Mike, "end I'd a leetle reether say it to you than to any o' them folks there, for they wunt believe it, they wunt."

"Well, Mike, what is it?"

"Wall, it's this hyur; you'd better get yer father to quit that plantation of his, and move up the country a leetle, or else down to Tampa, fur things ain't all right 'bout hyur."

"What is there wrong?"

"Wall, there's somethin' wrong with them copper-head snakes, the Injins. Yer can't see it yet, but things ain't right, and yer all so far away from everybody at the house that no one kin help you. Yer negroes ain't worth nothin' of any, 'count in case of a scrimmage, and yer father ain't over-liked in the swamp. Thar's nothin' wrong yet, and maybe won't be at all, but they are jist like painters, and yer don't know where to find 'em."

"Why, what have you seen wrong?" said the young girl, stopping by her boat, and looking at Mike inquiringly.

"Nary a thing, only them fellers have been down here, and I don't like it."

"But they come to the house, why not here? You are harsh in your opinion of them."

"'Cause they have nothin' to call 'em here. They've been about without showin' themselves, and that's suspicious. They knew we were here, for they can see our trails all about, yet they didn't stop, and they tried to leave no trail themselves, and that's a bad sign. 'Twunt do any good to say so to your father, but you kin make him do what's safe, end so I tell you."

"Thank you, Mike. I believe you know better than any one about such things, but I do not believe father would leave now, and I can't make him without a stronger reason than you have given."

"Wall, look out; and the time to look out is jist when everything is on-commin pleasant, for that's the blind with these sarpents. Thar's somethin' else I want to say, Miss Lou," continued Mike, after a pause.

Miss Jackson looked at the hunter as though inquiring his wishes. She

151

leaned against the prow of the canoe that was hauled up on the beach, but did not say a word.

"Wall, I was goin' to say that—that—wall, thar hain't been many tiger-cats in Floridy, and ef thar hadn't been *any*, I reckon I would hev got that one fur you, fur you know that ef a man—ef a man likes anybody—as much as—"

Mike here made a long pause. Lou Jackson had gathered up her cloak from the boat that she had apparently come down for, and turning slowly toward the tents, seemed moving away.

"Don't go yet, Miss Lou," said the hunter beseechingly.

"I am in a great hurry," said the girl; which, if so, was the first time she had been in a hurry since coming to the island.

"Wait one minute," besought Mike, brushing his hand across his forehead; "here's the tiger-cat skin you once said you wanted," unfolding, as he spoke, from under his hunting-coat, the flowing robe of an animal gracefully patched with yellow and black. "It's tanned as soft as store-goods," he continued; "I shot it this day two weeks, and an Injin woman tanned it for me."

"Thank you, Mike; that is the prettiest skin I ever saw," leaning her face down until it was hidden in the glossy folds of the robe.

"Wall, it is; but I wish it was a heap purtier for you."

Miss Jackson moved on toward the camp slowly, but Mike stood with his hand leaning on the prow of the stranded boat. She had gone a few steps, when, conscious that he was not following, she said—

"Come and see how they will admire it at the camp; that is the greatest trophy of the year!"

"No, it isn't no trophy," said Mike, in an extenuating tone, not moving from his place; "it is the best I had to give you, Lou Jackson. I'd give you anything you asked fur." His deep voice quivered as he spoke.

"Thank you, Mike, thank you!" said Lou, turning hastily to the hunter and seizing his hand, "it is everything I want!" and then as hastily dropping it, as though frightened at her own eagerness, she walked rapidly toward the camp, bearing with her the skin, and leaving Mike standing by the boat, with his eyes fixed on her receding figure. His stalwart frame was bent, and with the breech of his rifle he ground a hole in the heavy sand. A dog, one of the wandering curs from the camp, coming to the water's edge, set up a doleful cry near him.

"Shut up, thar, or I'll send a ball after you, and let the bark all out the wrong way!" he said, and tossing his rifle in the hollow of his arm, strode away down the bay. The words that he had been pondering over, had remained all unspoken; the robe that he had taken, with leagues of walking and weeks of waiting, that he had ornamented with all the taste of the woods, had only procured him a moment's gratitude, and the bold heart was frightened into hesitation and silence by a young girl.

The sun had gone down, the shadows lengthened on the long sandy reaches; it grew dark almost in a moment. Mike disappeared in the dusk, while from the knoll where the fires were lighted Lou Jackson was watching the way he went.

CHAPTER 16

Supper

"La découverte d'un mets nouveau fait plus pour le bonheur du
genre humain que la découverte d'une étoile."

— *Brillat Savarin*

WHO IS THERE, accustomed to American rural scenery, that cannot remember the summons that calls to dinner at the country farm? A stout housewife, when the sun-dial points to noon, walks out on the lawn, among the inverted milk-pans, where lies the house-dog stretched under the locust trees, and, turning her face toward the harvest-field, gives a long winding blast on the horn that wakes the echoes down the orchard, and over the meadow, and all along the hills, calling the farmers to their noontide meal. The watch-dog howls at the summons, and the workmen in the sultry grain toss their cradles by and turn homeward, the heavy oxen saunter away in couples, and the horses are unhitched and fastened in the shade by the trough of corn. The farmer, with his stalwart sons, and "the hands," crowd into the kitchen, with their necks bare to the pleasant wind, and the sweat of their labours on their brow. The laugh is light, the words are gentle, for they are confined to the simple subjects of the crops, the weather, and the farm news. The goodwife is at the head of the table, and pours out the tea or milk; the daughters sit among the men, coming and going as occasion requires to bring water, or bread, or pie. Their attire is plain, their manners are simple and frank. Before the old man there is placed a huge dish of stew; it is made of potatoes, carrots, chicken, and large squares of boiled fat pork, and he helps it out with no niggard hand, and when he has finished his own portion, he quaffs a huge cup of cider, and leans back in his chair, with a great sigh of satisfaction, to wait till his youngest daughter, with brown hair and blue eyes, just opening into womanhood, brings his pie. The brass candlesticks on the mantel-piece are filled with asparagus boughs, the oaken floor is polished with scrubbing, and the tall clock in the passage-way strikes one as the meal is ended.

There is another dinner scene that may be as often remarked in America, and equally characteristic of another class of eaters. A bell rings, or a jangling gong shocks the ear, while five-and-forty men rush past the waiter that is beating his brazen drum, and sit down at a long hotel table. On it are spread various small articles of food or ornament, such as celery, oranges, and figs, which are immediately seized, and appropriated. Waiters hand every person a dish of soup, of that consistency that is supposed to be proper to nourish persons in the last stage of disease. In a moment after the soup dishes are snatched away, and the guest is informed he can have his selection from any one of almost every kind of beast that walks the earth, or fowl that flies the air. Being a temperate man, he orders roast beef, and in a moment is supplied with a large slice of overdone, brown roast beef, flooded with a light-coloured gravy, a small dish of potatoes is slammed on the table beside him, and a plate of maccaroni. He tries the potatoes, but finds them watery and filled with lumps; the beef—it is tasteless; the maccaroni, and streams of water run out of the pendent pipes as from a dis-connected engine hose. The bread is dry and cut in small oblong pieces. He wonders, and, if he is a stranger, looks at his neighbours to see what they are eating. The upper end of the board is occupied by ladies that have ef-fected their entrance by some side-door, and they are arrayed in the colours of the rainbow, and seem to be busy talking loudly and looking along the table. The long rows of gentlemen are busy, without the interchange of a word, eating rapidly of everything placed before them. While our guest is remarking these things, his plate is taken away by the waiter, and he notices the gentlemen are all eating dessert, or leaving the table, having finished their dinner. The waiter asks him what he will have for dessert. He demands to know what there is to have. The answer is given so rapidly, it sounds as follows:

"Ap' pi—pi'-p—mi' pi—ca' pi—rat' pi!"

The guest gets confused, mildly inquires if they have any fruit.

"Yes, sah. Apple-dumpling, sah."

"Very well; I will take an apple-dumpling."

"Hard or soft, sah?" referring to the sauce.

"Oh, soft, of course;" referring to the dumpling.

The dumpling is dashed down in front of him, as hard as a cocoa-nut, and flooded in soft sauce, while the waiter disappears down the table, gathering up the plates with a clatter, and the room is deserted.

Once more an American table looms up through the mist of hungry years. A low frame-house, with a porch half covered with the trailing arms of morning-glories and columbines, stands on a knoll of a western prairie. That prairie is browsed by deer, and game birds of the choicest kind feed on it in millions. The river winds along the valley, teeming with fish, its banks margined with water-cresses and dock, and shaded with plum-trees and fruit-bearing vines, while from his cabin door the settler can see a hundred cattle cropping the wild grass.

Noon-time arrives, and the head of the house comes in from the ploughing to his meal, and finds the same food that was spread before him at breakfast, and that he will have for his supper, and has had at all his meals for years past. It consists of tea, Indian corn bread, and fried pork. The pork is cut in small slices, and fried until quite brown, and the bread is sopped in the gravy. There is no attempt at grace of service, no white cloth to hide the table, no dainty pat of butter on a grape leaf, such as tempts the eyes and palate in the Tyrolean châlet; but it is the simple medicine to cure a hungry stomach, administered without sweetening.

The refinement of a family is nowhere so quickly seen as at a table, or selfish instincts become more prominent. There is the centre of the family after the day's wandering, there its first meeting after a night of forgetfulness; there we give hospitality to the stranger, there the tongue is loosened, the wandering thoughts called back, and the heart is warmed into expression by generous wine. The feasts of Lucullus were celebrated for their wit, and the simple suppers at the Mermaid were the signals for intellectual tournaments. "He has eaten with me," is the Arab's talisman to protection, and the Christian has made a supper the emblem of his religion. Then what constitutes a supper, the food and its preparation, apart from its physiological bearings, is worthy of thoughtful study. Almost every one can remember having eaten of simple meals that were as good as any king's; sometimes they were found at a private table, where white hands that were dear to him have spread the cloth; sometimes they have been served in some out-of-the-way Gallic auberge, when the hungry traveller was even doubting if in a place so destitute he could find anything to eat; and again, it may be, they have been spread in that chief of all hostelries, that reckless home of self-reliance, the camp beneath the greenwood tree. Oh, dear beyond all cafés, and green when Verey's shall be forgotten, is that spreading blanket-cloth, those bark platters, and flashing fires, by which so many meals have been cooked and heartily eaten! Don't laugh, Epicurean, who reads these lines in a big city, where for years fancy cooks have manufactured spiced dinners at Midas prices, and do not say it was only the appetite, and not the dinner that was marvellously good. Though it is easy to cook when you have skillet and spider, bake oven and basting spoon, griddle, pan, sauce-dish, pot, skewers, rotary jacks, and a patent kitchen range, yet still there are more good meals cooked in this world without them than with them, and one of these was our last dinner on Bonda Key.

There had been a long hunt that had lasted from daybreak till almost sunset, and we were tired and hungry, and a certain feeling of approaching separation had come over us that made exertion necessary, and so we went to work with a will to cook a good meal. It is true, our utensils for cooking were few and simple; they consisted of one iron kettle, one tin coffee-pot, and a dozen tin cups and a dozen tin plates—a small *batterie de cuisine* for a legitimate cook, but they were ample for us. The fire had been burning for a week, and thus there were plenty of hard coals. The material consisted of some Indian meal, bear's meat, venison, wild ducks, wild turkey, red-fish, turtle eggs, and snipe. The cooks were Mike, the Doctor, Lou Jackson, and myself; the scullions were all the negroes of the island.

"Poke, you attend to the birds, will you?" I said, handing over a bunch of snipe that Rose had just picked as clean as apples and that were all nicely drawn, and had their bills stuck in their breasts as though trying to plume their lost feathers.

"No, *sir*," replied the Doctor emphatically; "*any* body can cook snipe, *I* am going to attend to the side dishes— *les entremets, vol-au-vents,* and the *pâtés.* "

"Nonsense! there are no side dishes, sir, and plenty of substantial food that can be roasted," interposed Jackson.

"Yes, yes, Doctor, give us an *entremet*

"Of candied apple, quince, and plum, and gourd,
With jellies soother than the creamy curd."

"Wait a while," said the Doctor; "I will show you a dish that will make you forget poetry."

As he selected a couple of flat stones, and commenced pounding up some biscuit that were so hard they had been declined by all the party since the commencement of the hunt.

"You, Sam, bring me a fork," said Jackson, as he approached the fire with a square of the loin of bear's meat nicely cut for roasting. The fork was produced, which was a stout branch of green wood, and carefully pushed into the sand at such an inclination that the meat would be between the fire and the wood; the roasting piece was carefully impaled thereon, and in a little while was hissing away before the heat as musically as if in a Dutch oven.

A red snapper of ten pounds weight that one of the boys had caught in the bay was drawn and wrapped up in green leaves, leaving the scales on, and carefully deposited in a hole in the ground under the fire, and the hot ashes were drawn over it. Mike had, in the meanwhile, plucked a pair of young mallard ducks, fastening their wings to their bodies with little sassafras skewers so they should not get burned, and tying them by their legs to long strings, hung them near the fire on high sticks. They looked like bales of cotton, or like horses when they are suspended by tackles to be hoisted on shipboard. The strings being then tightly twisted gave a rotary motion to the birds that presented every side equally to the fire, and prevented them from burning. A few fragrant leaves, and a dozen oysters being stuffed in each one, answered in the place of dressing.

Lou Jackson prepared the corn-bread cake called *pone* as only a South-woman can, and it was laid on a flat stone that had been carefully selected, and had served for this purpose for several previous dinners, and it would have been a pleasant amusement to see the white dough gradually becoming mahogany brown before the fire, had we not each been busy with the more delicate duties of the kitchen.

I made the boys cut some long wooden skewers, and Rose having cut a deer's liver in small square pieces, an inch in diameter, we impaled a half dozen of these little cubes on each skewer, and stuck them up before the fire at a safe distance from the coals. A piece of the bear's fat of the same size as the piece of liver was stuck on the top of each skewer, so that, as the heat of the fire gradually melted it, the liver was basted by the dropping fat, without any further attention being needed. Next a redfish, with its scales left on, but carefully drawn, and wiped dry, was rolled in green leaves, and buried deep in the hot ashes.

Poke, by this time, had completed his ship-biscuit powder, and been to the beach with Pompey Duffield Sah, from whence he returned with two large bivalve shells, resembling gigantic clamshells, which had been left by the waves on the beach, which he carefully washed, and greased with bear's fat, and then sprinkled with his ship-biscuit powder.

"That a poultice you are going to have there, Doctor?" said Jackson.

"No—gruel," I suggested. Poke maintained a scornful silence, continuing his labour, and making another trip to the beach with Pompey, from which they came with the tin pan full of oysters, which he proceeded to divide among his four half shells. When the shells were full, he sifted the balance of his ship-biscuit over them, and placed them in front of the fire.

"Scolloped oysters, sir, by the moustache of Soyer! you're a genius," said Jackson.

Lou Jackson made the coffee by boiling the water in the tin coffee-pot, and then tying up a sufficient quantity of ground coffee in a canvas bag, placed the bag in the pot which was kept simmering over the coals. Mike had cut several slices of venison, and laying them across two iron ramrods as a substitute for a gridiron, was carefully watching them cook, from time to time giving the ducks a twist, that made them revolve on their gallows like martyrs suffering two of the extreme penalties of the law at one time. Jackson set up the snipe as sentinels around one side of the fire, and the iron pot was hung over the coals, and in it was placed bits of bear's meat and venison, the breast of cranes, pieces of ship-biscuit, bits of pork, and all the little odds and ends of game, which being fit for nothing else, seemed especially intended for making a stew. To this was added a wild pepper or two, and some green leaves and roots that the negroes had gathered, and every time the water bubbled a savoury smell issued forth that made one entertain a more lenient opinion of Esau, in spite of the thousands of years of misjudgment that have been visited upon him. And lastly, as a crowning honour to the meal, a pumpkin was produced; a real golden pumpkin, with its honest ochre face wrinkled into lines of swelling rotundity, and suggesting the rows of rustling corn, among which it had obtained its plethoric shape. The boys had brought it from the plantation in the boat, and though some might say "there is an article that will bother these improvising cooks," it was hailed with exclamations of welcome. A plug was cut in its upper side, where the stalk joined the fruit, and when the piece was taken out it formed a cover to the interior cavity, to which the short stalk answered for a handle. The seeds were carefully removed from the interior, and in their place was poured as much heavy brown sugar as would fill the cavity; when the cover was restored to its place, and the emblem of plenty was seated in front of the coals, its jocund face reflected the bright flames with a pleasant glow, like that which shines on the countenance of an old patriarch, when down the Christmas table peer the bright eyes of long lines of merry grandchildren. The turkey-hen had been in the meanwhile transfixed on a stake, with its maw crammed with chestnuts, and was cluck-

THE CAMP-FIRES OF THE EVERGLADES

ing its despite against its warm roost, vapouring out its savoury humours, while Rose squatted behind it, screening her face from the fire with one hand and basting the bird with the other as the fire blistered its tender skin.

"Now for the omelette!" exclaimed the Doctor, turning away from a long survey of the various articles of food that girdled the fire; "bring me the eggs, Sam."

Sam approached with a grin on his face, and his hat full of soft shell turtle eggs that had been procured from the sand.

"You'd better roast them in the hot sand instead of trying to make omelette," I suggested.

"Or boil them in the stew, sir," said Jackson.

"No, gentlemen, an omelette soufflée I have decided upon. If you want some in the stew I can spare you six; don't put them in till the stew is nearly cooked or they will be as hard as bullets; but I am really suffering for an omelette;" and he began breaking open the little round eggs in one of the tin cups, singing all the while, with a merry tone—

"Who can help loving the land that has taught us
Six hundred and eighty-five ways to cook eggs."

When they were all broken he set one of the men at work to beat them up with a bundle of switches, and turned his attention to tasting the stew, that was being seasoned by the contents of the mess-box, and tasted by all the persons who expected to eat therefrom. Each one gave his opinion, and each one was finally satisfied; the Doctor threw in six turtle eggs for my satisfaction, and allowed an additional pod of red pepper for Jackson's taste for spices, while a fox squirrel, that is a dry kind of gymnast for cooking alone, was quartered, and thrown in to complete the mess.

"Round about the caldron go
In the poison'd entrails throw;"

began the Doctor in a declaiming voice.

"Hold your tongue, destroyer of appetites!" called out Lou Jackson; "don't mix bad ideas with the stew; that is worse than putting in tough meat."

"Poetry, ma'am, is never out of place," answered the Doctor, gesticulating with the forked stick with which he was stirring the stew. "Poetry is salt to life's omelette; poetry is the poor man's gold—the coffee to a

dinner.—You, Sam, twist the ducks; don't you see they've stopped?
—Poetry, ma'am, is suggestive of dinner and dinner of poetry, for—"

"Doctor, your *pâtés* are burning."

"Dear me, what a miserable operation! You, Sam, why didn't you see
that coal snap?"

"Didn't like fur to stop maussa's speechifin'."

"Ha! ha!" laughed Jackson, "you had better get the plates ready, Scip;
where are the plates?"

"All here, sah," said Scipio, bringing in a dozen or more pieces of white
birch bark rounded and smoothed with the knife; and behind him came
Cæsar with the tin cups brightly scoured. Some of the men had reared a
wooden table when we first came to the island; this unusual luxury for a
camp was elevated about two feet from the ground, and formed a convenient centre for the family that sat around on the sand where fancy
dictated. The plates were arranged on the table, one to each guest, and a
pile in store for other courses, for it was a thing unknown in this camp of
plenty to use a plate the second time.

"Turn the pumpkin, some one; don't you see it browning?"

The Doctor paused while measuring a handful of sugar for his omelette
to see the cooking progress. Rose basted the turkey, ejaculating from time
to time, "Gi, he hot!" Mike sat like a Turk on his crossed legs, gradually
withdrawing the venison steak from the heat, and Jackson, who never gave
himself much concern about the dinners, stood overlooking the coffee-pot.
It was a pleasant dinner in cooking, and when it was announced by universal acclaim that it was done, we all felt that we had earned our appetites.

First came out the fish from his hot bed, a black steaming mass, that
bore more resemblance to a sacred embalmed crocodile than to an article of
food; but as one by one the wrappings of wet rags and green leaves were
removed, bringing with them the skin and scales, and his fishiness was
gently rolled over on a piece of clean birch bark and placed on the table,
white, flaky, and steaming hot, a universal ha! from the convives heralded
the success of our first course. To talk of boiled fish, where half of the
peculiar flavour of a trout is left in the water, or *sole au gratin* that is
smothered in sauce and mushrooms, is a mark of gratitude for past
enjoyments; but if the nostril has ever inhaled the pure steam, the con-
densed just liberated essence of a cold-water fish, baked in the ashes, he will
forget those artificial combinations that have hitherto deceived him, and
believe only in the simplest cooking as the best. The fish was soon disposed
of, and Mike handed over his venison steak, hot and rare, just cooked

enough to make it tender.

"Ah! Mike, you rascal, it's not the cooking that makes that venison so tender, sir; you have had the selection of the whole deer," said Jackson.

"Would yer have me take the heels?" asked Mike sarcastically.

And thereupon arose a great discussion between them as to the best cut from a deer, as Jackson had some of the old yeoman's ideas of venery, and Mike was in no wise a stranger to this, one of the most considered arts of woodcraft.

"Hi, dogs!" called Lou, as the hounds crowded around her for the scraps of venison that we had not eaten, and licked the hand that fed them. "Down, Jip! back, Boz! back, Lady! Bring the turkey, Rose."

"And the bar," said Mike, tossing his wooden platter into the fire and taking another.

"And the oysters," said the Doctor.

"And some corn bread," said another.

"Ho! for a boar's head and a flagon of wine, and we would make a royal carouse!" cried Jackson.

"Were we kings, we would not have hunter's appetites," said I.

"And might have the gout," intimated the Doctor.

The turkey was placed on the table, flanked by the piece of bear's meat, and between them the oysters, and my brochets of liver. The corn-bread, brown and smoking, was broken up and piled on the board. And, finally, the tin pan, the only tin pan in the company, was half filled with the savoury stew, and put under the Doctor's nose, to his evident satisfaction, and his face broadened in spite of himself, as the delicate fragrance of venison, eggs, bird, and bear's fat, mingled with chestnuts and savoury herbs, ascended to his nostrils.

Hunting-knives were applied with vigour, and after a short interval of busy silence, there was nothing left on the board but a portion of Bruin's carcass, the stew, and one half of the turkey-hen, and these would have stood but little chance, had there not been the remembrance of the ducks and snipe that were still smiling by the fire. The stew had been pronounced good, but not as good as it will be to-morrow morning, for a stew is like wine, and improves by keeping, and a gentle cooking, oft repeated, makes it more grateful still.

"Now, Doctor, I think the time has come for the game, don't you?"

"I do. Let the game be served," said he, with a wave of his hand.

"You will have to serve it yourself, then," replied Lou. "Rose is eating among the men; just hear them laugh!"

Supper

The musical notes of the other party sounded from the farther side of the fire, where they were discoursing huge pieces of venison and bear's meat with a series of cachinnations that resembled the morning rejoicings of a gang of turkeys.

"You, Rose! the coffee!" shouted Lou; but the girl did not hear, and Lou had to bring the coffee herself, with the Doctor and Mike bearing the ducks and snipe. The birds were laid out in state on bark platters, and the coffee, after first removing the bag of grounds, was carefully poured out in equal portions, in the five tin cups that ornamented the table.

There are various kinds of wild ducks, and various sensations received from eating them. Sometimes they have been tough—leathery tough, these were the old-wives; it is generally only the young wives that buy them; others there are that taste like mackerel, these are the saw-bills and other fishy ducks; others that are dry, like corned beef, these are Pharaoh's lean kine; others again that are duck, but ruined in cooking, you would hardly suspect them, under their stuffing of acrid sage and rancid onion, to be duck, unless you saw their feet. The best manner of cooking a duck is to broil it. Large ducks like canvas-backs and red-heads are usually baked —picked dry, and not washed, a pinch of salt placed inside to draw out the juices, then baked not more than twenty minutes. Thus cooked, young fat wild duck of any of the good varieties is peer to any game that ever feasted a hunter. Nested in a tussock of grass, on some of the sedgy shores of the great northern rivers, it there lived on seed and succulent grasses, and making its first migration southward, it stopped at the wild rice-fields that fringe the shores of the big lakes at Sodus, or Sandusky Bay, the Thousand Islands, or the morasses of the Calumet River, in Indiana, and then for a day or so at the celery beds of the Chesapeake and Delaware, and then on the rice-fields of the Caroline or Georgia planter. It is so conditioned that its breast is flat, and its back is white with underlying fat, and by the colour of its feet you can say that it is its first winter out. Treat such a duck gently, pick dry, and don't wash it. Roast it or broil it rare, and when it is done, not crisp like a roast pig, but gently done, bear it away from the fire as lovingly as the Doctor carried the two that we had cooked, and flank it with nothing discordant and gross, but with some game bird, and nothing better than a English snipe, and then thank the Lord who giveth us our meat in due season, for never since man had dominion over the fowls of the air has there been cooked a daintier dish.

As the dinner progressed it had become dark, and then only the blazing fire lighted the foliage and the rippling beach, and only the faint call of the raccoon in the woods answered the heron and the duck in the marsh, and gradually we sank down to our usual places, talking in a low tone, and casting remarks back into memory, and away into the future, now telling a tale, now half singing a song, until we dropped asleep.

"But what of the pumpkin?" I hear you ask.

Oh! that we kept for the next day.

CHAPTER 17

Home Again

"Be thy intent wicked or charitable,
Thou comest in such a questionable shape
That I will speak to thee."

—*Hamlet*

IF THE READER WILL LEAVE for a short time his hunting acquaintances of the Key, and visit another contemporary camp, he can see, in fancy's eye, one of the chief men that at the date of our story controlled the destiny of the Floridas.

Halleck Tustenuggee was a Mickasukie chief of much repute, as well for his bravery and endurance as for his knowledge of the resources of his native land, his eloquence and his cunning in all the wiles of Indian diplomacy. Being born of the Mickasukies, the original owners of the soil, and being related by marriage to the principal men of the tribe, he possessed a wide influence that was sustained by his strength and manliness of person. Gaily coloured quills were plaited in the straight black hair that fell from the crown of the head, and his costume was more uniform than that of the savages of the northern tribes, and resembled the hunting-shirt of the frontier hunter. He was six feet two inches in height, and slightly made, with a sullen stolid face, that seemed in repose to be without intelligence, but which brightened into intensity when animated. Halleck Tustenuggee's favourite camp was located on the upper waters of the Ouithlacouchee River, on a live-oak island that reared itself, the only stable land amid leagues of morass. Here were erected neatly thatched cabins, and storehouses of food and ammunition, and here, guarded by the solitude, the quicksand, the tortuous lagoons, and the scaly reptiles of the swamp, were always to be found a company of little swarthy imps that played in the grass, and sober women that sat all the while with their blankets wrapped around them, as still as the dead monks in the Piazza Borgonona.

No white man had ever seen this island. The buzzard alone, from his slow circles in the zenith, had marked the camp smoke, under the long-hanging moss. Only the panther, from the labyrinth of the magnolias, or the alligator under the fallen trees, heard the children's laugh, or the squaw's song to her swart pappoose. So the stores of maize and powder were never burned by the enemy, and the dried and wrinkled scalps that hung to the tent-poles, some by their silken tresses and some by their short grey curls, continued to smoke and dry in the fire-light and the sunshine, unreclaimed and unavenged.

To explain the unconquerable aversion that has always existed between the white man and the Indian on the North American continent needs the description of many aggressions and revenges that each has inflicted on the most susceptible feelings of the other. The white man has colonised the lands of the savage by sufferance, and then, by reason of necessity of his position, kept them by force. By superior foresight he has bought their peltry at trivial prices. He has imported infectious diseases, has corrupted with alcoholic drinks, has cut down preserves of game, has amassed wealth, and power, and space, while his simpler-minded neighbour has been stunted under his shadow. All this happens even when the relations of the two races are amicable, and treaties are observed with fidelity, and the aborigine knows that, as the white man prospers he must decrease—that the white man's life is the red man's death. But the outward peace in a little while disappears. Some settlers' cattle or negro slaves have disappeared from the woods, and the Indian is charged with the theft; the charge is probably true. Some brave, in visiting the settlement, has been intoxicated, and killed or maimed a white man who has insulted him. The law claims a compensation. The law is made by the white man, who regards the Indian with contempt and dislike, and the compensation is graded by his judgment, and not by the meagre wealth of the Indian. Retaliation follows the distraining; a foray avenges the retaliation; then a burning village and the scalping-knife brightens the night, and brings on a campaign that for years converts the border into a debatable ground, like the Valley of the Shadow of Death. The white settler, at a distance from relief, and guarding his cabin only by force of arms, regards the sullen, wary, crouching foe with a bitter hatred that he bestows on no other enemy, and his hatred is handed from father to child, and perpetuated by tradition, picture, and song, and many a vacant place by the fireside. The chieftain looks back over a life of battles that were disastrous to him, and that has left his tribe a handful of broken men, and recalls the peace that was more injurious than war, the worthless bargains, hollow promises, poisonous gifts, discordant counsels, mock ceremonies, and cloaked hatred.

Little wonder is it, then, that when some chiefs of shrewder foresight than others come to power among the Indian tribes, they form combinations, recount their wrongs, and, urged on by the national enthusiasm, make a bitter burst for revenge and immortality! Such a chief was Halleck Tustenuggee, and such was the history of his people; and the settlers on the Gulf and the verdant bottoms of the Suwanee remember his last unexpected and bloody charge, as the fishermen of the Mexican Gulf remember the tornadoes that come out from the south in the middle of the summer afternoon, wrecking all that was basking in the tropical stillness.

Tustenuggee had consulted with all the divisions of the Seminoles. Runners had come and gone, some in canoes and some on foot, to all the different outlying parties. The women had been removed to the recesses of the swamps, extra quantities of lead and powder had been purchased, a census had been made of all the white inhabitants residing on the debatable land, and the forces had been appointed, so many braves to each department; at the same time no change in the demeanour of the red man marked their determination; they came and went the same as before, and bartered and hunted without a word of mistrust or dislike. The very day had been fixed, and the hour; and that night, while the laugh was so loud by the camp-fire at Bonda Key, and while soothed by the murmurs of the sea, we passed away to the land of dreams, the eye of the Indian was on us all the while, and we knew it not. While we were cooking and eating our meal, and when we had lain down to sleep, an Indian scout was watching us from a clump of thickly clustered trees that grew some fifty yards from our tents. It could not be seen in the shadows, and the land breeze that blew from us to it prevented the dogs scenting it. No motion attested weariness, no sound betokened its cat-like arrival. It was the skeleton at the feast.

As the morning brightened the east, the figure melted away with the warm colours of the sky, and when Mike left the camp to loiter around for his usual morning walk he found the dew disturbed on the grass, and following the slight trail he carried it to the edge of a bayou, where he noticed the rushes were divided as though they had been bent by somebody passing through. As he watched them carefully they still arose, closing more and more of the opening, showing that whatever had disturbed them, had but just departed. The hunter surveyed the whole bay and the opening bayous, and then followed back the trail to the clump of trees where the scout had spent the night, and examined the place carefully. He then made several casts around the camp, each one of greater circuit, examining as he went every indication of the presence, during the night, of any other person, and finally returned with his measured tread, and took his place by the fire.

From the survey he had made, he knew there was but one Indian on the island; he knew by the track, the new footmarks overlapping old ones, that the Indian had come and gone in the same direction. He knew that he was there to watch the hunting party, and for no other reason; and by the matted grass in the thorn-bushes he knew that he had passed the most of the night in the same place. It was no straggler, for he had an object; no hunter, for he was without dog or comrade. Whatever Mike's reflections were, he kept them secret, and smiled at Lou's jests and chatted as quietly with the Doctor, while he superintended the loading of the boats for the return trip, as though he had not left the camp.

The tents were struck and packed, our few skins and trophies were stowed away in the canoes, and when we had finished the hearty breakfast, and Rose had cooked sufficient venison and corn-bread to answer for our dinner, we embarked and started once again for "Far Away."

Mike had given directions at starting as to the course we were to take, and himself led the way. This was not the same route we had taken in coming, but deflected much to the southward. Soon the islands on which we had passed so many pleasant days were blue in the distance, and I envied the pelicans that were sitting on the sandy point, careless denizens of a happy land, to whom time brought no necessity for change, and who only migrated at their pleasure, a headland of water-oaks presently shut out our isola-bella, and the boats wound in among a group of islands that hid us from any view but those of the shores that immediately surrounded us. Mike's canoe, that led the way, paused for a moment, and as we rode abreast he spoke to Jackson, who was with his daughter and the Doctor, and asked them to row on slowly with the other boats through the channel that opened ahead, and await his coming in the first broad piece of water they came to. The boats all passed on, but Mike, who was paddling alone with Scipio, turned back and ran ashore on the low island we had just passed and that had shut out our view of Bonda Key. Landing on the beach, he bade Scipio wait, while he crossed over the narrow point of the island, and standing among the heavy moss that reached down from the trees, narrowly scanned the open water we had crossed. Bonda Key exposed its full length of blue; beyond were other lesser sandy keys blinking in the sunshine; nearer, the low tangled islands upreared their winter verdure, save when the magnolias or pines interspersed their green domes, or the gaudy creepers blotched them with scarlet. Long flocks of ducks crept along the horizon, or swam in nearer clumps; but it was for none of these the hunter was watching. At length from behind an island, that had momentarily hid the view, a canoe, impelled by a single paddler, glided over the water, apparently making for the place where the hunter stood. Mike returned to his canoe, and paddled to the point of the island where an old tree, undermined by the water, had fallen over with its load of vines and moss, and then pulled his boat under its shelter until it was completely invisible from any spot but the water in front. The canoe that was approaching from beyond soon reached the end of the island, on the side opposite to the one where Mike was concealed, and a young Seminole stepped to the shore, and crouching on one knee, cautiously peered around the point. A moment's survey satisfied him, and returning to his canoe he paddled on as rapidly as before, and turning the point of the island continued his course down the channel where our boats had passed, and where Mike lay concealed. He was dressed in buckskin breeches and moccasins; a belt supported a heavy hunting-knife, while the upper part of his body was completely naked. His head was bare, and a daub of scarlet paint ornamented each cheek and either breast. His blanket lay beside him, and with his eye fixed on the winding channel ahead, he was paddling rapidly past, when Mike, with a muscular push against the overhanging tree, shot out into the lagoon so far that the two canoes floated almost side by side. In spite of his training and his stoic blood, the Indian was startled, evincing his surprise by a quick motion and an aspirated ejaculation, as his hand involuntarily laid hold of his gun. Scipio was paddling the canoe, amd Mike's rifle was lying across his knee, while with an appearance of most simple assurance, the hunter said—

"Good-morning, brother, were you looking for me?"

"No—yes," replied the Indian, too much taken by surprise to collect his thoughts immediately; "I saw canoes ahead, I like company."

"My brother has been to the Keys hunting?" continued Mike.

The Indian answered by a nod of assent,—a gesture that he hoped the hunter would believe.

"And is now going up the river again?"

"Yes," replied the Indian, willing to favour the first supposition.

"Then we go together," said Mike, propelling his canoe a little forward in the direction the Indian was going.

"Yes, Indian is tired much rowing, he will not keep you back," answered the savage evasively.

The boats now lay side by side, and Mike, with his rifle in his hand, deliberately stepped from his own canoe to that of the savage, saying, as he did so, "Ingin Mike will help his brother paddle his boat if he is tired."

A keen glance and an impatient look proclaimed how much the Seminole was averse to this polite offer. His eye roved around the bayou as though expecting some treachery, and then rested on Scipio's face and his musket that lay beside him. There seemed to be no help for him, and if he had any suspicion as to Mike's intentions, he could not confirm them from anything he saw in the sun-browned face that confronted him. His hand left his gun, and the ill-assorted couple commenced paddling down the lagoon, while Scipio followed behind, his white teeth glistening as he laughed at intervals a low laugh, with a chorus of words and pectoral chuckles.

The surprise of our party was most unqualified as the strange boat paddled out from the winding lagoon to the open water, and took its place in the rear of the little squadron. The negroes' eyes opened with a language of ejaculation that was louder than words, and Jackson eyed it as a mallard drake would stare at a cormorant who should dare to sail in among his brood. Nothing, however, was said to our visitor, though from front to rear were passed many covert jokes at his expense. We kept on our course industriously, and by noon we were all in the mouth of the river, and stopped for our lunch and a little rest on an island, the smallest of a group of three that lay side by side. Jackson wanted to stop at a larger island that we had just passed, but Mike said that a little island with good company was better than a large one with bad company, and so we complied with his wishes.

The important feature in our lunch was the pumpkin that had been cooking all the previous night, and that had been carefully carried in Jackson's canoe. As Rose brought it up from the boat on her head, the Doctor smiled, I laughed, and Lou looked eagerly forward, as a child looks at an unopened Christmas box.

"Take off the cover of Pandora's Box, Lou," said the Doctor.

"It won't come off, it's glued fast," said Lou, tugging at the stem.

"Give me a chance," said Jackson, aiming a blow at it with his hunting-knife, which did not produce any impression on the shining surface.

At length, by the aid of a hatchet, it was split open, and the interior revealed itself to our admiring eyes. The pumpkin had baked soft, and imbibed the sugar melted by the heat, and candied in irregular shapes, like the interior of a crystallised rock hung with brilliants. The steam was pendent from the sides in drops, and a breath of sweets exhaled when opened that carried one's mind back to the dinner-basket of childhood, and as each one of the party possessed himself of a piece, and sat munching away, we must have looked like so many monkeys in a melon patch. Poke became poetical as usual and repeated Whittier's lines:

"Oh fruit of loved boyhood! the old days recalling
    When wood grapes were purpling, and brown nuts were falling,
    When wild ugly faces we carved in its skin
        Glaring out through the dark, with a candle within."

Jackson was disgusted with the rhyming. He had never lived in a land where every corn-field was bright with pumpkins.

An hour's rest and we were again on our course, Mike all the while in the Indian's canoe, and leading the van. The wild fowl were numerous along the river, though we did not stop to shoot, partly because we were loaded with game, and partly because Mike had requested us not, though he would give no reason, briefly saying in reply to our questions, "It's a leetle better to travel fast and hunt slow, than to travel slow and hunt fast." Large flocks of ducks were all the while being driven ahead of the boats, flying short distances each time they got up. Flamingoes and cormorants were winding from point to point, and knee-deep in the tide great blue herons waded, and snow-white cranes dressed their plumage. As vista after vista opened around the bends of the river, or up the lateral lagoons, new forms and colours opened to the eye. There the stately cypress-trees stood in the water, like the pillars of rustic Venice, and the mound-like cones their roots threw up extended all across the basin; while above, the swinging vine had caught its tendrils in the opposite tree, and thus back and forth festooned a royal *porte-cochère* to the forest mansion. On the other side a fallen tree shut in a passage and formed foothold for brier and creeper, and vines that aspired to the highest pinnacles of the forest and bowed the trees with their embrace. The lunge of the alligator, the cry of the bittern as he rose from the reeds, the scream of the fish-hawk, circling the air and chasing the tern, seemed fitting music for the scene, and soothed and interested the mind, while the low song the oarsmen sung did not disturb the wild inhabitants of the air, or mar the unity of the scene.

Nothing is sweeter than the negro songs, which they sing in perfect accord and with rich gutteral voices, sometimes low and sometimes swelling full and high with the emotion of the singers. While rowing they nearly always sang, and one refrain the hearer will carry in his mind until the dark river is crossed. It ran thus:—

171

"Roll, Jordan, roll, roll, Jordan, roll,
I want to go to Heaven when I die
To hear Jordan roll.
Oh! brothers, you ought to have been dare,
Yes, my Lord! a-sittin' in the kingdom
To hear Jordan roll."

The river grew familiar, and we recognised remembered trees and openings, and soon we saw ahead of us the bluff that marked the landing at "Far Away," and then the logs that formed the rustic wharf, and then the seat under the oaks, and then we landed once again on familiar ground; and leaving the boys to "tote the plunder," wound our way up the hill toward the house, Jackson taking the lead. The young Indian seemed to have made up his mind to accompany us, if not pleasantly, at least without any manifest reluctance, though I noticed Mike was always by his side.

As we mounted the hill I looked for the flock of sheep that usually fed on the bluff, but they were not there, though in a moment we passed one of the wethers dead by the side of the path. Before I could remark upon this, I heard a cry ahead from Jackson, and hastening forward we saw the house and the negro cabins were not there, but a pile of ashes that was drifting hither and yon by the wind, and a column of smoke that ascended from the ruins marked the place where they stood. The sheds were burned, and the sheep pen. The little kitchen, where so many pleasant dinners had been cooked, was gone. There was no voice or sound, no neigh of horses, or bark of dogs, or bleat of sheep. The only living thing there was a group of buzzards, that, heavily gorged, flitted up on the stones that formed the chimney. Looking to where they arose we saw a naked body, half-eaten and scalped. It was Aunty Blase, the old cook. Her eyes were protruding, her bare teeth were grinning at the spectator, and by her peeled skull we knew who had been the visitors at "Far Away."

After the first cry of horror that had escaped Jackson's lips, he turned around to Mike, and his eye fell on the Indian prisoner, who had taken advantage of the surprise of the party to glide away among the trees.

"Hound of hell!" shouted Jackson, "I know your work," and he levelled his rifle at the Indian, who was bounding away down the glade. A mocking cry answered the shot, and the spy disappeared in the woods.

"After him!" called Jackson, starting in pursuit.

"Hold thar, hard!" exclaimed Mike, springing after the planter and taking him by the shoulder. "You'll lose your own har in thar, and won't git his'n. Besides, I'm of the 'pinion that the sooner we get in fightin' trim the better for us. Them sarpents has made a clean sweep and thar is nothin' more for 'em to do here, and so I reckon they've gone arter us to the Keys."

Mike spoke earnestly, and Jackson stopped and returned to the rest of the party that by this time had collected together by the ruins. The negroes were moaning and making a noisy lamentation over the remains of Aunty Blase, rocking themselves to and fro, and throwing their hands up and down. The Doctor was examining the wound on the poor old negress with a professional eye. It was the first time he had ever had the opportunity to see this style of dissection, and Lou Jackson sat down on a log and wept as if her heart would break. Aunty Blase had been a friend of many years to her, and had baked the cakes at the feasts that yearly honoured her birth, and many a time had slyly cooked favourite dishes for her young mistress. It was no wonder then that Lou felt as though she had lost an aunt in reality, and not merely a slave.

A short consultation was had. Mike detailed the fact that the young Indian that had accompanied them back had been watching their camp last night, and stated his belief that he was there for the purpose of informing his tribe of our movements and of our return, in order that they might be prepared to surprise us, either at the camp or on our way back; that his un-expected capture had delayed the plan, and that there was no time to be lost in getting into a more open country, if it should appear, as he suspected, that there was a general rising of the savages along the coast. The reasoning was so correct that it was immediately adopted. A shallow grave, hastily dug, preserved the remains of the old cook from the buzzards, and a short survey and a "hulloo" satisfied us that the few other people that had been left behind had been carried off by the savages, and then, with the goods we brought home, we hurried back to the boats, and in a few minutes were speeding down the river. No song of oarsmen now; no laugh or jest; it was the hurried exodus from impending fate, "and the boldest held his breath for a time."

Tustenuggee, the Mickasukie chief, now commanding a band of the Seminoles, at the time of the return of Jackson's family, was lying with his men in one of the little elevations that raise themselves from the swamps, on the upper shore of the Ouithlacouchee, where he had retired after the sack of the plantation house to wait for the return of those whose unexpected absence had deprived him of half his revenge. Among the spoils he had carried away from the last night's sacking was a case of spirits that had created a debauch in the savage band, and from the chief to the youngest warrior they had all succumbed to its influence, and passed the day in alternate riot and stupor. But when the scout who had been sent down the river to watch the hunters, and whose fleetness of foot had saved him from Jackson's vengeance, arrived and told of the return of the party, the chief was immediately aroused, and shaking off his sluggishness, hastened to take such steps as were necessary to secure his prey. Runners were sent out, some to the site of the despoiled house, some to the river, and some to the country lying north of the river, and through which the settler's family would necessarily have to travel, if it sought to escape by land to the upper settlements, that at this time were but sparsely located, in the direction of Pensacola.

Hardly had the different scouts been sent on their errand before one came hurrying back with the word that the boats were descending the river again, and, like a pack of dogs on a fresh scent, the whole band hurried down to where a point ran out into the river. They leaped from root to root, and crossed the marsh where a hare would have floundered in the mud; they swung themselves, by hanging vines, over deep pools of black water, and their tawny bodies, as lithe as the copper-head snakes that slid from the logs they trod on, appeared and disappeared through the tangled woods until they at length reached the point of land around which the boats were sweeping, impelled by four oars each, and keeping well out in the river. Tustenuggee watched the flotilla coming with an eye that would have transfixed a lonely traveller, so much had it grown and brightened by excitement. He knew his prey was escaping, for it would be a long shot to those canoes, and no matter how strong his own force, he would be unwilling to hazard an open attack on sixteen men as accustomed to the rifle as those before him. The Indians were careful not to be seen from the boats, and crouched down behind any cover they could find, hoping that some of the canoes might approach near enough to afford them a shot. But Mike, who led the fugitive fleet, was too wary for that, but inclined the boats away from a point that he was conscious might afford a cover to a foe, and nearer the low timber that, growing in the water, would form but a poor footing for an ambuscade. The negroes bent to their oars, and the boats skimmed fast, making the curve in beautiful order, and had entirely passed the point, when the shrill report of a dozen guns sounded on the stillness of the forest, and the water near the boats was spattered by the bullets. Then followed the tremulous, fierce, prolonged war-whoop, and as it died away, Mike's taunting answer, with a gesture of derision, came back. Two or three of the savages had not fired with the rest of the band, but had reserved their shots for better opportunity. The opportunity came as the last boat, steered by Jackson himself, swept down with the tide. He had seen the futility of the preceding discharge, and regarding the boats as entirely out of range of the guns, had rather cut the segment of the semicircle than followed its outer curve. As he came opposite the point two guns were discharged almost simultaneously, and at the report Jackson dropped his steering-oar, and raised his hand to his side.

A taunting cry was echoed from the shore, and a number of the Indians ran out as far as they might come, mocking the fugitives, and delighted at the apparent effect of their shot. Jackson raised himself up, staggering, and attempted to bring his rifle to his shoulder, but could not; he spoke to Lem, his favourite servant, who put his arm around him, obedient to his master's command.

"Way enough, boys," he called out in a low voice.

The men paused on their oars, Jackson's lips compressed as the rifle came to his cheek, and at the sharp report, one of the two Indians from whom the last shots came, tossed his arms in the air and fell from the bank where he was standing with a splash into the stream and swirled off with the black water.

"Ha! ha! ye black devils," laughed Jackson, sinking down in the bottom of the canoe from the arms of the boy that was holding him.

"Oh, mars Andrew, you hurt; dear maussa, speak, maussa!" cried Lem, kneeling over the planter, and unbuttoning his vest.

The wounded man looked fixedly, and a guttural noise came from his chest at every breath and a perspiration dampened his iron-grey locks. The boat, unheeded, turned and drifted with the tide, and Mike's canoe, in which Lou Jackson was riding, seeing something was wrong, waited till they came up to them.

"Father," said Lou, as the canoes swung together, speaking in a low, hurried voice, "I am here, your daughter Lou."

Jackson did not speak, though he looked shoreward with a wandering eye.

"Dear father! God is good; he will not do this! speak to me, say it is not so!"

Jackson's lips moved, we listened, and low and faint, we heard a nursery prayer:

> "Now I lay me down to sleep,
> I pray the Lord my soul to keep,"

175

and then some words indicating that he was thinking of home and the garden walks. The stern heart was retracing life's steps again; it saw its childhood's home on the Altamaha, it heard its mother's lullaby, the evening prayer, it felt the good-night kiss, and smiled. The dangers around were forgotten, the war-whoop that was sounding mockingly along the shore was unheard, Jackson had retraced life's voyage to its source, and was home again.

We all saw the relaxation of muscle that followed the last hesitating word, and knew its meaning. Lou sunk back into her boat vacantly —listlessly staring, without a word or tear. The negroes wailed a low cadence of sorrow gazing on their master with streaming eyes.

"Wall, he's only got the start of us by a piece, it's a few days airlier or later; but them dogs don't get his hair—that's a comfort; and maybe it'll do him good to hear my rifle crack, if he hain't gone far yet—it used to make him smile." And saying this, Mike levelled his piece at one of the savages on the shore, who were watching in groups our movements.

At the crack of the heavy piece, that carried a ball farther than any gun on the coast, an Indian in one of the groups shivered, but by holding on to a branch above him he saved himself from falling, though we all saw he was wounded. Mike put his hands to his mouth and gave the war-whoop, but neither the ring of the rifle nor the wild cry of battle awoke the dead, and obeying the dictates of prudence we resumed our oars and hurried out of the river for the more open channels of the islands.

CHAPTER 18

The Burial

"Soft was the couch she had made for her lover,
White, white were the sheets and embroidered the cover,
But whiter his sheets and his canopy grander,
And sounder he sleeps where the hill foxes wander."
— *Campbell*

IN SOCIAL LIFE, the love of self and dread of others is not shaken off even at the grave. We bury our dead man with pomp and proper etiquette. There are invitations, and crape, hearse, monuments, and seclusion from society; even in our death we are worldly, draping the dead truth and its morals with living fashions. In the woods death is more direct in approach, and you less able to shun his company. There is no art to help the stricken, no luxury for the languid, no shrive for the dying. When the destroyer has left his mark on your comrade and gone again, the open eyes gaze at you, the stiff body is in your arms; no one speaks over it; it preaches in mute language for itself; there is no hearse, no mourners, no newspaper article, no hymn; you and your friend are alone together.

The night had well set in as we again caught sight of the low area of our camping-ground, after the hurried flight from the river with our sorrowful burden. We lay off in the open water until Mike had made an examination of the land to see that there had been no one there after our departure, and when we saw his fire-light signal we rowed to the beach and disembarked. The negroes spoke in whispers, the boats were half unloaded, the guns carefully examined, and lay ready for use; the very hounds felt the blow that had fallen, and crept listlessly to the fire, and laid down wondering, all save poor old Duke. Duke was a sterling dog, though somewhat aged; his bed for years had been his master's couch, his platter his master's hand; and now he kept by the blanket that was spread over the stern of one of the canoes, and licked a white hand that fell from beneath,

177

and at intervals half whimpered, as does a hound when dreaming of the chase.

Before establishing ourselves for the night, we made a thorough examination of the island, and posted one of the men on the upper end as sentinel in case any canoes were seen, as they would necessarily have to approach that way. Then one tent was raised for Lou, the smouldering fire was rekindled, being first sheltered from observation by the tent, and by a screen of bushes, and we addressed ourselves to sleep, though this was done more to encourage the men to take some rest than from any desire on the part of others for forgetfulness. Some lay down, and soon were oblivious to all earthly troubles; others dozed, and started, and mused by turns; only Lem, of all the negroes, seemed to keep fully awake, and his low moanings were pitiable to hear. The night was still, and the same familiar cries came from the marsh that we had so often listened to; but now they had a mocking sound. The "stars dreamed their path through the sky," and with the waning moon made a thin light that seemed cold and ghostly, and a mist arose from the sea— the sure precursor of a storm.

Mike presently left the camp, and walked down by the beach, and the Doctor and I followed him for the purpose of talking, and arranging some plan for the morrow.

"Well, Mike, what are we to do with Jackson?" said the Doctor, after we had taken a long look at each other.

"Thar aren't but one home for him now; but what's to be done with his darter?"

"Take her with us," said the Doctor.

"Where shall we take ourselves to?" I asked.

No one answered, and each looked at Mike as the surest adviser. The hunter sat himself down on the sand cross-legged, in the Indian fashion, and, after a pause, said—

"It's clair we aren't wanted hereabout, and it's mighty onsafe for the young woman. Thar has been a risin' of the Injins everywhere, and the only safe place for a crowd as big as our own is in the boats. The Injins wun't fight us by day; it's only when they ketch us on the sly, fur they know they aren't a match for honest folks, nohow. Ef it warn't fur this ere young woman, and Rose, and the boys, we might lay around and rub out some of those varmints, and like enough get back some of the people they stole from the house. But it's a mighty onsafe game to play, with a handful of niggers to bother one, and I reckon we'd best make tracks."

"But where shall we turn to?" asked the Doctor, looking around him.

"Well, ef we go north, it aren't a great way to Lorenzo's clearing, but I kind o' think Lorenzo lost his hayar night 'fore last, with the rest on 'em. The surest place would be Tampa Bay; thar we'd have the Fort, and from thar Lou Jackson could pass up to where she would."

"Poor girl! poor girl!" said the Doctor. "What is to become of her? She seems very calm; I was afraid she would feel it more. She has not shed a tear or made a sob since it happened."

"A hound don't yowl much when he's hard hurt," replied Mike.

"What of the body, Mike?" I asked. "We must bury it some time, and where?"

"Them sarpents won't let it stay buried long; they want his hayar."

"You don't mean to say they would despoil his grave for his scalp?"

"I mean they are 'bout among the islands, nosing us out this minute like wolves."

"O Mike!" said the Doctor, looking around anxiously.

" 'Taint likely they'll find us to-night, though they know pretty much where we be; but their spies'll be in all the passes at light to see where we go, and what we take with us, and they'll dog us to Tampa, and ef they can't get our hayar, they'll try to get his'n. We can't carry him four days' journey to the Fort."

"We could bury him in the sea," said the Doctor, "and there he would remain undisturbed."

"His darter wouldn't give in to that," said Mike.

"How do you know?"

"Wall, I reckon."

"Then how can we bury him, and when?"

"The sooner the better," I replied. "Bury him here to-night—'twould be least suspected."

"And how hide the grave?"

"Build the fire over it," said Mike.

And so it was agreed that the burial should be made in the night, and that the party should leave before light should expose their motions to the enemy. I was deputed to acquaint Lou Jackson with the plan, and to obtain her approval. I found her in her tent, that opened to the fire, half lying and half sitting against a roll of blankets. Her eyes were shut, and she seemed asleep, but when spoken to she answered without moving. I told her of our plans for the morrow. She answered in a low distinct tone that it was all well. I spoke of her father, and that it was necessary to have a burial so secretly as to preserve the grave from the knowledge of the enemy. She consented by a single word of assent in the same composed manner. I then spoke of its being done immediately, and asked her if she was willing. She turned in her habitual manner, as though deferring the question to some one beside her; it was her manner of asking her father that had always in the family been regarded as a question and answered by Jackson without a word. Then as if recalling to her mind that there was no one to respond, she looked around vacantly with a troubled look, pronouncing the name of Mike.

"Yes, child," said the hunter, bending his frame to the entrance of the low tent, and replying to the unasked question, "that's best."

"Very well," she said; and seeing her indisposed to talk, I left the tent.

In a few minutes the fire was removed from the spot where it had been burning for so many days, and the pile of ashes pushed aside. Then with sharp sticks for mattocks, and paddles for shovels, in a little while we dug a grave in the sandy soil. Four men took the canoe, covered with the blanket, and guarded by Duke, and carried it up by the grave. The fire waned and flickered and the moon was nearly set. The heavy gaily-coloured Indian blanket was wrapped around the dead man, and his hands were folded, "as though praying dumbly, over his breast." Nothing was said, but the plaintive moans of the negroes and Lem's wailing cry were the only sounds of sorrow. Lou looked on with eyes wide and staring, and followed every motion of the attendants, but no word or gesture escaped her. The body was then laid in the grave, and then followed a pause; so silently we stood, the very air in the trees seemed noisy, and the negroes ceased their lamentations and crowded round Duke, who stood at the end of the grave, looking sadly in, while his long ears touched the ground. We looked one at the other for a sign, and the dead man looked up at us from the grave.

The Doctor spoke with a voice so low, that but for the silence we could not have heard it: "Dust to dust, ashes to ashes." Then, as if seeking words to continue the service he could not remember, he broke forth in that great confession: "I believe in one God, the Father Almighty, maker of heaven and earth, in JESUS CHRIST, His only Son, our Lord." His voice, that was faltering, grew strong, the tears that were raining o'er his cheeks grew dry, and the triumph of his voice, as he proclaimed the resurrection of the body and the life everlasting, was like the march of a triumphal chorus, to which all responded, Amen!

Mike stepped into the grave and turned down the blanket over the face of his friend, our host and comrade, and laid beside him his hunting-knife and rifle—a kindly care he had learned from his Indian habits—and then the grave was filled up, all the dirt was carefully placed back, or thrown in the sea, the ashes drawn to their place, and the fire rekindled. The boats were reloaded, a piece of canvas was stretched on poles to imitate a tent, and one canoe that we did not need was left in plain sight on the beach, with a log or two half in the water to represent the others. This ruse was done to attract and occupy the attention of the Indians, who would be searching for us the next day, and who would thus be drawn away for a time from our real course. There lacked about two hours till daylight when we took to the boats and called away the dogs. They all came but Duke, who still sat by the fire, until one of the negroes carried him to the boat and placed him in; but as we started he jumped out and ran back to the spot where he had seen his master buried. The negro went back again, but the dog resisted and set up one of those long plaintive howls for which the true deer-hound is so remarkable, and which echoed from shore to shore like the call of a bugle. Lou was sitting in the boat, but at the sound of the dog's voice she sprang out, and running back to the hound, threw herself down on the sand with her arms around his neck, and broke out convulsively sobbing. It was the first tear she had shed since her father's death, and the torrent restrained was the more powerful.

"Oh! Missus! Jesus help us!" moaned Rose, swaying her head from side to side.

Mike rose up in his boat and, looking seaward, brushed his hand across his cheek, saying: "Thar ain't no show of light yit awhile."

In a little while Lou came back to the boat, leading Duke by the ear, and having taken her place with the Doctor, the boats glided off into the darkness and the mist, and, using only the paddles, passed like phantoms out of sight.

All that night we rowed, and the next day, and availing ourselves of the smallest of the open islands for resting-places, avoided surprise.

Whether the Indians ever followed us I know not, or whether they ever found the grave of the recluse planter by the sea. I never again visited the island, and the craft and ceaseless vigilance of our guide carried us safely amid the dangers by storm and warfare that constantly surrounded us during the four days that were occupied in getting to Tampa Bay. In the destruction of "Far Away" Lou Jackson had lost nearly all the property of every kind that she owned. Of the twelve negro men that had accompanied us on the hunt, only six were the property of her father and six had been hired, and would now have to be returned to their owner at Pensacola. Lem and Rose, together with five men, would accompany their young mistress and return from Tampa Bay to St. Augustine, where her father's relatives resided, by the first vessel that could be found. This was the meagre plan that she had laid out for herself, as we sailed down the coast. At length we made the point of Egmont Island, and entering the broad bay saw once more the American flag, and stepped ashore in security under the guns of the Fort.

CHAPTER 19

Indian History

"True, they have vices—such are nature's growth,
But only the barbarian's—we have both."
—*Byron*

WHEN FLORIDA WAS CEDED BY SPAIN to the United States, in the year 1821, it was inhabited by several powerful tribes of natives. The Seminoles, residing in the Alachua country, in the centre of the peninsula, were a branch of the Creek Indians, whose villages margined the Chattahoochee River, near Columbus, in Georgia, and the name of Seminole, or *Runaway*, originated with a secession of this branch, which occurred at a remote period. Micanopy was their principal chief. The Tallahassees inhabited the northern and western portion of the peninsula, their chief town being at Tallahassee, the present capital of the state. Thlock-lo-Tustenuggee, or Tiger Tail, was their head chief.

The Mickasukie tribe, under Ar-pe-ik, or Sam Jones, and subsequently, under an eminent warrior, Halleck Tustenuggee, had their hunting-grounds on the waters of the Ouithlacouchee, and the heavy swamps that border it.

South of Lake Okechobee another tribe found a secure home in the fastnesses of the everglades. They were called Spanish Indians, and their chief was named Chekika.

The Creeks of Georgia came down to assist their kinsmen in the wars that ensued, and were led by Octiarche, and subsequently by that chief whose name has added so much to the romance and dignity of the Indian character, Osceola. The whole number of Indians in Florida at this time was estimated at from fifteen hundred to as many thousands. To this was to be added an equal number of negro fugitives from the slave states, or the children of free Spanish negroes, all of whom were living with and adopting the habits of the Indians. So wide the extent of country over which they roamed, and so inaccessible their villages, that even the existence of some tribes was unknown until after many years of warfare. The tribes were different from each other in government and location, and some of them were hostile to the others.

After the cession of the province by the Spanish, the United States sought to control the haughty nations that peopled the newly acquired territory, many of which had never been subject to Spain, and to induce them to cede their lands and delegate their government to the Government of the United States, upon the condition of protection and alliance. To this end three Commissioners were appointed by the United States, at Fort Moultrie, near St. Augustine, in September 1823, who caused thirty-five of the principal men of the northern tribes to sign with their marks a treaty, denominated the treaty of Fort Moultrie. The first article of this treaty stated that themselves and their tribes have appealed to the humanity, and thrown themselves on the protection of the United States, "and do cede all claim to the whole territory of Florida." The United States Government in its turn agreed to pay six thousand dollars in goods, and an annual payment of five thousand dollars.

Immediately upon the execution of this agreement, settlers poured in and commenced cultivating the lands relinquished by the Indians, and many quarrels as to the intrusion and the rights of person and property arose between these two classes, so antagonistical in every element of character. Another difficulty arose from the desire of the whites to recover their negro slaves that had fled to the Indians and fraternised with them, sometimes inter-marrying with them, and the government records are full of complaints of these losses, and the war was largely stimulated on this account.

This difference of feeling led the United States Government to propose, and carry into effect, in May 1832, a conditional treaty known as the Payne's Landing Treaty, signed by seventeen chiefs, whereby the Seminoles agreed to emigrate to the territory of Arkansas, west of the Mississippi River, providing they should be satisfied with the country, after first sending some of their chiefs to examine the land, and to give up to the white claimants the negro slaves said to have escaped. Seven chiefs accordingly went, and in March of the following year, at Fort Gibson in Arkansas, the seven chiefs ratified the Payne's Landing Treaty, and without first making a report to their tribes, and thus made the original treaty irrevocable.

No sooner, however, had the delegation returned, and it was told to the different tribes of Florida that they had entered into an agreement to remove, than they, without dissent, repudiated the treaty, refused to relinquish their native land, or surrender their negro allies. They haughtily answered the different runners and Indian agents, commissioned by the whites, and withdrawing to their villages in the Cypress Swamps and hummocks, prepared to defend their homes as best they might, according to the ancient hereditary rules of Indian warfare. At a council summoned by General Thompson, when Micanaopy, Cooacoochee, Alligator, and other chiefs of high renown were present, Osceola, who was then a young chief, being called upon to answer if he would sign the treaties, strode up to the table in front of the officers, saying, "The only way I will sign such a treaty is this," and drove his scalping-knife through the parchment deep into the table, while the conference broke up in confusion. The call to arms sounded through the land, the Indians pillaged the settler to obtain military weapons, and burned his cabins, drove off the cattle, and waylaid the soldiers, and the United States Government threw her best armies into the country, to have them destroyed by the miasma and the Indian arrow, patiently renewing the losses in the regiments, and supplying millions of money for a period of over fifteen years. The amplest supplies were afforded for the prosecution of the war, and the first soldiers in the country, such as Generals Jackson, Clinch, Scott, Worth, and Taylor, led the armies.

This was the condition of Florida when, in the latter part of the winter of 1840 and 1841, we found ourselves involuntary prisoners at Fort Brooke, a low octagon fortress, with a palisade enclosure of sharpened timbers, situated at the end of Tampa Bay, and that formed the headquarters of the American army through the many discouraging years of the Seminole war. The temperate climate of the coast, and the commanding neighbourhood of the fortress, made it a pleasant and safe residence from the miasma and disorders of the interior country. It was also the depot for military stores, the arsenal for ammunitiion, and the harbour for the gunboats. Civilised and savage warfare here displayed their pomp and colouring in close relief. The painted savage allies with their wives camped daily by the walls or traded with the sutler; the Indian runners, who alone could thread the inner wilderness, came and went to distant outposts; and the little brown canoe of the savage, so thin in texture that a pin could pierce it, and so light in mould it left no wake in the water, floated side by side in the ripples with the heavy gunboat of the soldier that some day was destined to rake and crush to pieces its slighter opponent—fit emblems both of the power and feebleness of the people of which they were respectively the types.

Fort Brooke often contained within its casemented walls other and greater contrasts, and more stirring emotions than the material landscape and pageantry of war and race. Here came the young recruit, emulous of fame, with armour newly dight, and hither returned from the cypress swamp or the pathless everglade the soldier whose brief campaign sent him home wounded, wasted, broken, with his weapons untarnished, save by the rust, and his glory unmade, except by his sufferings. Here fled for shelter the settler's family from their burning home, the shipwrecked sailor from pursuing storms, here the Indian chieftain came with his armed band, wrapped in his wrought mantle and his stoic dignity, to treat for peace, or vindicate his race; and here the captured warriors in their damp prison ships shivered in sight of the warm life of their native forests. Here "talks" were had with the tribes, treaties signed, expeditions fitted out, forays revenged, and the barbaric life of the woods mingled and flowed side by side with the more complex forms of civilisation, as the Oswegatchie pushes its black current into the blue waters of the St. Lawrence.

The war that had been waging for over ten years through the length and breadth of the peninsula was apparently no nearer its termination than at any previous period. Small bands of Indians had been captured at different times, always by some *ruse*, and not by open warfare, and exported by ships to the far West. Several noted chiefs had been slain, and many villages and corn-fields laid waste, but braver warriors seemed to take the place of the old ones, and new retreats had been found in the more inaccessible swamps, wherein the Indian woman might nurse her babe and till her corn-fields, while the braves revenged their losses by some foray so distant, unexpected, and bloody, as to countervail all rules of warfare, and render useless all prevention, and impossible all redress. This was not one perpetual war, but a succession of wars, separated by treaties and truces more or less long, and more or less faithfully kept. During these truces, sutlers, relying on the promises made by the United States Government, made settlements in the territory, and with the temerity of the American borderer, pushed their outermost farms within the lines of the Indian territory. Sometimes, under favour of a particular Indian chief or band, they were protected for years, and remained safe while others were massacred. But at length some wrong done to their people would so excite the Indians that no individual favour could be a protection, and the outposts of the settlers would be whelmed in flame and blood.

"Far Away" had been an instance of this kind of reliance upon this uncertain tenure, and its existence had been prolonged by the hospitality of the planter; but courtesy could not avail in the hour of general retribution, and the revenge bred by years of accumulating wrongs swept over the homestead like a spring freshet.

In a few days after our arrival, a government vessel, sailing by way of Key West for St. Augustine, offered Lou Jackson a passage, with her people, which she accepted, and departed, carrying Duke with her and most of the negroes, and leaving Mike, Poke, and myself, again to our own resources, awaiting some opportunity for the indulgence of our roving propensities. But roving propensities were now only to be indulged under military escort, or else at the risk of our "*hayr,*" as the hunters pronounced it; so for the first few weeks we contented ourselves with the curious scenes that were daily transpiring in the enclosure of the Fort, or the limited walks directly around the pickets. Occasionally some scout would come in with the report of a soldier, or a runner, lying dead on some of the routes, and a guard of soldiers would be sent out to bring in the body, and give it a burial in the little burying-ground that was located just beyond the picket. The sight of the revolting exhibition of Indian warfare, however, soon passed by, and we forgot the terror that environed us in our desire for activity, and the enjoyment of the chase and the observations of the beauties of animal and vegetable life so prolifically developed.

It is strange that, when the morning *réveillé* of bugle and drum awoke the loud gobble of the wild turkeys not yet flown from their roosts on the cotton-wood trees on Hillsboro' River, we could not resist the call, but would occasionally steal out with our rifles, "jist to clair out our shootin' irons," as Mike said. Day by day these little excursions extended themselves, and we became so accustomed to the danger, that, like the villagers that build on the slopes of Vesuvius, we had forgotten the fires beneath.

CHAPTER 20

A Bear in Difficulty

"*Snout.* O Bottom! thou art changed: what do I see on thee?
Bot. What do you see? you see an ass-head of your own, do you?"
— *Midsummer-Night's Dream*

ONE MORNING MIKE AND I left the Fort in our canoes, with Scipio and Cæsar, to look for some game on the islands that were scattered along the beach in the many indentures of the bay to the southward of the Fort. An hour or two of paddling brought us where a low island was fringed with the tangled roots of the black mangrove. This peculiar tree frequents the salt-water shores, and springs up from a multitude of roots that raise the trunk of the tree above the water. The pendent branches then droop until they touch the water beneath, where, clasped by oysters and other parasite shell-fish, they are anchored to the earth, and, taking root, send up many shoots that thus ramify and interlace like miniature banyan-trees. A large portion of the peninsula of Florida is fringed by this hardy hedge of vegetation. Behind a border of this kind we saw the towering forms of some gumbo-limbo-trees, and the oval leaves of the sea-grape, and, finding an open place wherein to conceal our boat, landed and commenced to hunt down the island.

It was early morning, and the dew was still on the grass, and the mocking-bird had not yet finished his matinal song.

"There's a dog's track," I said to Mike, directing his attention to some footprints fairly marked on the sand; "there may be some Indians camping here."

"No," said Mike, following the tracks with his eye for a moment; "a wolf."

"How do you tell?"

"A wolf's got two long fore-toes on each foot, d'ye see?" pointing to the mark on a piece of clay soil, where the animal had leaped over a pool of

188

water, leaving a deep scratch on each side that showed plainly the formation of his foot; "he passed some time in the night; they are great travellers, they be, and like enough he's now on Topolika River."

A little creek ran into the island, containing about an inch of water at low tide, but into which, with the flood-tide, fish were accustomed to feed, and the shores of this inlet, at its narrowest part, were strewed with the heads and tails of small fish, such as the young of bass and redfish, while the whole shore was tracked with the prints of some animal. We stopped before the signs, and Scipio, his natural instincts fully alive, exclaimed—

"Gi! dere be shocks ob coons here o' nights fishin'."

A closer examination satisfied me that such was the case, and that some raccoons were in the habit of repairing here when the tide was ebbing, and heading off the fish that had ascended the stream, to seize them on their return to the sea. Scipio and Cæsar consulted long over the marks, with an air of much importance, and then informed us that such was "de fac'." Moreover, Scipio assured me that he had seen, on moonlight nights, raccoons engaged in these industrious pursuits, and standing knee-deep in the retiring tide, using their broad fore-paws for hands, scoop out the fish and throw them far up on the beach, while a fellow-fisher of the same family, wading down the creek from above, with splash and squeal, would drive the fish into the very paws of their cunning foe. Cæsar indorsed the same story, which I would readily believe from the nature of the animal, but which I cannot think that Scip and Cæsar ever had the forbearance to watch, while they had the means of pouncing on the raccoons.

Not far from the creek lay a hollow log that Scipio judged might be the resort of his friends, the raccoons, and, trimming a willow stick for a probe, after one or two careful examinations into the different knot-holes, he began a vigorous series of punches, while Cæsar stood at the end with a club elevated to knock over the prize. Instead of a raccoon, to our great amusement out slid a huge rattlesnake, disturbed in his morning nap, and shaking his tail with a whirring sound, like a grasshopper's buzz. Over went Cæsar in his haste to get away from his dangerous prize, exclaiming, as he ran—

"Gord a'mighty bress us! what's for you call ee coon? you purty nigger, dun know snake fur coon!"

There were no signs of deer on the island, though quantities of birds of every description, that roosted in the mangrove bushes, and resorted to the pools and the beaches of the island for food, and made the bushes laugh with their various notes. The Key West pigeon was here, with its burnished colours, and the ground dove, with its plaintive note; the oriole gleamed in the willows like sunrise, and the mocking-bird so peopled the bowers with his many-tuned throat that the stranger would believe a hundred voices were singing at once. When, through vistas of the mangrove, we caught sight of the sea, the porpoise was rolling in pursuit of the fish on the bar, and the pelican and cormorant were following his motions in rolling circles high in the air. All created things in their multitude of ways were fulfilling their destiny, and each grade of life, by the other fed, ran its appointed round to make its part in the measured whole of that great cycle of animal life, of which man knows but a few members, and whose rules of revolution seem to his dull vision to be the mere instinct of appetite.

"Bar!" said Mike, interrupting my reflections.

"Where?" said I.

"Smell him."

"Nonsense!"

"Yah! ha! ha! ha!" said Cæsar, tugging at the leathern leash by which he held Mike's hound; "Yowler smell him too!"

Mike took the strap in his hands, and we silently followed the lead of the dog. In a moment we passed a tree that had been stripped of its bark for a distance of five feet from the ground, and the bark scattered all about, while the hard inner wood of the tree was furrowed by the nails of the animal.

"An old He," said Mike.

"How do you know that?"

"The she ones are 'bout havin' young, and are hid in the big swamps," replied Mike; "and he's a fat one; see, his hind-toe marks don't touch his front ones. If he'd been a real lean one, they'd a well-nigh overlapped."

The marks we saw soon led us to the edge of the bushes, and then out on the open sands. We followed carefully until a roll of sand affording a cover we crawled up behind it, and carefully concealing our heads behind bunches of grass that grew scattered about the summit, beheld our game in the undisturbed pursuit of his morning avocations. The surf was rolling in, and there were many things lying about on the sands that had been stranded by a recent storm: here a tortoise-shell, and there a cocoa-nut, and farther on a board, and some fragments of a vessel. Bruin was busy inspecting these flotsam that had drifted into his domain. He would first look at the article, then smell it, then touch it with his fore-paw, and then he would deliber-ately seat himself in the sand on his broad posteriors, with his hind-legs projecting in front, and his toes turned up, and, lifting the article under consideration to his mouth, turn his head on one side, and try to crack it with his teeth. The indescribable air of burlesque gravity with which this was done was laughable. Added to the individual awkwardness of the animal was the fact of our unsuspected observation, and the scene appeared doubly ridiculous; and when the negroes chuckled aloud, the bear would only discontinue his investigations for a moment to take a survey, and then renew them again. The cocoa-nut he found too hard to bite, and so, after rolling it over two or three times, threw it into the sea again. Then he examined a large tortoise-shell, and putting his claws in the side, with his arms a-kimbo, pryed it open, to find it empty. Next he picked up an orange, and sitting down as before, ate it with evident satisfaction, his fore-paws resting during the time of mastication, on the toes of his hind-paws. Occasionally he would reach around and scratch himself in the same manner as a negro, whom he laughably resembled in very many of his manners.

Presently he discovered a small cask, and after applying his nose to the bunghole to scent the character of its contents set to work to arrive at the interior. But the half-barrel was strongly coopered, and in spite of bites, and boxes, and hugs without number, it remained intact, though an oily juice ran from the bunghole and smeared Bruin's paws, who eagerly licked them dry. At length, by a good deal of biting, he enlarged the bunghole so that he could get a paw in, and by this means fished out the sweets, holding the cask up with one arm, and dropping the other into it, and then into his mouth, like a little negro on a molasses barrel. But this mode of getting at the contents did not seem sufficiently expeditious to little Tommy Horner, who presently getting up on his feet, inserted his nose in the barrel, and then his head. A bear's nose is very sharp, and goes through a small place very easily, but does not have the same facilty for coming out, owing to the hair and ears being set backward, and the heavy folds of skin that hang around the neck. In this instance Bruin made the discovery of this difference, and soon gave symptoms that he was fast. He began to pull back, but as he pulled the barrel came with him, until he rolled over on his back, pawing ineffectually with his hands at the convex sides of the barrel, which revolved around his head as on a pivot, but would not come off. Mike smiled out loud, and the negro yelled with laughter. The bear, hearing the sound of our voices, probably increased by the reverberations in the hollow barrel, took fright and ran for the woods, making directly to where we were lying, and carrying the cask on his head like a helmet. We could not have shot at that half-barrel, even had we been able to fire guns, which we were not from laughter, and therefore scattered right and left as the animal rushed up the hill; as he crossed the conical peak he lost his foothold, and rolled head over heels in our midst. Then picking himself up, he started in the direction he happened to be when he regained his feet, and ran directly into the sea. This turned him about again, when Yowler, who had escaped from the negroes, seized him by a leg and forced him to halt. At this he reared himself on end, and commenced growling and waving his paws all the time, resembling more a picture of Bacchus than a wild animal. We ran down to where he was standing, when Scipio, with a blow of a club over the head, broke the barrel, scattering the remains of mackerel with which it had been filled, and released the animal from his confinement, who rewarded the negro with a blow from his paw that knocked him on the sands, when Mike and I, with a simultaneous discharge of our rifles, laid him lifeless. This was a large bear, and from the abundant mast still hanging in the woods, and from the quantity of shell-fish on the island, was very fat. We brought our canoe round to the beach, and in a few hours we were again with our trophy safely back to the Fort.

CHAPTER 21

Turtle-Spearing

"Man's life is warm, glad, sad, 'twixt loves and graves,
Boundless in hope, honoured with pangs austere,
Heaven gazing, and his angel wings he craves;
The fish is swift, small needing, vague yet clear,
A cold, sweet, silver life, wrapt in round waves,
Quickened with touches of transporting fear."
—*Leigh Hunt*

SOME FISHERMEN COMING IN reported many turtles in sight off the coast, and we arranged a turtle hunt for the following day. At early dawn two dug-out canoes with negro boatmen pulled down the bay to the outer islands. The boats were shapely, the oarsmen good, the water smooth, and with song and story we sped out to the islands, and leaving our luncheon and heavy impedimenta on shore under the shade of a cabbage-palm, we emerged into the open gulf.

There are several varieties of tortoise in the gulf, the chief being the logger-head turtle, which is the largest in size, the hawkbill-turtle and the green-turtle. The hawkbill produces the shell that is so valuable in commerce. The females of each variety come to the sandy beaches in the night-time, more frequently in moonlight nights, and crawling up above high water-mark, dig a hole with their hinder flappers a foot deep in the sand, in which they deposit their eggs twenty to thirty in number, and covering them with sand, and smoothing down the surface, they crawl back again to the sea. The same tortoise lays eggs several times the same season.

One often sees the easily recognised trail of the turtle with its equidistant stub foot-tracks in each side, and the mark of the tail between. By following the trail one soon sees where the shoreward journey is ended, and the animal has turned again toward the sea, and by probing there with a sharp flat stick, can unearth the whole nest of eggs. The eggs are spherical, and the size of a guinea-fowl's egg, of a dull white colour, with a soft but tenacious shell. They are good eating, and when boiled for one minute, make a charming addition to a soup or a stew. Other hunters besides men appreciate them, and one often finds the tracks of raccoons, wild cats, and bears following those of the turtle, and an empty gathering of egg-shells tells the tale of a stolen supper.

In the spring-tides when the moon is at its full, it is a frequent sport to lie hidden on the beach, and when a turtle, if found crawling on shore, to run rapidly to him, and throw him over on his back, from which position he can rarely recover himself. If he is a large one it requires the strength of two men to turn him over, for he violently resists the indignity.

In pleasant weather it is their habit to lie asleep on the surface of the sea, with their backs and nostrils just above the water, cradled by the gentle movement of the ocean. Then the fisherman steals on him with muffled oars. As the boat nears him it moves slowly and in absolute silence. The harpooner stands in the bow of the boat with his lance-like harpoon in his hand. The point of the harpoon is a blunt heart-shaped lance-head about two inches in length with a ring attached to the side near the upper end, and to this ring a long cord is fastened, which is wound up at the bow of the boat. This lance-head has a hollow socket in which is inserted loosely a light wooden shaft eight feet in length.

When within fifteen feet of the tortoise, the fisherman casts his lance in such a manner, that it describes a curve in the air, and comes down perpendicularly on the back of the tortoise with a thud. The lance-head penetrates through the shell, and its further progress is stopped by the ring. The tortoise dives, the shaft floats away, and the strain of the cord comes latterly upon the lance-head, and therefore does not pull it out. A gentle strain is put upon it, the boat gradually gets headway towed by the turtle. As he dives, more cord is yielded to him, as he tires and comes to the surface, the boat pulls up to him—he dives again—another race and then another —each shorter than the one before—the boat pulls closely along side, and an oarsman catches a flipper, another oarsman catches another flipper, and the prize is drawn on board alive, and only slightly injured, and can be transported alive to market.

With us the sea was large and the tortoises small, and our eyes were tired with watching. One sleeping turtle was espied, and we rowed towards him with all the skill we could use. We fairly crept towards him, and held our breath to lighten the boat. A little-looking negro man stood on the forward grating. He was dressed in a pair of pantaloons and a straw hat of other days. His mahogany skin shone with sweat in the hot sunshine. Another soft stroke of the oars and the boat would have been within striking distance, when an oarsman, in his anxiety to witness the blow, turned his body, making a slight grating noise. The tortoise raised his head. A wave of his flipper, and he disappeared in the blue depths of the sea as quickly as a seal could have done it.

"Dah! you—wah fur you dun kum' to sea fur," ejaculated the lancer, "you tink turtle got no more sense 'en you be! Eh?"

It was not an hour before we espied another turtle, and this time the lancer drove his spear into his back plumb up to the ring, and diving, the tortoise carried down shaft and all. This was unfortunate, as he turned after diving and wound the cord around the shaft. A moment more he rose near the boat, and seeing the cord snapped at it, cutting it off as a pair of shears would have done. It was a large loggerhead-turtle, and their bite is sharp and vicious, sufficiently so to take off a man's fingers. As he swirled down under the boat the Doctor cried, "Good-bye, my friend, I'd much rather you'd go down there than into this boat."

We retrieved our shaft, and fitting in another lance-head were prepared for further warfare. But the wind had freshened, the sea was ruffled, and we turned homeward setting a little sail that pushed us along merrily, while now and then a flying fish rose out of the water, and like a little white bird flitted over the sea for a hundred yards, and then sank back again into the waves.

On one of the islands covered by mangrove-trees we saw what appeared trees with snow upon them. As we neared it, we found it was a pelican's breeding-place, and the grey pelicans had adopted it and built their coarse nests in the low trees. Their droppings made tree and island white as marble, and the dead young and the wasted fish brought by the old pelicans for food for their young made the odour intolerable. Many soft, fat, pulpy, downy young, with mandibles so disproportionately heavy that they could not lift them horizontally, sat in the nests, or on the sand where they had tumbled from the nests, and gulls and fish crows had assembled in crowds to feed on them. The squalling of the gulls and the ludicrous attitudes of the young birds produced a comical effect. The mother birds kept high in the air, flying about with distended pouches waiting to feed their young, and yet shy of their uninvited spectators.

The two varieties of pelican seem to keep apart. The white ones in large flocks follow in long parallel lines the schools of small fish, the hinder birds flitting and tumbling over the front ranks in pursuit of the fish, scattering the water in spray and making a turmoil that could be seen for miles away.

The grey pelican pursues his solitary way, flying low over the water with a pendent bill like a gigantic woodcock. Every few moments he drops with a splash into the water, seizes the fish, and throwing his bill into the air, gobbles it down. A little black diver duck followed him around, and after his plunge swims around him with great vivacity, picking up the crumbs that fell from the huge jaws of the great bird. When the pelican arises from the water the little diver follows him to pursue his chase, like the jackal that follows the lion.

We saw the anhinga or snake-birds with their long thin necks and tails sitting on the dead trees, and two men-of-war birds high in the air veered to the freshening breeze. The anhinga are of the cormorant family, and seem to swim under water as readily as on it. Plover of many varieties, and roseate spoon-bills and other wading birds stood on the sandy spits, and whirled around us as we reached our island where the luncheon was stored.

A hearty meal gave us contentment, and a long pull to land delighted the eye as we rowed over fields where

> "The sea-flag streams through the silent water,
> And the crimson leaf of the dulse is seen
> To blush like a banner bathed in slaughter."

Negro songs, and the setting sun and the rising moon, and many a tale and joke, made the day memorable, but the beautiful tortoise shell that was to adorn our camp and serve as a punch bowl was never captured.

CHAPTER 22

Tarpon-Fishing

"The generous gushing of the springs,
When the angler goes a-trolling;
The stir of song, and summer wings,
The line which shines, and life which sings;
Make earth replete with happy things
When the angler goes a-trolling."
—*T. T. Stoddart*

"KEEP HER STEADY, dod-rot your woolly head," yelled the captain of the *Avenger*, as the gallant vessel moved out of Tampa Bay with the last of the shore wind in the grey of the morning. The captain hauled the peak of his mainsail taut, looked with a threatening eye at a fluttering jib that was beginning to shake on the close-hauled course, emptied a soda bottle of whiskey, the last he would have for many a day, threw the bottle overboard, bit a large piece off a roll of tobacco of the kind called nigger-head, and then deposited himself by the tiller elbowing the negro away without a word. He was a bold buccaneer, that captain—that is, in language. In spirit he was as gentle as a calf. His vessel, a sloop-rigged centre-board scow, was littered up with barrels, nets, small boats, and miscellaneous rubbish. The fierce name of the *Avenger*, spelled *Avengeher,* on her stern belied her peaceable errand. The captain explained the name by saying, "Yer see, my t'other boat was clean stole, and I built this 'ere, and named her the *Avenger,* fur if I ever ketch that miserable Yank that got away with the *Rosebud*—tar and feathers—he'll ketch,"—emphasising the unfinished sentence with a sounding jab with his fist that would have knocked in the head of a flour-barrel.

In the interim of his pursuit of the thief the captain had agreed to take us down to Charlotte Harbour, and back again to Tampa, so that we might see a new fishing-ground. The craft had six bunks, but we generally

198

slept on deck, and wind and weather favouring, we found ourselves in two days in Charlotte Harbour, then an absolutely unsettled country. The great diversity of an indented shore like this afforded unlimited enjoyment of game and fish of every description. Not only were there fresh-water rivers emptying in the bay, but wooded islands and sandy beaches were full of migratory birds of every kind. Some we knew, many we could not name. The tropics and the frozen zone seemed to contribute their out-pouring of feathered game, while fish were so abundant, and of such varieties, that every species of sea-bird seemed to gather there to feed upon them. The waters of the Gulf of Mexico, discoloured in the nor-therly portion by the great detritus of rivers, like the Alabama and Mississippi, became clearer near the Caribbean Sea, and often we could see skates of great size wabbling in the water, while the sword-fish with his lance, and lazy Jew-fish and shark were hourly to be met. Mullet in shoals bred in the shallows, and as the boat passed by the tangled roots of the mangroves they would scud out in hundreds. Weak fish, red-snappers, sheepshead grunters and channel-bass were easily taken. The pompano also were occasionally hooked, and in the night we could hear the boom of the drum-fish under the boat. One feels how little he knows when he sees around him so many families of the unknown.

There was one fish that most excited our attention; we had never before seen it, nor even heard of it, and here it was we caught our first tarpon.

This fish runs from ten pounds to two hundred, and our captain as-sured us he had seen them double that size, but the captain in regard to fish and women was a gallant liar.

He would have made a good President for that Long Island Shooting Club, where the members were all liars, and the one who, at the annual dinner, told the biggest one, was elected President for the ensuing year. A fisherman desired to join the Club, but they declined to have him, saying they didn't want professionals.

The tarpon carries a double dorsal fin, the forward rays of which are long and high like the peak of a lateen sail, and gracefully cut the surface of the water as the fish goes cruising along, while the last ray is immensely elongated, reaching backward and nearly parallel to the body, a graceful or-nament or crest. The ventral fin is similar in shape, but pointing downward. The tarpon is shaped like a herring, its mouth is cut in from the top of the head. It has a large, full eye, but its great beauty is in its burnished silver coat of mail that gleams white as it turns its side to the sunshine,

or leaps from the water when it is hooked. This beauty of scale gives it its local name of *Grande Ecaille.*

Among the lumber on our deck was a bunch of a dozen green bamboo poles sixteen feet in length, and cutting off the too pliant tips, and mounting guides of copper wire, and lashing on our reels with the same, we were soon provided with suitable fishing tackle, a little rough to the eye, but service-able as any. Taking each a canoe with a paddler, we drifted along among the islands in about ten feet of water, and with a piece of mullet for bait, we cast here and there, letting the bait sink to the bottom, and then drawing it slowly upward. Reaching the end of an island that faced the open water we steadied our boats, and cutting up some mullet, "chumed" the water with the pieces. This soon brought visitors. The first was a catfish, a sullen-look-ing fellow with a mouth like a half-shut door, and barbed with cord like whiskers. He came up heavily, and after prying open his mouth with a handspike he plunged back sullenly in the bay. The next visitor was a channel-bass. Bright and quick, with a rush and a jump, he brought life and light to the boats, and was welcomed with a cheer. Away he sped with forty feet of line, turned a somersault, and flew off in the opposite direction, and when the weight of the line pulled too heavily, jumped again to clear it, then came to the boat, and was nicely gaffed by the negro oarsman. He was a fish of twenty pounds, with a bronzed back shaded into silvery sides, and two spots of black appeared one on each side just forward of the tail. And so the day wore on. Bass, spotted trout, catfish and red-snapper, in varied order, but the tarpon came not to our hooks.

"If you un's waren't so green you'd ketch 'em two at eh time; them fish kin smell a man what lives on shore, and they steers right away," said the captain on reaching our boat again.

The next day, with a new supply of little mullet, and provisions for staying out all day, we rowed down to one of the little inlets that are formed by Gasperilla Island. The day was quiet, and only the faintest breeze ruffled the sea, gulls on the water loomed large as swans, and the cocoa-nut palms on a distant island stood up in the sky with the mirage.

"Hi da, maussa, see," whispered my paddler behind me, and following the direction of his eye, the tall sharp fin of the fish we were seeking cut slowly this way and that the surface of the water. Our canoe drifted slowly towards him, and, casting the line, the bait dropped a dozen feet ahead of the fish. The fish's fin paused in its motion: I drew the bait towards me. My hand trembling with excitement doubtless lent naturalness to the motion.

The fin subsided beneath the water, and in an instant the line was seen running out. I threw back the rod heavily and felt the weight of the fish, and he, feeling the hook, dashed away with a yell from the negro behind me. "Yah—ha! he gume off, and a hook in he mouf sure." My slim rod bent with the strain, and the canoe followed rapidly, so that it saved some line. In a moment after the fish made his first jump. Up like a big plate of silver he shot in the air, lifting his whole line from the water, and then with a thwack fell back and started again on his race. How the line thrilled through the water! How my heart beat in the race! Then again came his leap, not so high this time, and straight away,—a water spout—a flash of a gun—a spirit—a mirror—all of these at once! Back he went into the sea, and my line came in parted; my hands fell limp at my side, shame covered me, and darkness was upon the face of the deep.

"O Gorra mighty maussa, he's guone!" quoth Jeptha the boatman.

If it hadn't been for the boatman I would have cried, and when Poke called from the neighbouring boat, "Whare, oh, whare are the Hebrew children?" I was angry.

We caught other tarpon since then, but I am convinced that there never was one so large, so strong, or with such a resplendent coat of silver mail ever fast to a fisherman's line since that day.

The tarpon runs up to two hundred pounds in weight. One we captured weighed one hundred and fifty pounds, and measured six feet six inches in length. It may be there are larger ones, but if so the writer has not met them. In colour it is pearly steel on the back, but the sides are the most lustrous silver. The scales are two inches in breadth on the large fish, and are pure silver as a pearl, and are frequently used as ornaments. Sometimes they are drilled and sewed on to a belt, making a conspicuous girdle of studded silver. The beauty of the animal is its vigour and power in the water, and the daring leaps it makes when hooked, accompanying each leap with a shaking motion, which sooner or later throws the hook out of its mouth.

While we were slowly drifting, my paddler had baited a hook attached to a cord-like codfish line and it was trolling behind us, but he caught nothing. Tired of holding it in his hand, he wound it around one of the thwarts of the boat. Presently the line payed out rapidly. Before it could be thrown off the thwart it drew taut and snapped with the sound of a fiddle-string. The negro seized the line, and hauling it in came to the frayed end, he looked at his broken line and then across the water the way the fish had gone, and said with the most melancholy air, "Dun gone." An instant after, the fish, with the broken line still attached, leaped twice from the water, it seemed a mile away shaking itself to free the hook, and then we saw it no more. A few moments later my paddler called "Da he's hook 'em," and I saw Poke's canoe going to sea, as if impelled by a submarine screw. The boatman held his paddle firmly in the water for a rudder, and the line, where it came out of the water, cut a furrow of spray. A moment later the fish broke water with a rush. It jumped five feet clear of the surface, and the wire snell attached to the hook rattled as the fish shook himself in the air. It fell back with a splash, the line still held, and the race began again. Three times in quick succession it came out of the sea, and once turned a somersault. Then it too was free, and the idle line came in with a broken hook.

"Have you seen anything of those Hebrew children?" I called. No answer. Poke was thinking of his sins. I felt sorry for him, and said no more. We fished with varying fortune all the day. Sometimes we had a channel-bass, a most lively and merry leaper, and sometimes a caralli, a hard fighter, and once I hooked, but pulled out from a Jew-fish, about the size of a pork barrel.

It was not until towards evening that we found a better ground for tarpon. We saw their back fins above the water before we reached them. A careful approach, a gentle lateral swing of the rod, and the bait fell some fifty feet from the boat, and between two fish whose fins we could see above the water. How I held my breath until I saw the line pay out, and knew the fish had the bait in its mouth. It made a short run, and then stopped. I paused and counted eight, and then threw up the tip of my rod and bore my weight upon it. Away, as if a lance had struck it, darted the fish, and before the canoe got fully under headway the fish arose from the water looking as my boatman said, "jis like a marble headstone." It then turned at right angles and rushed away, nearly crossing the line of the other fisherman who also was hooked to a fish. Many times it jumped, fiercely shaking itself, and even when tired out it tried to leap and was unable. At last it rolled heavily to the side of the canoe and Jeptha laying down his paddle drove a spearhead through its spine just back of its head. It died instantly and with much care we lifted it aboard, a more precious ingot than was ever dug out of a silver mine.

This was a fish of five feet in length and weighing about ninety pounds.

Poke had captured his, of a little lesser weight, and both of us tired out with the excitement stretched ourselves in the canoes and the boatmen rowed us back to the sloop singing—

"In de old swamp, behind de hill,
De night-bird sings hes song,
He singin'—singin'—whip-poor-will,
An' he sing it all night long.
Den hoe de cotton, hoe de cotton,
Hoe de cotton, boys,
Ole maussa listenin' on de hill,
An' he lub to hear dis noise."

"Ef you'd like to see a mermaid, would yer?" said the captain in the morning, as he sat drinking his black coffee out of a tin cup as black as the coffee.

"A what!"

"Eh mermaid—er a merman—er a big pollywog—bigger than that nigger. Got arms and no legs, and a flopper fur a tail."

"Yes, of course we would," and learning by further questions that it was a manatee of which he spoke, we were soon under way, and after an hour's sail our sloop was anchored at the mouth of a river emptying into the southern end of the bay. It was a sluggish river of small size, and the tide rose and fell in it as we could see by the markings on the mangrove bushes that fringed the shore about three feet.

Taking to our canoes we paddled up the stream with the flood of the tide for several miles. The river broadened here and there into lakelets or shallow pools filled with grass of various kinds, and in one of these pools we saw our first manatee. We were lying quietly at the point of reeds that fringed the entrance to the lake, watching some swans that were disporting in the water, when I heard a noise like a sigh. Looking in the direction from whence it came, we saw the head of a manatee that had come up to breathe. Nothing is stranger than its physiognomy. Its muzzle, dark grey, almost black, seems to be divided perpendicularly into parts like a rabbit's, with a third part fitting in from below. Each part is shaped like a pad or a fat pin-cushion filled with black pins, and the three parts open and shut like valves. When the nozzle is directed toward one the eyes are not seen, and the animal, having no visible ears, seems to be all nose.

The skin wrinkles around the neck like the skin on a fur seal bull, and the little eye is black, and would be unnoticed but for the wrinkles that surround it. Its tail, shaped like a beaver's, lies flat with the surface of the water, in order to aid its rising and diving. Two large flippers are in the place of fore-legs, each having four little toe-nails upon them, and a large pulpous almond-shaped tail completes an animal that for lazy, innocent self-indulgence has no counterpart in nature. Those we saw were about ten feet in length, and the fishermen say they catch those that are larger, weighing one thousand pounds. They feed exclusively on the various grasses that grow in the bottom of the rivers, chiefly on *fuscus vesiculosis*. They have thirty-two teeth, all of which are molars. Sometimes they descend to the mouths of the rivers, but never go out into the salt water. They are freshwater seals, fat and gentle, slow in their motions, perpetually gathering grasses with their flippers, and drawing their food into their mouth with an in-and-out motion of the three lips. They seem to sleep on the muddy banks in the lake and are quick to hear or see danger, and their only refuge is in diving through the dark waters to a distance where they come to the surface among the weeds and grass to take a breath and watch their pursuer.

Their flesh is eatable, and the tail soaked in brine is like the beaver's tail, considered an article of great luxury in the West Indian Islands. They are mammals, the female having two breasts just under the flippers. The fishermen harpoon them for their flesh and oil, and occasionally one is taken with nets of rope to sell to museums. But they pine in captivity for their accustomed food, and rarely live long. They are one of those conspicuous and helpless races, which, like the moa, the dodo, the great auk, the mammoth, the Irish elk, the rhytina, and the bison, are destined to extermination, and presently will only be known by their skeletons. In the great pools of the everglades, these simple-minded beasts have found for ages a suitable home, but as population increases, and the devices of man for destruction are multiplied, they become extinguished.

Presently the male manatee came to the surface, and, exhaling its long-contained breath, paused to look around. It did not see us, or if it did, paid no heed, but munched the grasses that still hung to its mouth and used its flipper to aid it with a ludicrous resemblance to a negro finishing dinner, and wiping his mouth with the back of his hand.

As our canoe moved ahead they both disappeared making little disturbance in the water, and slipping away like a seal.

Continuing up the river we saw another lying with its head supported on the oozy bank of the river apparently asleep. The motion of the oars disturbed it, and drawing off a young one, that was lying near on the bank, with a sweeping motion of its flipper, the young one disappeared and the mother followed it.

The skin of these animals was of an olive colour getting greyish with age, and having a few scattered hairs like the skin of the hippopotamus.

Their gentle ways plead for them, and one of the sweet remembrances we have of the Florida rivers is that we never shot at, or attempted to hurt, one of these gentle beasts during our visit at their homes.

Some years after the time of our story one captured on the St. John's River visited New York. It was about six feet in length, and occupied a tank in the public market. It was fed daily on sea-weed gathered in Wellabout Bay, always taking its food from the bottom of the tank. Its gentle life ended after three months of captivity.

A few days later, in a sou-sou'easter, we set sail, and in a day and a half saw again the flag at Tampa Bay.

CHAPTER 23

How We Conquered Halleck Tustenuggee

—— " 'but,' quoth he,
'It was a famous victory.' "

THE WINTER HAD PASSED AWAY and spring had come, opening the pyramid of silver tulip-flowers of the palmetto royal (the *yucca gloriosa* of the naturalist), while we were watching a chance to leave Tampa Bay. One day the commanding officer detailed a company of men to cross over the peninsula to the forts on the easterly side for the purpose of keeping open the communication, and learning the situation of the enemy, as well as of the troops operating in the interior.

We accepted the chance, and the next day found us with our packs slung on a mule, two canoes for ferrying across rivers, and a company of about forty men winding through the pine lands that lie east of the bay. There had been an old trail cut through, marked by blazes on the trees in the open woods and here and there a log felled bridge-like across the creeks that intersected the swamps; but the trail was only useful as a guide, although it is marked on the charts of that day as a military road.

The dear-bought experience of the American troops had not been profitless, and the company was as well organised as it was possible to be. The men were frontiersmen, quick in the use of the rifle, unterrified by the sights and sounds of Indian warfare and—what was of vital importance—accustomed to the country, and skilled in woodcraft. They could support themselves, if need be, in a swamp, or build a town there without foreign assistance. The rules adopted for crossing the country were as follows: No more baggage to each man than was absolutely necessary, and this baggage to consist only of food and ammunition; each man to carry his own share. One guide was placed ahead of the detachment about three hundred yards; within sight of him and of the column, another. These men

208

were the most experienced of the hunters, and generally one a friendly Indian. To their knowledge of the geography of the country the party was indebted for the directness of its route, to their quick eye for its security from ambush, and to their observation of every passing footstep on the land, marks of paddles on the shallow bottoms of rivers, or the slimy projecting logs, its acquaintance with the movements of out-lying parties of Indians, or the recent passage of friend or foe. How small these signs might be, and yet be detected, how blind and yet be read, is one of the mysteries of those woods that are disclosed only to the observant and the practised. Their very description excites incredulity. The passage of one of these scouting parties through the Indian country was a curious scene, and impressed one with a feeling of awe. The old tokens by the way, here a ford named after some bloody massacre, and there a little log-pen whitened by the bones of those who fell there at bay together, hemmed in by the pursuing savage, were so frequent and well-remembered, that the soldier crossed the woods with a ceaseless watchfulness. He travelled all day with his utmost speed, lest his pursuers might come up on his trail, and at night lay down in the darkness without his fire, that his covert might not be disclosed. The celerity of the passage was the safety of the party.

Thus we crossed over to Fort Fraser, on the Hitchipucksasi, and two days more brought us to Fort Gardiner, on the ford of the river that connects two of the largest of the lakes of central Florida, Lake Kississimee and Lake Tohopekaliga. These forts were nothing more than heavy cabins built of logs, and defended by palisades, sometimes garrisoned by a company of men, and sometimes only houses of refuge. The one last named was in the margin of the cypress swamps, one of those huge shallow tarns, whose black waters, encumbered by logs and cypress knees, and encroaching into the dense forest by interminable arms, were more intricate than the labyrinth of Crete. The Indians excelled in the navigation of these lakes. Their canoes left no trail, and they could be hovering about for weeks without the scouts discovering their presence. If they wanted to leave, they knew of water connections through to a score of other lakes, or they could flee away to the south down the Kississimee River, to the great Okechobee Lake in the everglades.

Some portion of the land around the fort was of the same nature as that commonly known as everglade. Properly, the everglades are confined to that portion of the peninsula lying between the uttermost southerly point, Cape Sable and Okechobee Lake, a space of about two degrees of latitude, though some are found farther northward.

No language save that of the painter's brush can depict the desolate immensity of one of those treeless swamps. There league after league of rank grass waves on every side, unrelieved by hope, to the explorer, of termination or prospect of change. Here and there a thick-leafed cactus, or cabbage-palmetto, or a clump of leafless cypress, grows upward, draped in the moss the dampness has bred. Fallen trunks of old trees are tangled with palmetto roots beneath the grass, having drifted in the summer rains from the place where they grew, or gaunt dead water-oaks hold out their arms, from which the flesh of leaves has dropped away, or still clings pendent from the fingers. Strange birds fly over, screeching in foreign tongues, and trees and reeds show by green deposit on their sides the different heights to which the water that floods the waste had arisen at different times. The rattlesnake and the water-moccasin are abundant.

In the dry season this broad extent of country is nearly dry. During the rainy season of spring and summer the water lies over it in varying depths from two to twenty inches. Through the grass are seen winding channels made by the prevailing currents and lagoons, from whose black muddy bottom grow the pond-lily and floating grasses which intersect the prairie and turn back the pedestrian. It would seem as if the rolling of the sea had built an embankment of sand around all the coast, shutting in this low-lying tract as does the cushion on a billiard-table, so that it could be only drained by evaporation, or settling in the shallow lakes and lagoons.

Through this Stygian pool the haunted Indian doubled and wound, or turned to strike the pursuing soldier whose toilsome march he had been watching for days, or he disappeared into its mirage with his family, like ghosts, without a trail and beyond all successful pursuit.

The story of this war has yet to be written. On the one side were Generals Scott, Clinch, and Worth, names that were dear to their countrymen, and millions of money, and loving chroniclers of gallant deeds. They hunted the Indians and their negro allies with troops, boats and dogs, and renegade spies crueller than the hounds, entrapped their chiefs at the council board, and broke up the organisation of their bands. On the other side was a people deriving their weapons only from their foes, insufficiently provided and suffering every want. They resisted attack with patriotism, and battled in swamp, and water, and reedy fastness, for thrice as many years as the Americans were fighting their War of Independence, with no historian to record their protests, their councils, their sufferings, or heroic deeds. It is well known that Molly Starks were there at every battle, for their bodies lay on the field when the fight was done. Bunker Hill was represented in every cypress gall. The cruel winter at Valley Forge they underwent, though their torture was the miasma and the heat. Their capital was burned at Palacklickaha, and their fruitful fields were destroyed. The old prison-ship lay moored for them in Tampa Bay, and their highest chiefs were captives in its hold. They had their Sumpters and Marions in Chekika and Hospetarke, their Pulaski in Holartoochee, and their Washington in Osceola; and had their Arnolds been discovered, they would be living still, an independent people.

If men are to be esteemed for high virtues in proportion to the obstacles they had to overcome in attaining them, and if the praise of comparative great deeds is due mostly to those who have from lower life made themselves eminent, the brave resistance of the savage in his swamp is a higher chivalry than the war of a civilised people, with its wealth of reason and example; and if it does not stand on historic page in brighter light, it is because the page is written by the civilised race more as a defence than a veritable history.

One morning as the sentinels around the fort were changed, a stranger came up to the relief, was recognised, and then sauntered into the camp,—a huge, rough, talkative fellow, a hunter by trade, and now following the camp, like many others, half for the fun and half for the gain, a sort of cousin to Mike, not in blood, but in position. Mike was a little more gentle and observant, Potter a little rougher and jollier, more rollicksome, hailing everybody, singing wherever there was eating and drinking, and running every danger to be present at a fight. His leathern suit, rifle, and knife, were the prominent features of his dress, and a keen eye and huge mouth and limb, the first points noticed in his person.

Mike knew him, and recognised him with a smile and a question—

"Up?"

"No, down."

"S'Gustine?"

"Wall, you bet."

"Seen Injins?"

"Stacks of 'em— slinkin' about like coots on the S'Johns. Squaws, too; somethin's up—reckon they're agoin' to purr a little; sent a letter to the old man. Who's your old man here now?" continued the hunter, pulling out, as he talked, from his bullet-pouch at his belt a little roll of birch-bark; "took 'em an all-fired time to write it, and had a big pow-wow to read it when wrote. Scissors! I saw some good-looking squaws at that camp. Came as near being tuck that time as I ever did; felt my hayar jist fallin' off; thought I

211

was wolf's meat that run. Yer see I'd been dodgin' tracks all day, so's to git to this clearin' when night cum on. I sez to myself, 'Go it, boots!' and made a bee line. Fust thing I knowed I had walked right into an Injin camp. No fire—fire'd gone out—cuss the fire! Pitched slam-bang over a red-skin asleep, and in a minnit there was forty atop me. 'Hold up!' sez I; 'I'm Injin, don't you know me? I'm come with a letter from the great white chief,' and I held up an old bit of paper that Jake had given me in S'Gustine, with the writin' on about bringing some stores. They swallered the bait, and I sot there half an hour readin' off in Injin the cussedest lot of nonsense you ever heard tell on. Then they wrote this answer, and I started fur here. Didn't I make dirt fly for the first ten miles betwixt us?"

Having rattled off his account of the adventure, that left no more mark on his danger-loving mind than an every-day encounter would have done, he tossed his rifle in the hollow of his arm, and lounged over to the cabin occupied by Colonel Worth.

The missive he delivered was on clear white birch-bark, and pictured a broken hatchet, and a half-circle of Indians sitting around a council fire. Being translated, it read: "We have broken our weapons of war, and are now consulting about peace; only half our chiefs are here—we are waiting for them at the council."

This message was on a par with many others that were constantly passing between the Indians and white leaders, always on the part of the Indian procrastinating and guarded.

From Potter we learned many items of news from the east coast, but none that served to interest us so much as the information of Lou Jackson. It seemed that a month before Lou Jackson had been in St. Augustine, and had embarked in a revenue cutter to go down the coast with a relative who had been appointed light-keeper somewhere in the neighbourhood of Key Biscayne.

It seemed strange that after the danger experienced at the plantation she would so soon go off to an equally exposed and lonely life. Could she not find a better position than that of a light-keeper's assistant? Or did the lonely life it promised agree with her disposition and her feelings of sadness?

Mike expressed his feelings, looking southward as if he could see the light-house, by the words "Wall, wall!"

However, there was no explanation to be had, and after talking it over, we turned to the frolic of the camp and the Indian negotiations, which seemed rapidly approaching a definite result.

A few days more at the lakes, and we found ourselves at Fort King, having accompanied Colonel Worth with a detachment of troops by the way of Warm Springs, where there was a collection of Indian chiefs who had come in for a conference.

This was one of the occasions of periodical truce, so common in this war. Each party was glad of cessation of fight—the soldier to be relieved from marching and incessant watchfulness, and the Indian to gain time to recruit and purchase a stock of ammunition. At such times the precinct of a fort was the scene of a pageant. The chiefs came in under the white flag, without their arms, bringing their wives and children, and pitching their camps right under the guns of the fort, and the sutlers traded with them as with the soldiers. These chiefs retained all their stoic dignity of manner and gaudiness of dress. Regarding themselves as in a measure in council, they dressed with care, and studied to impose on the respect of the whites or each other. Some of them were men of much influence and honour among their own people, nearly all of them were objects of great curiosity to the troops who had been so many months in their pursuit, and who connected each of their names to some bloody massacre, or hard-fought battle.

The leader of the present band was our old friend Halleck Tustenuggee, who had left the marks of his black fingers at Far Away on our last visit there. He was standing at the gateway as we came in, the war-paint washed from his face, and his heavy black hair drawn back from his head, and plaited down behind with the feathers of the roseate spoonbill; a heavy blue blanket hung from one shoulder, in which was wrapped one arm, and the other hung freely at his side. His bearing was noble, his words were few, and if there had not been in his eye the glittering cruelty of his race, something akin to the fascination in the tiger's eye that stops you as you pass his cage, he would have stood with credit for a Roman general. His wife and children were with him, and two subordinate chiefs with their wives. The main body of his band, twenty-five in number, were a few miles distant, near the camp at Warm Springs, participating with all the abandon of the native character in games of ball and quoits, wrestling and dancing. Nothing was omitted on the part of the officers to make the truce pleasant. Provisions were distributed and presents made, and to crown all, a great feast was prepared, to which all the warriors were invited. When at the table, at Warm Springs, the commanding officer announced to those there gathered that they were prisoners; the soldiers, already instructed, sprung to their arms, and the band, that no force could conquer, were bound prisoners for life.

A messenger was sent from Warm Springs to convey the tidings of the capture to Colonel Worth, who was entertaining Tustenuggee and his family at Fort King. The rider came fast through swamp and woods, for his life would be little worth should the day's proceeding be known to Tustenuggee, or any outlying Indian, before he reached a secure shelter. He approached the fort at a moment when the commander was sounding his Indian guest upon the ever-recurring subject of their emigration. The officers were seated in front of their quarters, within the palisades the Indian chiefs stood before, and the idlers of the camp were gathered around listening to "the talk."

"A horseman is coming from the south," called out the Doctor, relieving his pockets of one hand to shade his eyes.

"Come as ef he was sent," remarked Mike.

The sentry challenged, and the rider came in with his report through the open gateway in the palisades and up to the doorway where Colonel Worth was sitting, and delivered his missive. Tustenuggee stood before him in his Roman attitude until the despatch was read, and watched the while the countenance of the colonel, but the hard-bearded face gave no sign.

The rider dismounted and stripped his saddle. A brief order was given by the colonel to the orderly who stood behind him, and the Indian chief resumed his talk.

"My heart and the hearts of my chiefs are white, not from fear, but in love. You sent me the flag of the five fingers (white flag, with white and red hands clasped). I know you want friendship. I trust you. Tustenuggee is here. Listen, white man; what he says is true—listen, Great Spirit; what he says is true. His answers are the answers of his people. He is the chief of the chiefs."

The colonel—"The chief has spoken like a brave man, and his words in council are like his deeds in battle. We all honour him, for he will listen to reason. He has lost many men in the wars, and the rest are weary. But the white soldiers still come, and will come on for ever. The white man has many soldiers, and many weapons, and much ammunition. It is not good for the red man to fight against him, for he will waste away, no matter how brave. The white man has offered his red brothers land in Arkansas many times. Some have gone there—Tustenuggee has refused. The white man now offers for the last time, and he wants to know if Tustenuggee will move at once with all his people."

Said the chief: "Hundreds of winters ago the Great Spirit gave to us this land, its woods, its waters."

He enunciated emphatically and pointed slowly to the sky above him, and waved his draped arm around with a slow majesty peculiar to the oratory of his race.

Old Primus, a snowy-haired Indian, translated into English as he spoke, and a secretary at the table wrote down the conversation.

"Where was our white brother then? Where then was that shadow?" pointing to the shadow of the flag on the officer's quarters, as it fluttered back and forth on the green sward. "Forty years ago, God made Tustenuggee. Then our white brothers lived to the north. Did the Mickasukies war against our white brother, and ask him to go to Arkansas? The Mickasukies were big then, the white man little. The white man was so little he could not do his own work, but had black man to help him.

"Tustenuggee has always lived here. Tustenuggee's people always lived here. They loved the soil; they dropped their seed here, and their seed has taken root. The roots have gone down far into the earth. The white man is a great wind. He comes from where we can't see. He blows against the red tree. If he blows hard enough the red tree will break down, but the red tree has grown too long to take root elsewhere. My people are like deer—they have been hunted, and they are shy. They start when they hear a twig break. They hide when it is day. The white man has hunted them for many winters. He has burned their cabins, he has rooted up their cornfields. They are sick at heart. The women can find no covert to bring forth their young. The men dare not light a council-fire, or come together to talk. The chiefs cannot know the minds of the people, for they are scattered. Let there be peace. The red man will hide his hatchet, and take his hoe. The white soldier may go home. Then, when the tribe comes in from the hummocks, we will talk of moving. Runners will go to Sam Jones, to Octiarche, and to Tiger Tail. Our hearts will be open—the sun will shine on them—the smoke of powder shuts out the sun now. When that is gone, we can see clear. Tustenuggee will not promise what he cannot perform; Tustenuggee is too great a chief to lie. His tongue is straight. When peace comes he will see clear. Then he will read the white chief what is written in the hearts of his people about moving. Tustenuggee has spoken."

The Indian stepped back, and wrapped his blanket around him.

The colonel arose, and said: "Halleck Tustenuggee, I read your thoughts. You have wanted a truce to buy ammunition and provisions. You would then do as you have done before—take to the swamps and renew the war. This stratagem is now to be ended. At Warm Springs, to-day, all

215

your warriors have been taken prisoners, with their wives and children, and will be sent forthwith to Arkansas. You and your chief are also prisoners, and will accompany them."

Tustenuggee looked around him with a quick gesture. The gate in the palisade fence was drawn, and the soldiers were under arms. His eye flashed, his breast heaved, and, as his young chief made a desperate but unavailing attempt to escape by scaling the palisades, he quietly drew his blanket over his head and sat on the ground.

No word was said by the bystanders. The intense interest of the scene chained every tongue. The sentinel stopped on his round. The soldiers gathered from their avocations. The orders given by the colonel for the security of his prisoners was delivered in a low tone, and as they moved away to the guard-house our hearts seemed to beat again as if after the spectacle of some great tragedy.

Thus ended the career of this great chief. The woods knew him no more. His race lost his fiery valour, his vindictive vengeance, his far-sighted policy, and the influence of his name. He was one of the most uncompromising foes the white man ever had, and was only taken by the same means that Osceola had been before him.

That night, while most of the camp had retired, or were sitting by the fires that lighted the enclosure, a savage scene was enacted in the guardroom where the prisoners were confined under a guard of soldiers. A large fire was lighted and the captives sat around it, among them several of the Indians taken at the other camp, that had been forwarded for security. It appears they had been canvassing the means by which they had been made captive, and one of them had intimated that it could only have been effected by the treachery of their chief.

The words were no sooner out of his mouth than Tustenuggee was on his feet. Bounding over the fire, he struck the bold speaker in the breast with both feet, then seized him by the throat, and as those in the yard, attracted by the tumult, reached the window of the building, they saw him almost strangled in the tiger-like clutch of the raving chief. Before help could be rendered him, Tustenuggee had seized the ear of his antagonist between his teeth and bitten it off, then throwing aside his prey, he ground the ear between his teeth, and spat the clotted flesh in the faces of the guard, then, raising his sinewy form to its grandest height, and waving his arm, he gave the Indian whoop, and called out with a wild voice twice, "Halleck Tustenuggee! Halleck Tustenuggee!" and fell back to his seat, trembling with excitement and the rush of his passions.

The strange accessories of form and colour, the armed guard, and red fire-light, the savage act of the barbarian, impressed the scene on our minds as the acts of a demon. It held us enchained, and we looked on the actor as a caged lion.

On the morrow he and his chiefs were on their way to Tampa Bay, to be sent by ship to New Orleans, and beyond to the reservation of the Arkansas.

CHAPTER 24

The "Painter" in the Pig Pen

"I was with Hercules and Cadmus, once,
When in a wood of Crete, they bay'd the bear
With hounds of Sparta; never did I hear
Such gallant chiding."
— *Midsummer-Night's Dream*

THE DAYS WERE GETTING RAPIDLY WARMER in the interior, cut off as we were a large portion of the time by the close woods from the free winds. The ducks had gone to the northward long since, and with them the snipe and the rail. To take their place, the flowers were opening to the spring on every side.

Hunters are rarely botanists. Few of their wants are aided by its science with the exception of the knowledge of the points of the compass, told by the moss, or an acquaintance with the texture of different woods, or the medicinal properties of a few plants. They are equally unused to the description of flowering plants. The pointed cutting of a deer's hoof on a cactus leaf to them is a greater study than the most radiant flower that ever fringed its pulpous leaf. They cannot give technical descriptions, and but few natural ones. They may not call the stars by their names, or classify the active life that peoples every muddy pool, or makes a decayed tree a miniature world.

Yet, for all this, there is no race on whom the sweet influences of the Pleiades fall who are more open to their soothing—none to whose eyes the radiations of the flower afford a keener pleasure—none to whom the fragrance of the woods opens a more vivid association, or who are more observantly drinking in, night and day, those Æsop lessons that man puts into a fable, but that God talks with in letters of life. The constant observation of what is around him makes his recognition quicker; his natural active life makes his senses keener, and the soft, damp, fragrant wind that touches his

cheek in passing, may tell him of a change of weather, of the wet swamp
that he is skirting, and may even whisper the kind of trees and plants there
growing, and whether in bloom or no; the plants will tell the soil, and he
may know the very animal life that lives in the woods before him, by what
on another cheek would be a passing wind, and nothing more.

Even the roughest hunters at the Fort would show this observant taste.
Mike had it to a great extent. Potter had it, though burlesqued by the wild,
random manner of an impulsive boy. We would often get them talking in
order to lead them out. Evening was the ordinary occasion of many tales
and practical jokes. The men would gather around the huge fires, sitting
and lying in every attitude—negro interpreters, Indians and soldiers, the
volunteer hunters, that gained their living by supplying the garrison with
game, and the officers, in uniforms that the swamps had left no longer
uniform or neat. Names well known in the Florida wars were often there
under flags of truce. There were Primus and Gopher John the Indian scouts,
and Holatter Mico, the royal chief, and Vose and Wilcoxson, officers, and
Mike, Potter, and a score of others whose local fame there ran as high as
Maréchals of France, though in a narrower sphere.

There were drinks of government whisky, and smokes from pipes
shorter and blacker than a Killarney man could fix in his hat-band, and
Irish jokes, and yarns of monstrous length, that were roughly criticised or
excelled by some other more incredulous still.

Potter gave us one. Seated astride of an empty barrel, with his rifle
across his knees, his buckskin cap pushed back on his head, his blue flannel
shirt-collar rolled back, exposing a breast as broad and shaggy as a bear's,
he told us the following story with gesticulations and amid peals of
laughter:—

"Wall, you see how it was, Squire, is this."

The speaker took a long pull at his pipe, gave a hitch to his suspenders,
and then, ejecting the dense smoke in volumes through his nostrils, commenced his narration.

The Panther

"I was livin' that year on the coast, purty nigh St. Augustine. It was late in
the year and the night was oncommon dark—wall, it was— and the wind
roared ugly. Yer could hear the trees smashin' up in the woods every five
minutes when it buckled to a little extry, and when yer put yer head out o'
the door, as I did once in a bit to see, you couldn't have seen Talyhasse

Capitol House ef you had rubbed your nose agin' it. The big breakers were poundin' on the bar, and yer could see 'em one by one whare they struck, for the phosper lit 'em up like blue paint. We had a screechin' fire in the chimney, and it was right good to look at. The old woman was a-mending clothes in the corner, and I thought it war a cussed sight better bein' a home body and turnin' in by the side of one's own wife than a-roosting all night in the open range, as I had bin a-doin' for a month back.

"Parson Smith war thar, too; he had dropped in goin' up to Pelatky on a revival trip, and seein' the blow comin' on stayed all night, and he was talkin' religion to Marthy by the fire, drying himself and convartin' a soul both ter once. Parson Smith was a likely man and a rael talker. They called him Doctor, and he wrote his name Rev. Eliakim Smith, M.D. M.D. stood for Medicine Doctor, though that war somethin' of a lie, for he war a horse-doctor before he took to religion, and he had a kind of oily way of rubbin' his hands down his legs as he sat by the fire and talked away that would take the spavin right out of a woman, and convart her in two-forty.

"Wall, there he sat a-rubbin' away and watchin' the taters roastin' in the ashes and the bacon frying in the pan, and talkin' of Election and Delilah, and them other holy women folks in the Bible, till I begun to feel holy myself, and I thought I was in the land o' Canaan, when I fancied I heerd a painter screech. I was to hum in a minnit. 'Holy Moses!' sez I. The Doctor hadn't heerd the painter, so he thought I was getting grace, and he right away buckled into me with all sorts of Bible sayin's, and my wife jined in, but I just riz up and went to the cabin wall, where there was a little winder that I had cut to look out toward the woods. I pulled out the shut-ter and put my head through, but yer might as well have looked into the Kentucky cave, it was so dark. The wind come in, too, so strong and chill-like, that it made the Doctor and my old woman draw up a little clusser together. I listened a while to see if I could make out any signs of the critter, but it war no use. What between the surf a-hammerin' on the bar, and the branches a-crackin' in the woods, and the squalling of the gulls that had blowed in from the sea, you couldn't 'a' heerd a neighbour asking you to take a drink, and I reckon that is what a man hears quickest. Once in a while one of the big water-oaks would topple over in the woods. I knowed it had *blowed over,* for it makes such a smashin' of little branches when a hull tree comes over, and then a short tug or two as the roots break. Then agin yer could hear one of them tall pines on the ridge break. There was no give there; it would break short off with a crack like four or five rifles. I would have bet I could have told the very trees that snapped, I knew 'em all so well. Then agin the wind would die away, and you didn't hear nothin' but the rain.

" 'Jist the night fur them varmints,' says I, drawin' my head in again; 'they allers come down in a storm, kind of unsuspectin' like; that's their natur'.'

" 'Yes, nothin' so decaitful as the 'Piscopalians,' says the Doctor.

" I knowed what he was after; the Doctor went tooth and nail agin the 'Piscopalians, and so did the 'Piscopalians 'gin him. That's the natur' of religious people.

" 'No,' sez I, 'it was the painters.'

" 'Painters! where?—have you seen a painter?'

" 'No, but I heerd one just now.'

" 'You don't mean it,' sez he, and went right over to his saddle-bags that was a-lyin' on the bed, and tuck out two of the longest kind of Spanish pistols, and primed 'em up, sayin' all the while somethin' about how with the jawbone of an ass he had slain a thousand men.

"I didn't believe the critter, for he was given to blowin'; but Marthy, she jist swallowed it all like batter-cakes.

"I seen old Boz, who was asleep by the fire a-whimperin' away—you know how dogs take on when they're dreamin'—raise his head quick like and make a straight p'int for t'other eend of the cabin, whare the logs was a little open like. He stood there for about a minnit and then came back and laid down agin. I knew somethin' was up, and that screech I heerd war true music. The old woman seed the dog, and she broke in with—

" 'Yes, that's so; when my old man, and the dog, both smell painter, I knows there is a painter. Two dogs don't both make a false p'int to once.'

"At this Doctor Smith he walks to the door and unlatches it; the wind blew it wide open. I saw a pair of long white horns outside, and that minnit the Doctor gave jist one of the biggest yells yer ever heerd a wild Injin make; one of his pistols went off; I don't know ef he fired it off, or it went off of itself, and the preacher went over backwards as my yoke of young steers came a-rushin' right in the cabin. Lord! yer could 'a' heerd me larf a mile.

"The critters was a-frightened in the storm, and maybe had smelt the painter, and were mighty glad to get in the house where the light was; but they weren't half as frightened as the Doctor was. He hadn't any more pluck in him than an old hen on a rainy day; he was right wilted down, though he tried to show how the bullock had hit his arm and that had fired the pistol.

"We got the critters out again presently, though they didn't want to go and I sot a-thinkin' about it, and wonderin' how it was they were so onusual skeery, and the old woman had fixed the Doctor somethin' warm, and I hadn't heern any more of the painter for an hour or more, when all of a sudden, queek, quee-ee-ee-ak, we heerd the old sow go, and a thumpin' noise, and the cattle bellowed and run around the house.

" 'Thar, I knowed it,' says I, as I grabbed my rifle, upsettin' the teapot, 'cus the painter, he's got the old sow.'

"Lord, you should ha' seen that cabin empty itself. Boz and the other dogs first, and then the Doctor and his pistols, and then the old woman, though she was the smartest man of the lot, fur she brought out a big pitch pine knot all-afire, to see what we were goin' after.

"I put right for the pig pen; that was about eight rods off from the house, and where the pigs were a-squealin' bloody murder all the time. That's what bothered me. I knew if the painter had got a pig he must have killed it right off, and then he would up and away with the carcass. That's the natur' of the varmint. Could it be an old she-painter a-havin' one of her cubs out exercisin' him, and the cub couldn't lug off his share of the game!

"We got up to the pen. It was a log-cabin about twelve feet square, built of heavy logs, jist to stop such doin's as this. The dogs had their noses to the cracks baying away like all-fired, and the pigs were a-snortin' and squealing inside; but the strangest thing was, that the door was tight fast, the chain across it, and the big oak pin drove in as tight as ever.

" 'Whar's the painter?' says the Doctor, as he came sidelin' up, looking behind every stump.

" 'That's jist what I want to know,' says I, as I cum around the buildin' to look fur his hole, but without findin' it. The pigs were a-squealin' away as if they would split their throats, and the dogs were a-dancin' and a-howlin'. The old woman was a-sayin' somethin', but you couldn't hear what it was, for the wind blew as bad as ever; it only wanted that cussed painter's screech to make it all complete; and jist then, as I am a livin' sinner, the varmint gave his screech, and it was inside the pen!

"I say, Squire, it would ha' done yer good to have heard that screech, and ha' seen that scrimmage. I've hearn the varmints screech many a time when they and I have been in the woods all alone, but then it was kind a soft-like, as if he was a-doin' it for his amusement when he was lonely; he puts it then in the best metre, of course, and it isn't disagreeable, unless he might be too close to you. But here he didn't smooth it down, his dander was evidently riz, and he yelled out as if he was filin' a ninety-horse-power saw with the Rocky Mountains, and wound up with a spit that jist took the hair off a steam whistle. The young pups drew back a little and howled, and the old dogs went nearly mad because they couldn't get through the cracks between the logs.

"The Doctor was fur settin' fire to the cabin and burning him up. The old woman was fur cuttin' a hole in the door and shootin' him. That was kind of onfair to the varmint, I thought. Sez I, 'I'll show you a purtier trick than that; I'll jist open the door, and then, Marthy, if you hold the light steady, I'll take him with a poke in the ribs that will stop his stealin' my pigs. There is no miss fire to my gun, and that won't be imposin' on a varmint that's down.' I put my hand to the peg that held the chain, when the Doctor, taking the ends of the logs that stuck out at the corner of the cabin for a stairs, jist put himself on the top of the pen in a shake of a deer's tail. I smiled softly to myself, but I didn't say nothin', for, thinks I to myself, if the varmint does come out here, and I do miss him, or only wound him, the dogs will be on him like a shot and then he'll go to tree right on top of the cabin, that's sure.

"So I tugged at the peg, and every time the chain rattled, the Doctor edged back on top of the cabin, gettin' up to the ridge, I s'pose, for a sure seat, when all of a sudden he disappeared. Heavens and yearth! he had come backwards onto the hole the painter had dug in the roof, and had tumbled in.

"Yer should have heerd that man scream! The painter wasn't nothin' to it. Painter might have been some louder, but then it wasn't so skeery. It fairly made me shaky to hear him. As he come down to the ground inside, there was such a hustling around in that little building! pigs and painter and man, all seemed to be stirrin' about pretty lively, and to all the other noises the old woman set up a screechin' that made me more shaky than anything else.

" 'Quick!' she hollered, 'pull open the door—quick! O Eliakim! oh dear!'

"I pulled as hard as I could, but the cussed peg had swelled with the rain, and yer couldn't budge it, and the chain was the ox-chain, as went all across the door.

" 'Tear it down, you old pirate!' says the old woman to me, and she took hold of it with both hands, but she might as well have tried to pull down the cabin. And all the time, between the howlin's of the dogs and the squealin's of the pigs I could hear the Doctor a-prayin' away one minnit as loud as he could bawl, and at another minnit callin' to me to come and help him.

" 'Run,' sez I to the old woman, 'run to the house for the axe.'

"Away she started, leaving the torch with me, and she run like a wild Injin. I kneeled down so as to get on a level with them, and puttin' the pine knot so it would shine through, I peeped in at the varmint. Lord! he was a beauty. Crouched up in the fur corner of the cabin, he stood with one foot on the wall, ready for a jump. His glossy bay coat shone like a horse. His eyes looked like two blue lights out on Florida Keys, and his open mouth all the time dropped water down on his whitish chest and on his feet. Once in a while he'd take a look up at the hole in the roof and lay down his ears, as if to jump at it, but it was a leetle too high for him, and he couldn't get enough room to make the leap. Oh, he was a purty critter. His feelers were as long as a ramrod, and when he looked up at the roof they lay so far back that they reached the wrinkle that crossed his shoulders, the only wrinkle on his body. I wanted to take a shy at him, but it warn't no use, the cracks were so narrow I couldn't begin to sight over my rifle, and knowed if I wounded the beast it would be all day with the Doctor. 'Oh,' thinks I to myself, 'ef I could get my pigs and the Doctor out, I'd manage some way so as to take him alive, and make a spec out of a real live painter. 'Twould be the first ever seed in Ameriky, I reckon.'

"Just then the Doctor broke out afresh, half a-screechin', half a-prayin'; he seemed to be kind o' confessin' to the painter, for he was goin' over what a sinner he had been, and talking about Daniel in the lions' den, and the sword of the Lord, and somethin' about Gideon, and Samson and the young lion, and yer never did hear a critter get out so much that was pious in so short a time. I think if I wanted to convart a sinner I'd shut him up with a painter—I would.

"Just as he was sayin' somethin' about reposin' on the protectin' arm, the painter gave a jump for the hole in the roof.

"Jehoshaphat! what a jump! he got his fore-claws on to the shingles, but the shingles guve way and down he cum with a spiteful screech. With that the pigs rushed round in double quick time, and Eliakim, forgetting his prayin', hollered for me and Marthy to come and help him. He was like the old woman who trusted in Providence, when her horse run away till the britchen broke, and then she guv up.

"Poor fellow, I felt sorry for him; every time the painter moved, he and the pigs moved too, and they were hazed around that pig-pen in double-quick time, for the painter is a restless brute, and can't abide standin' still.

"Soon the old woman came back with the axe, and I commenced cuttin' the peg that held the chain. This riled the painter, and he commenced runnin' round livelier than ever, and away went the pigs, gruntin' and squeakin', and away went the Doctor, runnin' and jumpin' over the dead sow the painter had killed, prayin' away and callin' to me by turns. 'O Potter! quick—be merciful to me—a—a—painter's comin'—as you hope —to—be—saved—blasted sow—oh, ough—salvation!'

"A stroke or two of the axe cut off the plug. 'Stand aside, Marthy,' sez I, as I pulled down the chain and threw open the door. I had my rifle to my shoulder. The first thing that come out was the Doctor; he nearly ketched the bullet, for I was just a-pullin' on him when he said somethin' and saved himself; then came the painter quicker than greased lightning; as he struck the ground outside after his first jump, I pulled on him. The ball struck him just in the shoulder, breaking one leg; he fell, but was on his feet again quicker than a wink, and every one of them sixteen dogs, pups and all, a-top of him.

"Phew! what a tussel! 'Go it, pups!' sez Marthy, holdin' up her light. 'Go it, yaller-backs.' That old woman was clear grit—well, she was. Gone now, poor soul!" and the frontiersman wiped his eye with the sleeve of his hunting-shirt; "killed herself larnin' to read.

"The painter fetched himself up on his hind legs, like a bar, hissin' all the while. One leg hung down—that was the broken one—the t'other one he fetched around among the dogs, and knocked 'em over like nine-pins. Old Boz took some of it, and it keeled him up straight, and then Tinker, and Sumter. I seen 'em getting cut awful, and so I walked into the muss with an axe. One clip did the business. It took him just over the ear and druv into the brain, and I got his skin now,—aint it a beauty?

"Wall, the Doctor was in the house when we cum in with the painter, and he was still holdin' on to his pistol. He was just used up, and all my larfin at him, and all Marthy's Schiedam Schnapps didn't cure him. He took the fever and agee and couldn't leave the house for a week, and when he went he war so weak in the back that he could hardly sit on his horse.

"He stopped there purty often agin that winter, goin' and a-comin', but ef we ever heard anything out doors nights he would always coax me to go off and see what it was, but he never left the house, and was purty sure to lock the door when I was gone, to keep the varmints from comin' in. That's the natur' of a doctor."

CHAPTER 25

The Sand-Hill Crane

"Fond of the speculative height,
Thither he wings his airy flight,
And thence securely sees
The bustle and the raree-show
That occupy mankind below,
Secure and at his ease."
— *Cowper*

THE NEXT DAY WE SPENT on the marshes and sandy reaches, gathering roseate spoonbills, curlew, and plover. Long lines of white pelicans sat on the islets, and several varieties of shore-birds ran along the shallow water feeding on the little white sand-lice that hopped out of the sand after every receding wave.

Our great find was a flock of sand-hill crane that, unconscious of the foes that were concealed in the rushes, flew over us, and as we raised, received the contents of four barrels, which brought down five of those birds as large as an adjutant stork. We gave them to the Cherubs to tote home, and at night their breasts served as steaks for supper, tasting and appearing much like venison. This bird migrates from the gulf to Hudson Bay, and, singular to relate, nests equally well south or north. I recalled a day's hunt in northern Iowa, near where Spirit Lake spread its several sheets of water to the autumn sun. It was before visitors were frequent there, and when hotels were unknown. A friend and I drove up from our camp at Lost Island Lake, with the dawn yet invisible, and a mist filling the hollows. The team, after a fast run, halted on a high prairie hill, and smoking horses and men paused to reconnoitre. The lakes lay before us, and the slough stretched away to the east, yellow with rushes and dotted here and there with big musk-rat houses, while wild rice marked the deeper water. In the distance a red light showed where Olsen, the squatter on section ten, thirty-two, forty, was lighting his fire.

Listen! You can hear the "qua-a-a-k, qua-a-k, quak" of the mallard drake, the "eonk" of the goose, and the squeak of the widgeon. There is another sound, more pervading and more difficult to locate. It is the guttural roll of the letter R repeated three times. Some sentinel of the plains is calling *gru-r-r-r-r-ur—gru-r-r-r-r-r-r-r—gru-r-r-r-r-r-r-r*—and another is answering, and a third from the grassy embrasure of his fort responds, heralding the sunrise. Yet you cannot see the fort, nor locate it, nor say whether 'tis near or far. But you feel it is one more new association with the prairie, and a call you cannot yet answer. It is the sand-hill crane *grueling,* to coin a word. It may come from a mile away, or three miles, so deceptive is the distance, and yet it pervades all the air.

When the horses are unhitched and tied to the wheels, and Billy the driver has wrapped himself in his blanket, and is smoking his pipe with his back against the tongue of the wagon; when you and your comrades, incased in india-rubber leggings, are hid away, one in a blind of sedge, and one on a musk-rat house, with the oozy waters of the slough half-way up your thighs, taking what is called "the enjoyment of ducking," perhaps you may see the cranes come over you, moving their broad wings like geese, and with their legs stretched out behind them, flying high in the air to some corn-field or open grass land. You may hold yourself coy, but they will not come lower, but in a long irregular line, gurgling their note from front to rear of their cohort, they will take their course to their well-known feeding ground.

When corn or wheat is stacked for the winter they visit the stacks, and with their strong beaks and legs scatter and waste more than they eat, until the farmer has to set a guard on his stacks. In the late autumn they frequent the corn fields, and placing sentries on the most prominent places, the remainder of the flock will feed for an hour, when the sentries will be relieved, and other sentries take their places.

Their bright colours, tall forms, and stately walk, make them conspicuous on the prairies. Their shoulders stand three feet high, their heads two feet higher. The upper part of the body is a light blue or slate colour, with a line of chestnut where the primary feathers of their wings show along their sides, the under parts light grey, their chins white, their legs steel blue. The upper part of the head is bald and the skin on it rough and red, and, like a cap of Fez, it surmounts the head, reaching to the lower mandible. From this red head-dress peers out a hazel eye, noticeably strong and bright, with a yellow iris. The motion of the bird is vigorous. If wounded it fights dangerously against dog and man, using its bill as a lance, and aiming it at the eye of its antagonist. The flesh is dark, like venison, and in the young, delicate for food.

The Indians have a legend, that in the early days when the crane first came to their land he found the eagle there before him, disputing his way. There was a great fight, and the crane was struck down to the ground and the eagle took his scalp. The crane, however, drove his lance-like bill through both the eagle's thighs. Since then, the crane has always borne his gory head, and the eagle has, when walking, limped like a deformed beggar.

Sometimes the weary traveller sees on the distant prairie knoll, a fellow-traveller. Welcome sight! He turns his horse towards him. As he nears him, two or three more appear on the knoll, and the traveller finds it was the crane sentinel watching while the others slept.

In common with the grouse family, living on prairie land, the crane dances for amusement. On a bright day, when a dozen are loitering together, one ancient maiden will apparently lift up her skirts until she shows the whole length of her spindle shanks, and then hop on her toes a dozen paces, when, dropping her skirts, she will assume the demure air of a Quakeress. Another will do the same; then a red-capped gallant, after a rattle of dry nuts in his throat, will extend his neck, fly up in the air a few feet, and come down, repeating this movement until he advances thirty or forty yards. And then another and another will lift up their skirts, and twirl and hop and flit, without rhyme, and with what reason we know not. Perhaps the stately gallants and dames who performed their minuets a hundred years since could, if living, give us a reason, for the dances are wondrously alike.

"Billy," said I to the driver, who was with me watching one of their hops, "why do they do that?" (I always make a point of gleaning knowledge from the natives, they are so familiar with birds.) "'Cause they are cranes," quoth Billy.

The sand-hill crane is a land bird. He feeds essentially on grain and grass roots. Sometimes he takes snakes for variety, or snails found along the marshes, or a frog, to feed his young. But he likes best the upland, the breezy hill, and the wide-reaching corn-field, and at night he seeks some shallow lake, where, at a distance from shore and prowling enemies, on one foot, alternating with the other, he will sleep away the darkness.

His nest is built in the deepest sloughs, where acres of reeds and floating grass make a barrier against his enemies. The nest is large and rude, and built of broken reeds and rushes, supported by a log or musk-rat house. The eggs are generally two and very rarely three. They are yellowish-white, rough and punctuated and patched heavily with dark irregular brown, and are hatched in June.

The young, at first yellow, leave the nest as soon as hatched. Presently they become a dun colour, which they retain until autumn, feeding for a little time in the slough on snails and frogs, but soon getting out on the unprotected prairie. Cranes fight the moment they are hatched, the hunters say, and as their bills are sharp, and strength is great, one is slain, and the surviving Cain is usually found alone with his two parents. But this is theory, the singleness of the offspring being more likely due to marsh enemies of other species. When captured young they are easily domesticated, and come to the call. They will make friends with the house dog. They select some spot on the ground to roost, and always occupy the identical spot, with the head facing always the same way. When any one moves in the yard at night, they make a low grating noise like a challenge, and clatter with their mandibles, then relapse into silence. When troubled, they get angry and strike viciously with their pointed bills. When spring comes and their kindred are flying overhead with their old familiar cry, they will, if unwatched, forget the master's crib, and fly away, never to be seen more.

Like many birds they acquire, in their wild state, a certain knowledge of men and his ways. A man with a team ploughing, troubles them not. A slow-moving double wagon is but little noticed. A man with a gun is a walking terror, recognised across the township.

The writer once was driving in a double team with a driver and two sportsmen, when three cranes were seen on a hillside nearly ahead. Our course was changed so as to pass along the foot of the hill and a gunshot away, and the horses continued their walk while the sportsmen sat with their guns in their hands but their faces turned toward the horses. In this way we drove until opposite the birds, when they attempted to rise, but necessarily, in rising, had to face down hill, as they could not rise and surmount the hill together. Each marksman selected his bird, and we thus secured all three, although one fell a mile away.

This bird migrates late in the autumn, seeking the Floridas, the gentler prairies of Texas, and the Gulf of Mexico, and reappears in the latitude of the Great Lakes in May. They are scattered over the whole continent of North America and are found as abundant on the Pacific coast as on the prairies of Illinois. They migrate in large flocks and fly in irregular lines, often so far aloft that they seem like tiny drifts of smoke which the eye can barely see. Sometimes a snow-white crane is seen among them, and hasty writers have assumed this to be a bird grown white with age, while, in fact, it is one of another species.

One other habit of the bird deserves record.

If, on a still October day, in city or on prairie land, you hear that gurgling cry, so faint that though at first you pause, yet you will say to yourself "that is only sweet memory," and walk on. It may be you will catch it again. Stop short, and look the sky all over. Far up against the blue welkin, so high that you can just see it, you will find a moving circle, no larger to you than your lady's finger-ring. You cannot count the number of feathered jewels in that ring, there may be fifty or more, but you can see it sway, and move, and slowly float along, dropping as it floats, that grueling cry that will fall from Heaven right into your heart, telling you that the cranes are moving south, and that, idling on their way, they have paused to call to you and make you look Heavenward.

CHAPTER 26

Poke Receives a Cur'osity and Tells a Yarn

"Oblivion here thy wisdom is,
Thy thrift the sleep of cares;
For a proud idleness like this
Crowns all life's mean affairs."
—*Emerson*

THE INDIAN PRISONERS HAD GONE with most of the garrison to Tampa Bay;
the fort looked desolate in contrast with its previous crowd and excitement,
and we were anxious to start for the east coast.

Our party had made preparations to descend the Ochlawaha to Lake
George, and thence down the St. John's, and Mike had employed his leisure,
with our negro boys, Scip and Cæsar, in building two dug-out canoes.
These "dug-outs" are cut out of a solid log, and are often beautifully made
with lines like a racing boat. In these our "plunder" was carefully stowed,
and with a store of salt provisions from the fort, one pleasant day we embarked and swept away down the current.

There is something of unusual novelty in descending a Florida river. An
aspect of dreariness that only long habit overcomes, quiets the tongue and
awes the heart. The black turbid river boils in circular eddies, or spreads in
motionless lagoons, far into the neighbouring woods. The stiff cypress-trees
stand naked with their feet in the water, and knobs like toes rising around
from their roots. Their foliage was the grey Spanish moss that hangs from
every branch in tresses of wondrous length, sometimes reaching from the
upper limbs into the water, and marking the direction of the current. Where
the lagoons opened into the river there was constant doubt as to the course
of the channel, for the lagoon might be broader than the true course, or the
latter totally shrouded from sight by the draping moss or jammed trees.
Sometimes the leading boat would wait for its fellow, calling to it a few feet

off to come through some curtain of vegetation, where it had just found a passage. There was no animal life here save reptiles, and little vegetable beauty. It was a waste of water overhung by the dead growth of ancient times.

Then, too, there was a watchfulness against Indian cunning that made our passage seem more like a flight than a hunt, and when some alligator rushed from the bank to the water, the noise would startle us and bring back the scene when Jackson died on just such a passage down the Ouithlacouchee. Two or three days brought us into pleasanter life, and our eyes were greeted with the open water of Lake George and the varied vegetation of its low-lying shores.

It was curious to watch Mike make his entry on the lake. As we approached, our boats came nearer and paddled slower. We hugged the shore closely, and when the first faint roll of the waves of the lake came into the river, he motioned us to stay, and glided down among the rushes in his own canoe, watching the broad open water with a keen, careful eye. We slowly came up and followed him as, parting the reeds, he wound along the shore some quarter of a mile, till where the grass began to grow thin. Then beaching the canoes where they could not be seen from the lake, we unpacked our provisions, and, seated where we could overlook all the water, and yet not be seen, ate our dinner and took our noonday nap.

The propriety of Mike's caution in a little while became apparent. A canoe came out from one of the outlets of the lake a mile down, and crossed over to the side where we were sitting. In it was a single Indian. This was followed at a short distance by another with three women, and both boats disappeared in a cove. Had we been on the lake we should have been seen, or had we continued our course we must have met them.

"What's that mean, Mike?"

"Injins."

"Yes; but what are they doing? Is there a tribe of them here, and are they a war party, or what?"

"No; it's a band; they've got their squaws with 'em. They're travellin', fur they paddle, leastwise the squaws do, as ef they were tired. And there's more on 'em somewhars, for there's too many squaws there fur that one red-skin. Keep quiet and they'll show their hand."

Before night three other canoes passed the lake in the same direction, and turned round the projecting point where they first disappeared.

The evening came on apace. The sun set—a globe of fire. The pencillings of red on the lakes shortened; and then disappeared. The birds that had fished all day in the shallows settled in the trees to roost. The earth wrapped itself in darkness as a mantle, "and left to dews the freshened air."

"Wall," said Mike, after a big yawn, "let's do somethin'."

"Yes, and that something must be to get out of this place as soon as possible," quoth the Doctor.

"No!" replied Mike, with a comical accent.

"It's very well for you, Mike, who have *a gift* for Indians, to hang about them, but I don't think I care to have my ears bitten off, like Tustenuggee's aid-de-camp."

"We're all right so long as we squat here, and make no fire, or any trails, but when we come to go away we may meet more Injins in the river."

"But the faster we go, the less likelihood of meeting."

"Wall, we will go.—Shut up, Yowler, you dod-rotted dog!" to the hound, who was attempting one of his houndish yelps. "But first I must see who them creeters is, and ef you'll keep quiet here awhile, I'll go look."

So, in spite of the general dissent, Mike took one of the canoes and disappeared in the darkness, while the negroes crept up close like monkeys, shivering with fear of the darkness and danger, and we chatted in low tones of the scene around us. There was a steam on the water that looked like a gathering fog, and made it dark close to its surface. The night was hushed, and the heavy booming of the alligator bull came down the lake like the muffled roar of a lion.

In an hour Mike returned, with his quiet salutation, stepping ashore and tossing something in the Doctor's lap, saying, "Thar's a cur'osity for your c'lection."

The Doctor picked it up, but it was too dark to tell what it was. It looked like the boy's toy called a sucker, made of a circular piece of leather, about three inches in diameter, with a string fastened to it.

"What is it, Mike?"

"Somebody's heyar."

"A scalp?"

"Reckon."

"Where did that come from? It is not a fresh one."

"Stole it from those beggars; too lazy to watch their own boats!"

"How many of them are there?"

"Nine, and five squaws. I stole the only scalp they had, and jist marked my cross on their canoe with my knife, so they'll know 'twas me. It's that cussed old Tiger Tail. Drat his red skin! won't he swear some to-morrow! I

234

reckon we'd better go. Marbee it wouldn't be safe to be loafin' 'beout here when he finds his canoe punched and his scalp stole."

No one obeyed this suggestion to depart with more alacrity than the Doctor, who already felt Tiger Tail's fingers clutching his own scalp-lock in revenge for the lost one, and a few minutes found us on the lake pushing fast and silently for the St. John's.

The next morning we learned the cause of the movement of Tiger Tail's band. The flight of several flocks of water-birds, and the chattering of the blue jays, gave us warning of the approach of some stranger, and, taking to the bushes that fringed the banks, we watched for what would appear. Soon we heard the measured stroke of oars, and then several Indian and negro scouts in canoes passed without observing us, and then swept along six barge-loads of soldiers—a part of the Second Regiment moving up the river on one of their forays, by which they sought to disturb the security and destroy the products of their foes. The American flag was flying at the bow of the leading boat, and the merry laugh of the men, and the loud joke and call passed from front to rear showed how inadequate they were to catching their fleeter foes.

"Hulloa!" said Mike, pushing out his canoe from the reeds, "goin' a-fishin'?"

This sudden satirical salutation brought the boats to a halt, and sent half the soldiers searching about for their muskets.

"Where are you from, and where to?" was the answer of the officer.

"Oh, cross country, goin' a-pleasurin'," responded Mike.

"Seen any Indian signs?"

"No signs in partickalar; stopped at Tiger Tail's camp a piece back," replied Mike, gradually moving down the river, and away from the boats.

"That's the band we are after. How soon do you think we will come up to them?" The boats getting further off all the time.

"When the river freezes!" responded Mike, paddling down stream at full speed. "Ketch a fish-hawk jist as soon," he continued in an undertone.

The boats had resumed their course, when the officer, who seemed to know our hunter, hailed us once more.

"Hulloa!"

"Hulloa!" said Mike.

"Come and guide us, and you will be well paid."

"No; you're too many of you, 'taint no use;" and a turn of the river carried us out of sight.

That night we camped early, secure from annoyance, for the passage of the troops up the river had, we judged, driven away any lurking Indians. Indeed, the only band in the St. John's which we were approaching had been Tiger Tail's, the rest being occupied with treaties and negotiations that had been in progress on the west coast. So we kindled our fires and cooked our meal, and laid down to talk and dreams.

Mike assured us that he had no tales to tell, mumbled about Tiger Tail, and wondered where he was leading his band, then ventured some remark about Lou Jackson, half to himself and half to his hound, and then fell asleep. The Doctor being called on for a story, gave us an account of a fire-hunt in the woods of the Adirondac. As nearly as I can remember, it was as follows. I can't repeat the words, only the ideas. They were pleasant; he was a poetical fellow, that Doctor, when it grew late in the evening.

Fire-Light Hunt

"Beyond Little Tupper's Lake, some three or four miles further on in the wilderness, toward the Racquette, lies Little Rock Pond, a mere dot of glass set in the emerald woods that stretch for miles away in every direction, unbroken by human thrift and unmarked by the fruits of that primal curse that caused the thorns and the thistles to be brought forth. Connecting these two sheets of water is a narrow stream so insignificant that it joyfully runs its way nameless and unknown. The hills stand back on firmer bottom, and the little valley bordering the river is filled with succulent grass, reeds, swamp alders, and rose-trees that blossom and bud for the wild game alone. Here Stalknecht and I had a camp and were spending a month together, keeping house in the only decent manner there is of living in this free country, where the servants are all a little better than their masters." (Poke was violently opposed to Irish servants.)

"Hank, my guide, and I one night paddled our boat up this stream to its source in Rock Pond, and when darkness had come we lighted our jacklight, and, setting it in the bow of the boat, he took his seat in the stern with the paddle, and I mine in the bow with my double-barrelled rifle, and we commenced to descend the stream. A jack-light is so arranged that it throws a bright light in front of the canoe, while it leaves the boat in utter darkness, and the hunter, thus sitting in obscurity, is enabled to see anything in range of his light with perfect distinctness. So we began to descend the stream. Our voices, subdued to a whisper, we were presently hushed altogether. Not a sound disturbed the stillness; no splash of the paddle in the dexterous hand of the guide; no noise of motion; we floated on the water as the moon floats when 'with white fire ladened' she sails out into the still night. The weird trees, naked of leaves and shirted in moss, flashed out in light, and then fell back in darkness, save when their tops marked the sky beyond. Bush and flower, reeds pendent with their heavy seed, and lancifoliate lilies, with their deep blue plumes, lateral lagoons, gemmed with water-plants and bordered with their larches, came out into the light, dropped into the darkness, and were succeeded by others in clumps and clusters, and festooned by blackberry vines. Ghostly-looking sights, stumps that had supernatural shapes, and tombstone trunks, blanched white by rain, marked the banks.

"Kee-honk! kee-honk! screams a blue heron in aspirated accents, as he springs into the air, fanning the night with his great wings in measured beats that can be heard long after he is beyond sight. The musk-rats come out in the circle of light before the boat, in wonderment at the pale fire that awakens them, and dive beneath the waters when the boat is on them. The boat swings around in the turning of the stream, and I see the erect head and large ears of a deer. It is a doe, for there are no horns. A moment of pause to be sure that I am right, and the ringing shot awakens a hundred echoes, and clouds the air with smoke.

" 'Why, ye'nt seen no deer, did yer?' asked Hank.

" 'Yes, a doe.'

"A dip of the paddle sends the boat to the shore and then discloses to my mortified gaze the blanched limb of a tree, standing up in the grass, the veriest spectre of a deer.

" 'Well, your doe is dished now—ha! ha!' laughs Hank.

"I load my rifle rather humbly. 'Ready—push on!'

" 'Don't you want to see if you hit it?'

" 'No; push on, will you?'

"The boat glided forward again, mile after mile, in the same spectral journey, as still as the dead. My mind floats along with the water-bugs that run ahead of me and the shadows. I see the stars floating in the water, and those overhead likewise, and many more stars than ever shone in these latitudes. In fact, I fell asleep. I don't think I had slept long when I was awakened by a shrill noise, resembling the letting off of steam from a small steam-engine when the valve is suddenly opened and as suddenly closed again. I have heard such noises in a country church before the commencement of exercises, when some plethoric deacon blowed his brazen nose,—only, if anything, the night-bugle was a little more emphatic, and several times repeated in quick succession. 'What's that?' I whispered.

" 'Deer,' responded Hank, in a whisper, swinging around the canoe so that, as the light moved against the woods, the motion of the boat brought forth two or three more sneezes, and then we heard a heavy crashing through the bushes as a deer dashed up the hill, awakening the echoes with his nose, more terrifying than Bardolph's fiery beak to all the bottom land: for immediately, from the other side of the brook, another buck took up the cry, and rushed up the hill to the summit, where he stood some minutes stamping the ground and startling the darkness with that most singular of alarums.

" 'Two big bucks,' said Hank. 'There be'ent much good huntin' here any longer; we've got ter get back to the lakes agin, fur them bucks has called off all the others.'

" 'But it won't do to give it up so, Hank; we must have a deer, or we won't go home till morning. Think of the hungry mouths in camp.'

" 'Wall, I suppose we can try them sand-beaches round on the south shore. I kinder think the bucks fodder on the sand-beaches more'n on lily pads this time o' year.'

"So around we went, glaring our Cyclopean eye over the open lake, and causing the loons to laugh like monkeys. One or two islands stand out in the open water where the brook makes in, and we passed around their jutting rocks to the southern shore. The water began to shoal, and I could see the white sand on the bottom, from which here and there the osiers reared their taper wands, and, as the air came wafting from the land, it brought the odour of the white water-lilies, the queen of all the water flora. Skirting the osiers we could see the sword-grass growing rank beyond, and presently we heard a splash in the water. A moment more of slow drifting motion and we heard the tramp, tramp, of some animal wading in the water. A little nearer we floated, the rifle in hand and the senses concentrating on the grassy marsh. A little nearer, and the eye caught a motion. Brighter grew the light as the canoe floated up and reddened the grass and reeds, and we caught, in the darkness ahead, a bright blue light, and then another, the reflection from the deer's eyes. Then we heard a suppressed snort. Another push of the paddle, and a deer stood out in the grass, his head thrown up, and his eyes shedding pale light. The boat is directed straight toward him, and the paddler is as still as a statue. I aimed and fired. From beyond the smoke I heard the splashing and dashing of water, and a big buck dashed past me, and then two others, all rushing off together for a belt of timber that arose close by us on our right. As they ascended the bank, I aimed at the hindermost with my remaining barrel and fired, and at the sharp ring of the rifle he fell back convulsively dead.

"We hastened to the shore, and, carrying with us the light from the boat, we found the deer I had first fired at lying with a broken shoulder, just dead, in the high grass. The second was lying among the lily pads, where he had fallen, the ball having passed through the centre of his neck, breaking the spine and killing him instantly. They were both large bucks of six tines, with their horns fully grown. It seemed a marvel—something that was as supernatural as the weird scene around us—to see those two noble beasts that, a moment before, were the wildest forest things that range the earth, so still and heavy, in among the lilies and the sword-grass.

" 'Wall, wall, that was purty well done,' said Hank.

"But Hank's praise could not lighten the dull leaden weight of the stags, nor relieve my mind from the lurking impression that the coming by night into these solitudes, to shoot down two of the lords of the soil while at their food, was not the part of a brave man. But what is the use of moralising? Some men sin without thought, others with much; but I opine that the much thought don't deter from a repetition of the sin.

"With a good deal of labour we hoisted our two deer into the canoe, and paddled home to the sleeping camp, and then——"

"Tuck a drink," said Mike, whom we all thought fast asleep, from under his arm.

"A drink! no, sir, I was more intoxicated with my hunt than a gallon of whisky would have made me."

"All who believe Poke's story, signify it by saying I."

"I," said Poke.

"I'se sure maussa tell fur true 'bout firin' in de stump part," suggested Scip.

Potter turned to Mike, and while filling his pipe said—

"Yer didn't hear tell of that horse-showman when you was up to Pensecolee, did yer?"

"Naary," said Mike.

"His name was D. Villars, ef he didn't lie about it. A thin, black-eyed, razor-nosed cuss. I want to get track of that fellar."

"What fur?"

"Wall, he cum it over the boys up there a leetle too strong. He had a sort of show, and advertised that a horse of his would go around the ring on the run while a dog was all the time a-sittin' on his tail. Wall, we all liked horses some, and dogs too, and we all calkelated we'd go in fur that show. We pinted up our half dollars, and said we'd see him. The grocery was empty that night, and so ware Gorzalz cock-pit. Jim Lane was thar, and Dusty Jake, one-eyed Bill from St. Mark's, and Captain Spinks and his gaal Lize—Lize that used to be maid on the Nancy Belle when she busted—and a pile of fellars from the coast.

"That chap raked in a jack-pot o' money that night. Wall, he had a sheepshead-lookin' roan mare with a wicked eye, and a thin tail. When she showed up, we all said that dog can't sit up on that air tail, nohow! The dog cum in too, and this Villars man raked in the chips from the till into his pocket, and then commenced to ride around the ring. He rode, and he rode, and he rode, until Jake Billins yelled out for the dog to get up. 'Gentlemin, gentlemin,' said the showman, a-smilin' as a monkey,—'gentlemin, I beg you will not disturb the ladies.'

" 'We've got enough horse now, show us the dog a-sittin' on his tail,' called out Jake.

" 'Gentlemin,' said the showman, 'I always fulfill my promises; I'm a man of my word; you have seen my horse go round the ring on a run, and now look there and you can see the dog a-sittin' on his tail.' Sure enough the dog was a-sittin' in the middle of the ring on his own stumpy little tail. There was a yell. 'Gentlemin, gentlemin!' sez the showman, 'respect the ladies.' He couldn't say more, fur jist then Hell broke loose. The crowd piled over into that ring like a drove of buffalo bulls. Sticks flew, pistols blazed, and the showman on his horse cut out of the back fly of the tent that he had left open, and ef he hadn't had a smart beast under him, he'd had his neck stretched. I 'spec't he's a-runnin' yit. Lordy, I wish I could ketch him!"

As no one could suggest any means of finding him, no one spoke. The fire flickered, the negros laid themselves down with their heads to the fire and their feet bare. Potter sprawled out on his back with his fur cap over his face. Every man chose his own position, and first one, and then another travelled into the land of forgetfulness:—

> "A pleasing land of drowsy head it was,
> Of dreams that were before the half-shut eye;
> And of gay castles in the clouds that pass,
> For ever flushing round a summer sky."

CHAPTER 27

Woodland Choruses

"In the long nights of winter when the cold north wind doth blow,
And the howling of the wolves is heard amid the snow."
— *Macaulay*

AS WE DESCENDED THE ST. JOHN'S RIVER, the water views gradually enlarged and became more characteristic. The wider volume of water set back the forest to a further distance, and not only removed all question of Indian bullets, but the change from the heavy woods to the open vista made us freer in feelings and more rapid in our motions. The boats moved faster, and wind and current in our favour, with trolling lines astern for sea-trout, and the negroes singing their Methodist air—

"In a few days, and a few days
We're gwine to glory,
In a few days,"

we rapidly sped northward to our final destination and the scenes of civilised life.

One day we passed an Indian canoe. Mike said the paddler was an Indian, though he looked more like a negro, and had a long talk with him. They used the Indian language and we could not understand them, though from some names we heard spoken we judged their conversation went back to Tiger Tail. The Indian, we thought, once mentioned Jackson, and once gave the native motion for taking a scalp. After he was gone Mike seemed moody for a day, and then the meeting with the Indian was forgotten.

The jumping mullet were frequently seen and at night we could catch them in abundance in our canoes by carrying a torch. They sprung from the water toward the light, frequently two or three at a time, and fell in the boat, their pearl-coloured scales flashing in the torchlight. In some places they are called moth-fish, from this peculiar instinct. In later years the raftsmen on the river availed themselves of this habit, and placing lights on the sides of their rafts collected quantities of fish that readily leaped the low edges of the raft.

The nights were very dark during a portion of the time we were descending the river, yet as we were in haste to be home, we kept on on our way sometimes till late in the evening, making our course by the black line of forest that margined the shore. Some of those nights were exceedingly solemn. The mystery of the darkness, the splash of the leaping fish, the murmur of frogs and newts, the rushing wings of the night-birds, and now and then the heavy bassoon of the alligator, in whose bosom the spring of the year had awakened tender recollections of his mate, all added to the awe and novelty of our voyage.

Sometimes, too, we could hear the plaintive whine of the panther or the howlings of wolves, that, scenting us from shore, challenged our distant passage that left them no bones for their supper.

These wolves are funny fellows. You would hear one howl away down the river just audibly above the insect hum. Then an instant's pause, and another answers from the opposite shore, and then one close at hand gives a yelpish whine as though he had been intending to howl, but a bone that he had in his mouth stopped him, until he laid the bone down and hurriedly had his howl out. Most of the wolves on the Gulf coast are black. In the northern part of the continent the grey wolf predominates and the black are rarely seen.

We pitched a camp one night at dark in a grove of orange trees a little up from the shore with everything to make us comfortable. Opossum, venison, fish, and doves were hanging before the fire; the night was dry and pleasant, our camp was well located, and we had every anticipation of a cheerful night, until the Doctor, who could never resist the chance of throwing a line, must needs hook a small alligator in the river on his night line. It was all very easy as long as the animal was in deep water—he was a caught fish,—but the moment the Doctor dragged him up to shoal water where he could obtain a good footing, then the Doctor was caught, and had either to be pulled in the river or let the line pay out and the brute get back to four-fathom water.

Soon we heard a call for help, and, after a number of facetious suggestions offered and refused, one of the negroes paddled out a few yards, and, when the animal came up to the surface, put a rifle to his head and killed him.

The hook was cut out of his mouth, and the body floated down the river a few yards, and, as we learned in the morning, lodged against the bank.

The discomfort of the Doctor's fishery now became apparent. Supper being despatched, every one rolled over, pulling off his boots for a pillow, or laying his head on his arm. The first sleeper had just begun to emit a hoarse breathing which a listener would call a snore, when we heard, "Ah-ha—whoo-a-whoo-oo-oo!" from a little way down shore. "Bow-ow-ow-owe-owe!" said every dog in the camp, in different tones of shrillness, depending upon the acidity of their tempers. Up on end came every sleeper.

"What's that?" queried some one.

"Cuss the wolves!" quoth Mike.

"Dar's a prime psalm-singer, settin' de tune," added Scip.

"'Cause he settin' tune, yer mussent kick around like all-afire," says Cæsar, holding on to his bruised shin.

"Wag, here Wag, don't go there!" called the Doctor to his cur, that had not the least intention of venturing beyond the circle of the firelight.

Everybody turned over; wolves are never dangerous, unless to your provisions, and in a moment more there was silence and a sound of strangulation from the Doctor that foreboded his profoundest sleep, when "Ooh-ooh-ooough," came the old note, followed by the rush of the dogs and the same series of questionings and yawnings and objurgations.

There seemed to be a concert near us; for the moment one wolf would get tired, another would take up the refrain until it was soon apparent that there was no more sleep for that night.

We only took cat naps, eating a little now and then and sometimes taking a drink, talking, conjuring up all the old stories of wolves that we had ever heard or read of, good bad and indifferent, they were all repeated,—wolf had no mercy shown him that night. If he could have understood our language I am sure he would have howled louder in anger at the character we gave him than ever he did in hunger or melancholy.

Mike's opinion of him was that he was a "dratted mean cuss, feered to hunt deer alone and fodderin' on his own young ones when he can't ketch nothin' else."

The negro boys entertained the belief that the luminous appearance from their eyes at night arose from their feasting on the slain in battle, and a suspicion that they sometimes visited graveyards for other purposes than pensive meditations.

The Doctor told how the power of a wolf's jaw was greater than that of any animal, that it had a power of—I have forgotten how many hundred pounds—and something about his facial muscles that no one understood.

I told the following story of an adventure. It don't seem now half as natural as when the wolves were howling an accompaniment, but it is true, nevertheless.

The Wolf Chase

"During the winter of 1834, being engaged in running a line in the Aroostook country in the northern part of Maine, I had much leisure to devote to wild sports. To none of these was I more passionately addicted than to skating. The deep and sequestered lakes of this State, frozen by the intense cold of the northern winter, presents a wide field to the lovers of this pastime. Often would I bind on my skates, and glide away up the glittering river, and wind each mazy streamlet that flowed beneath its fetters on toward the parent ocean, forgetting all the while time and distance in the luxurious sense of the gliding motion, thinking of nothing in the easy flight, but rather dreaming as I looked through the transparent ice at the long weeds and cresses that nodded in the current beneath and seemed wrestling with the waves to let them go; or I would follow on the track of some fox or otter, and run my skate along the mark he had left with his dragging tail until the trail would enter the woods. Sometimes these excursions were made by moonlight, and it was on one of these occasions that I had a recontre, which even now in a warm climate, and with kind faces and bright fires around me, I cannot recall without a nervous looking-over-my-shoulder feeling.

"I had left my friend's house one evening just before dusk, with the intention of skating a short distance up the Kennebec, which glided directly before the door. The night was beautifully clear. A peerless moon rode through an occasional fleecy cloud, and stars twinkled from the sky and from every frost-covered tree in millions, and the great zone of the milky way and the lucid planets were all copied in the mirror-like ice, till your foot seemed treading the jewelled vault of heaven. Your mind would wonder at the light that came glinting from ice, and snow-wreath, and incrusted branches, as the eye followed for miles the broad gleam of the Kennebec, that like a satin ribbon wound between the dark forests that bound it. And yet all was still. The cold seemed to have frozen tree and air, and water, and every living thing that moved. Even the ringing of my skates on the ice echoed back from Moccasin Hill with a startling clearness, and the crackle

245

of the ice as I passed over it in my course, seemed to follow the tide of the river with lightning speed.

"I had gone up the river nearly two miles, when, coming to a little stream which empties into the larger, I turned to explore its course. Fir and hemlock of a century's growth met overhead, and formed an archway radiant with frost-work. All was dark within, but I was young and fearless, and as I peered into an unbroken forest that mirrored itself on the borders of the stream, I laughed with joyousness, my wild hurrah rang through the silent woods, and I stood listening to the echo that reverberated again and again, until all was hushed. I thought how often the Indian hunter had concealed himself behind these very trees, how often his arrow had pierced the deer by this very stream, and his wild halloo had here rung for his victory. And then, turning from fancy to reality, I watched a couple of white owls, that sat in their hooded state, with ruffled pantalettes and long ear-tabs, debating in silent conclave the affairs of their frozen realm, and was wondering if they "for all their feathers, were a-cold," when suddenly a sound arose; it seemed to me to come from beneath the ice. It sounded low and tremulous at first, until it ended in a prolonged yell. I was appalled. Never before had such a noise met my ears. It seemed more than mortal, so fierce, and amid such an unbroken solitude, as if a fiend had blown a blast from an infernal trumpet. Presently I heard the twigs on shore snap, as if from the tread of some animal, and the blood rushed back to my forehead with a bound that made my skin burn, and I felt relieved that I had to contend with things earthly, and not of spiritual nature; my energies returned, and I looked around me for some means of escape. The moon shone through the opening at the mouth of the creek by which I had entered the forest, and considering this the best course, I darted toward it like an arrow. 'Twas hardly a hundred yards distant, and the swallow could scarely excel my desperate flight; yet as I turned my head to the shore, I could see two dark objects dashing through the underbrush at a pace nearly double in speed to my own. By this great speed, and the short yells which they occasionally gave, I knew at once that these were the much dreaded grey wolf.

"I had never met with these animals, but from the description given of them, I had but little pleasure in making their acquaintance. Their untamable fierceness and the untiring strength which seems part of their nature, render them objects of dread to every benighted traveller.

> 'With their long gallop, which can tire
> The deer-hound's hate, the hunter's fire,'

they pursue their prey—never straying from the track of their victim—and as the wearied hunter thinks he has at last outstripped them, he finds that they but waited for the evening to seize their prey, and falls a prize to their tireless cunning.

"The bushes that skirted the shore flew past with the velocity of lightning, as I dashed on in my flight to pass the narrow opening. The outlet was nearly gained; one second more, and I would be comparatively safe, when my pursuers appeared on the bank directly above me, which here rose to the height of ten feet. There was no time for thought, so I bent my head and dashed forward. The wolves sprang, but miscalculating my speed, sprang behind, while their intended prey glided out upon the river.

"Nature turned me toward home. The light flakes of snow spun from the iron of my skates, and I was some distance from my pursuers, when their fierce howl told me I was still their fugitive. I did not look back, I did not feel afraid, or sorry, or glad; one thought of home, of the bright faces awaiting my return, of their tears if they should never see me, and then every energy of body and mind was exerted for escape. I was perfectly at home on the ice. Many were the days that I spent on my good skates, never thinking that at one time they would be my only means of safety. Every half minute an alternate yelp from my fierce attendants made me but too certain that they were in close pursuit. Nearer and nearer they came; I heard their feet pattering on the ice—nearer still, until I could feel their breath and hear their snuffing scent. Every nerve and muscle in my frame was stretched to the utmost tension.

"The trees along the shore seemed to dance in the uncertain light, and my brain turned with my own breathless speed, yet still they seemed to aspirate their breath close in my ears, when an involuntary motion on my part turned me out of my course. The wolves close behind, unable to stop, and as unable to turn on the smooth ice, slipped and fell, still going on far ahead; their tongues were lolling out, their white tusks glaring from their bloody mouths, their shaggy breasts were fleeced with foam, and as they passed me they glared, and howled with fury. The thought flashed on my mind, that by this means I could avoid them, viz., by turning aside whenever they came too near; for they, by the formation of their feet, are unable to run on ice except on a straight line.

"I immediately acted on this plan. The wolves having regained their feet, sprang directly toward me. The race was renewed for twenty yards up the stream: they were already close at my back, when I glided round and dashed directly past my pursuers. A fierce yell greeted my evolution, and the wolves, slipping on their haunches, sailed onward, presenting a perfect picture of helplessness and baffled rage. Thus I gained nearly a hundred yards at each turning. This was repeated two or three times, every moment the animals getting more excited and baffled.

"At one time, by delaying my turning too long, my antagonists came so near that they threw the white foam over my dress as they sprang to seize me, and their teeth clashed together like the spring of a fox-trap. Had my skates failed for one instant, had I tripped on a stick, or caught my foot in a fissure in the ice, the story I am now telling would never have been told. I thought all the chances over; I knew where they would first take hold of me if I fell; I thought how long it would be before I died, and when there would be a search for the body that would already have its tomb; for oh! how fast man's mind traces out all the dead colours of death's picture, only those who have been near the grim original can tell.

"But soon I came opposite the house, and my hounds—I knew their deep voices—roused by the noise, bayed furiously from the kennels. I heard their chains rattle; how I wished they would break them, and then I would have tried 'turn about is fair play.' The wolves, taking the hint conveyed by the dogs, stopped, and after a moment's consideration turned and fled. I watched them until their dusky forms disappeared over a neighbouring hill. Then, taking off my skates, limped up to the house, half cured of romance in the woods and tired of the name of wolf.

"But even yet, I never see a broad sheet of ice in the moonshine without thinking of that fetid, snuffling breath, and those fearful things that followed me so closely down the frozen Kennebec."

As the tale ended, an unseen auditor, who from his covert in the bushes was indignant at my account of his people, yelped out, Oo, who-oo, who—oo—o—ah, aigh.

"Hear the vowels," said the Doctor, "a, e, i, o, u, and sometimes w and y."

"Drat the cuss!" quoth Mike, throwing a blazing knot into the bushes, "has he got no decency?"

CHAPTER 28

Life in the Light-House

"The rocky ledge runs far into the sea,
And on its outer point, some miles away
The Light-house lifts its massive masonry,
A pillar of fire by night, a cloud by day.

"The startled waves leap over it; the storm
Smites it with all the scourges of the rain;
And steadily against its solid form
Press the great shoulders of the hurricane."

FAR TO THE SOUTHWARD of what has been the scene of our story, forming one of the barriers between the coquina-fringed coast of Florida and the Atlantic, lies Key Biscayne. Southward still, innumerable little islands of white shell show their backs above the tide, and then Key Largo, Indian Key, and Key West, sweep in a curve around the point of the continent, warding off with their coral arms the blows of the angry Atlantic, and the soft allurements of the Gulf Stream. To the westward on the mainland stretches from ocean to gulf the labyrinth of the everglades.

There were no permanent settlers in this country at this time, though at Key West was congregated a reckless company of men whose boats found shelter from the storms among the islands, and who gained a livelihood from the shipwrecked vessels that monthly dashed to pieces on the coast. Most of them were desperate men without families, only cultivating the soil to plant cocoa and plantain trees, and relying upon the sea for the supply of the rest of their wants. Their low craft could be seen among the innumerable reefs at the beginning of every storm, like sea-gulls foreboding the tempest, and hovering for its waifs.

In the interior of the peninsula the Indian still remained secure in his morass, and from Key Biscayne at times his camp-fires could be seen against the midnight sky.

The only thing that was human on the coast, contrasting with the cruel shore and the more cruel wreckers, was the light-house on the Key. The great charity reared itself between the wilderness and the sea, an oriflamme over the strife. It stood on a jut of beach at the lower end of the island, where the palmetto trees dried out in the shale, and only the long sword-grass grew around in scattered spears. A boat with a mast lay on the shingle, and a log canoe, and close by the light stood a little low white house, with two square windows and a door toward the sea, and two square windows and a door toward the bay. A tiny porch covered each doorway, and the little windows were opened and closed by heavy wooden shutters. The only vegetation near the light was one tall, twisted cocoa-tree, whose fronded leaves were so high in air they formed no shelter from the sun, but crackled with a shardy sound, and when the wind blew fresh from sea, from time to time the tree loosened one of its large cocoa-nuts from its stem, letting it fall to the ground with the thud of a cannon-ball.

The prospect to the eye from the lantern on the tower was a weary stretch of sand islands between the sea and the bay, and beyond the bay the desolation of limitless swamps. Heavy surges beat on the shore, long hot days made the land glimmer in the mirage, and the tower and the little house cowered before the breakers, or danced in the white heat.

Here Lou Jackson had come, and with her father's brother was living in the house and keeping the light.

It is difficult to explain the motives that in some persons lead to their course of life. Was it necessity, was it adventure that brought her here, or was it a secret longing unconfessed to be near some one of the comrades of our many hunts?

Lou had a little foot, and it was laced over its high arch with an Indian moccasin. The wrought buckskin became the foot, as it was tapping the uppermost step in the lantern, while its owner, with her arm on the window-sill, sat looking seaward. Here was her accustomed seat as the sun fired the everglades at his sitting, and left the ocean still as a child tired with its romping, and every evening, for the month that she had lived at the Key, found her in the same spot dreaming away the twilight, and when it was dark brightening the eyes of the passing mariners with the expectant flash of the lantern.

Life in the Light-House

The spits of sand that ran up and down along the coast were margined with little rollers that broke in foam along their seaward side, and then fell back to renew the attempt, while doe-witches and sand-pipers with nimble tread pursued them back and forth. The blue line of the horizon, where it cut the roseate sky, was marked by the sail of a ship, that Lou was watching. She was conning over her past few years of life. Figures came up to her misty eyes, dead friends, and other homes, strong men, and patches of wood, and camp-fires and old longings. There were tears in her eyes, and her foot ceased to tap the iron step, and she leaned more over her arm and looked harder out to sea. Then appeared her lonely life, and the wild imaginings and romances it had created, and her form straightened again. Her short lip curled, and the tears dried up.

She thought of her kinsfolk in the States, and how with haughtiness she had thrown back their proffers of assistance. She thought of her own active life, her self-educated tastes, her superiority to her sex of the same age, not boastingly, but proudly and justly. Old dreams of romance came over her, dreams that had been dreamt and re-dreamt, and had awakened old fancies of a desperate, whole-souled love, proud as her own, that was to meet her own and make surrender—that was to woo, plead, strive, and die for her, and be accepted. She thought of Mike, and in the daring mood she was, the patient, gentle, watchful hunter was swept away with a rush of scorn. Too timid or careless to plead for her, too simple for an ideal, his love was the likings of a man, but no love for such as her. A man that she couldn't understand at times, a man that was too cautious to praise, too weak to dare anything for her, even a refusal—out on such a man! The consciousness of a secret liking that had made her leave Mike so hastily at Bonda Key when he had proffered the cat-skin, made her pride revolt and her scorning bitterer. Then she was too proud to let him come nearer her because she was the daughter of a planter and he a vagrant hunter. Now she was too proud even to think of him, for she was poor, and an orphan. Yet she could not rid herself of that unconfessed regard. There were other men that were bolder than he, many more refined. Had this immense world no life and form in it that was perfect to her ideal?

"Fool—fool! I am a fool!" she said aloud, springing upon her feet. Taking a cloth from a locker, she began polishing the reflectors of the light, whistling between the pauses of her duty.

"Donald, isn't it time to light up?" presently called her voice from the gallery of the lantern.

251

"Yes," answered her uncle from below, scanning the horizon with a long look to note the gathering shadows.

In a moment more it was dark, and the sailor pacing his watch on the ship in the offing called from the fore-castle deck to the mate: "Cape Florida light, sir, on the port bow, ten miles away."

CHAPTER 29

Tracking the Enemy

"For it is with feelings as with waters—
The shallow murmur, but the deep are dumb."

"NINE INJINS AND NO SQUAWS," quoth Mike, seating himself on one of the rolling sand-hills that border Indian River, a little south of Cape Canaveral, after a long examination of the surrounding shores.

On the same evening that we pitched our camp on the well-marked trail leading from the St. John's River across to St. Augustine, Mike had disappeared. He had given no notice of his intention, unless the purchase of powder and ball from a trader camping at the same place might have been a notice. The place where he slept at the fire was vacant, and the dun hound and heavy rifle had disappeared with their owner.

We were safe from all doubt as to our course, and from all danger, for St. Augustine was but sixteen miles away, but we speculated much on the cause of the sudden flight. Had the trader or his men given him any bad news? No, they were only talking of the wars, of Tiger Tail's forays, and how the troops were drawing down in concert to destroy the Indians or drive them southward. We thought at first he had gone over to the town, but a missing canoe showed he had taken to the water. We mentally bade him farewell, and started over to St. Augustine, and were soon pacing its narrow streets, beside the quaint old Spanish church with its chime of five bells, and the moss-grown walls of the old fort, builded, as saith its inscription, by Field-Marshal Don Alonzo Fernando Hereda, of noble fame.

In three days Mike had retraced the course he had brought us in descending the river. Over the broad water of Lake George, where the great pearl-shell mussels grow, he passed like a gull before a northerly wind, holding up his blanket for a sail, and made the orange tree point where the St. John's enters the lake from the southward.

Following the St. John's beyond Lake Monroe, he passed in the night, and unobserved, the company of soldiers we met in descending the river. Their camp-fire was bright on the beach, and he could hear the sentries challenge as they marched to and fro under the stately trees, according to what Mike thought their unnecessarily ostentatious rules of camp government.

"Hulloain' like that in the woods when they ought to be hidin' away," said he to himself, as he noiselessly floated by; "that's all some folks knows."

Mike was like a good many quiet people—he liked his own company, and would talk to himself, little by little, in disconnected sentences, even when he refused to talk to any one else. The many days he passed alone encouraged the habit.

Thence still up the St. John's, through all its winding course, he paddled, warily watching the shore and water, and often visiting either bank to look for signs. Wherever there was a bend in the river, he kept close to the point around which the curve made, creeping around so slowly and cautiously that his eye took in all the reach of the river ahead before he could himself be discovered. He visited many old Indian camps, wandering around them, looking for little signs indicating the intention the occupants had at parting. Wherever there was a trail across the river he seemed to know or divine it, approached it warily, and only left it after a careful scrutiny.

When he built a fire to cook his food, it was made back from the river, and the fire was lit of the driest twigs, so that it raised no smoke, and at leaving he covered it over with ashes, and stamped out the mark his rifle had made in the sand. Sometimes he would not let his dog come ashore, or if he did, carefully rubbed out the tracks of his feet. He did not travel at night, unless in the early part of the evening, and never struck a light after dark, but carrying his canoe on shore, filled it with moss, and laid down in it with his dog at his side.

At the far upper end of the St. John's, after the explorer has passed through innumerable expansion-like lakes, and crossed the beautiful waters of Lake Poinsett, he will find the St. John's winding and twisting, overflowing the prairie here in shallow marshes, and running off into deep long tributary lagoons, fringed with canes, reeds, and flags of the most graceful shapes and dense growth. Some of the canes totter over, leaning their tall tips against the others for support, and so they reach entirely across the narrow creeks, shutting out the sun and air, and leaving the boatman to push

"Tried to dodge—landed back and walked around. Somethin's up—wouldn't have been so pertickalar ef they'd been actin' honest."

The hunter followed the trail both back to a branch of the lagoon, where they had left the ordinary course, and then over the sands till where the footsteps faded out in the ripples of Indian River.

"Seven days out, jist!" he said musingly. "Scratchin' along fast."

Seating himself on the sandy hillock, among the rough swaying grass, he mused on the thoughts suggested by the trail, and after a very long silence again repeated with a sigh, looking southward—"Nine bucks and *no* squaws—that means mischief."

He laid off his cap and drew back his matted hair, leaving his forehead open to the caressing air. "Seven days," he said. "Wall, seven days are a deal of time, and what's wrong done, is done bein' helped. I might as well go over and see. Somehow or 'nother, it don't seem nateral for that critter to come this way. Ef he's runnin' from the soldiers he'd gone west; he knows too much to be bothered by them. He's sent off the women folks for no good, but it mayn't be he's goin' so far. She'll think I'm 'spectin' danger when there ain't none.

"Wall, wall, I might as well be down thar. She won't be any the worse for my bein' nigh her. Poor child, poor child! And ef thar's nobody about, why, I can come away again without her knowin' it. It does a fellar good to know she is near, and maybe it'll turn up, as times go she may need me."

That night Mike with his dog slept among some willows, kindling his fire from the half-burned brands that had served before to cook the food and dry the moccasins of the band he was pursuing. Travelling, as they both were, by canoes, there were no signs left save where landings had been made to cook or sleep, or to carry over the little portages, the traversing of which so shortened the route between Indian River and Jupiter Inlet. But it was the knowledge of native character that guided the pursuer. He could tell on his day's journey just where such a band, impelled by Indian cunning, would land to conceal their fire. Had they been running carelessly, landing where accident led them, their course would have been more difficult of detection, but Mike was tracking them mentally, more by reason than by a trail perceptible to the eye, and as he ran his canoe to the beach, it would sometimes strike on the very footprints of the savages, and the hunter would give his satisfied ejaculation of "ha!" and quietly sit down to his meal without further examination.

Mike travelled faster than his predecessors. When he carried his canoe over the portage connecting Jupiter Inlet with the next creek to the southward, and examined the tracks where they had not been drifted over with the sand, he smiled, saying—"Gained a day." Presently his dog dug up from the sand a broken paddle. Mike patted the hound, and examining the paddle knew why they had travelled so slowly that day; and a little search showed some shavings where a new one had been cut. His suspicions as to the leadership of the band and the direction they were taking had become confirmed, little by little, and now he baked his corn-bread, and rolled himself to sleep on his Spartan couch, satisfied to a certainty that his journey was not a needless one.

A boat is usually sent by the government, at regular intervals, to visit the different light-houses of the United States coast, and supply them with stores. Such a visit had just been made to the light-house at Cape Florida. Two barrels of oil, provisions for the light-keeper, a little powder and shot, some tools, cordage and oakum, a few fishing implements, and some books that had been sent for Lou Jackson, had been delivered and were lying in front of the little house, and the white sails of the schooner were again low on the horizon, leaving the light-house keeper and his niece to another month of solitude.

Lou's uncle was busily engaged storing the goods, some in the house, and some in the light-house, and the girl was in the lantern with a book on her knees and her eye wandering away along the reaches of the shore and of the past. The evening was lull, and even the gulls had settled down on the waters of the bay. Presently her eye caught a motion from over the palmetto bushes that ran down the island, and she watched for the cause. In a moment she saw a naked Indian creeping over the sands, running from a clump of bushes to one nearer the house. The fellow's face was painted vermilion and black, and from his gaudy colour and crouching motion, looked like a leopard more than a man. Lou was not so ignorant of Indian ways but that she knew the meaning of the war-paint and the subtle approach that never could have been seen from below. The blood rushed to her heart with a bound, and then her thoughts were as cool as before. This had not been a totally unforeseen contingency, and they had discussed the course to be followed, and had in a measure prepared for it. The door of the light-house had been made heavy and strong, and the arrangements in the upper story had been such that a person would find it a comparative shelter.

Lou leaned over the rail and called to her uncle in her ordinary voice, "Uncle!"

"Well, child?"

"Look up here, uncle."

The old man leaned over the coil of ropes he had in his hand, and looked up at the lantern.

"Don't move fast," said she, in a measured voice, "but come into the tower quietly; there are Indians in the palmetto bushes."

The uncle was not capable of self-control. He cast a hasty look around him, dropped the coil of rope, and ran to the light-house. It was well for him the door stood open wide, for as he ran a ringing shot came from the palmettoes, the bullet cutting his jacket, and another shot from another covert shattered a pane of glass beside Lou Jackson, and from every side broke out the war-whoop, while half a dozen savages, whooping with their hands to their mouths, sprang from the palmetto bushes, and rushed across the opening to intercept the fugitive.

The old man slipped in, slamming and bolting the heavy door behind him, and was safe. The savages crowded up against the doorway, as an angry wave would sometimes do on a stormy night, and then fell back, baffled for the nonce.

CHAPTER 30

Smoking Out the Enemy

"The creeping tide came up along the sand,
　　And o'er and o'er the sand,
　　And round and round the sand,
　　As far as eye could see;
The blinding mist came down and hid the land
　　And never home came she."

—*Kingsley*

IT WAS EVENING when Donald Laidlaw, Lou's uncle, effected his escape into the light-house, and the next morning found the two prisoners in the upper floor, vainly seeking to spy out their foes, who had disappeared like the uncouth shapes of a dream. The prisoners had listened and waited all night long, but there was no sound on the air but the low wash of the sea, and nothing could be discerned from the apertures of the tower save the sand and the trailing gleam of the lantern on the ocean.

Hour by hour glided by in perfect hush. The cormorants flew past to their daily fishery, the gulls came in from sea, and the shore birds ran in and out with the ebbing tide as they were wont to do. Laidlaw emerged out on the upper floor of the light-house, and turned out the lamp, cautiously peering about him. He saw the goods strewn on the sand, just as they had left them, and the half-open door of the cottage still ajar. He descended again to the tower and told what he had seen; but his escape from the enemy had been so narrow on the previous evening, and Lou's knowledge of Indian character was so good that they concluded it was far from safe to venture out of their place of refuge. So they opened a bag of biscuit and made a frugal meal, from time to time peeping out of the crevices between the plastering and the floor above, and then turning again to each other to talk or dream away the day.

Noon had long passed when they became conscious of some one calling

260

from below, and saw an Indian standing in front of the house, waving a white rag, and indicating by his motions a desire to speak. Laidlaw mounted the steps to the platform on which the light was placed, and which extended some distance over the tower, and, moving cautiously to the edge in such a manner that only his head was exposed to observation from below, called out to the Indian to inquire his message.

"Indian wants to talk."

"Well, what is it? Go on," answered Laidlaw.

"Indian going away—he wants peace. Indian will do no harm. Give him one blanket and he goes."

"Why did you fire at me last evening?"

"Indian was wrong—Indian much drink—Indian is sorry. Give Indian one blanket."

The savage held up one finger to denote the smallness of his wants, and his other hand he pressed to his breast. His face was free of paint, and he carried no arms and spoke very pleasantly, and with a graceful gesture.

"What shall we do, Louisa?" asked the uncle, turning around to the trap-door, through which his niece's head had appeared, as she listened attentively to the conversation.

"Tell him to take the blanket and go. We will see if he will do it."

Laidlaw told the Indian, who, after a pause, replied: "Indian can't take blanket—say Indian stole blanket."

"Uncle, it is all a cheat. Look out for them," whispered Lou.

"No, we will not come out to bid you good-bye. Take the goods you want and be off."

The Indian seemed disappointed, judging from his manner as he turned on his heel and disappeared in the bushes, while the old man descended to the securer retreat of the tower.

The light-house in which Lou and her uncle were entrenched was the ordinary columnar-shaped edifice that may be seen at intervals all along the coast at the present time. It was built of unhewn stone, to the height of about six feet from the sand, and then of concrete—a composition of broken shell and mortar—for forty feet more, slightly decreasing in size, until within a few feet of the top, when it suddenly expanded to receive the bell-shaped lantern of glass that covered the lamps.

Under this lantern was constructed a stone platform, overlaying the tower, and extending out till it formed a narrow ledge, and a single handrail ran round its exterior edge, so that the light-keeper could walk the outside, polish the glasses, and keep undimmed the light. In the lantern stood the lamps on a pedestal, with their metal reflectors, a can of oil and a bundle of waste, for polishing.

At the base of the tower, and on the side from the sea, was a heavy oaken door, entrance to which was gained by a little flight of stairs, and the door was placed above the stone-work, so as to be free from any extraordinary tides. On the level with the door in the tower was a pile of stores of divers kinds, some provisions and some necessary implements for the station. From this, winding stairs of wood ran up to the narrow opening that led to the lantern.

When Lou and her uncle took refuge from the savages, they remained at the bottom of the tower, reclining on the cordage or bales, save as they were occupied in trying to make discoveries of the savages through the narrow windows that here and there were cut, like arrow slits, into the walls for the pupose of light. It was hither they descended when the unsuccessful Indian diplomatist departed, and they were left once more to their own anxious expectations, and to the renewed machinations of their foes.

It was not a great while they had to wait before they heard on the exterior the guttural voices of the savages, and felt the door vibrating under their tests of its strength. Presently they heard heavy blows as though from a stick of timber, and then the sharp rap of a hatchet. Laidlaw started up, and arming himself with the only weapon he possessed, an old fowling-piece, prepared to do battle, when the door should no longer be a security. Lou retreated up the steps toward the lantern. But the door was of live oak, studded with nails, and the Indians did not care to risk their hatchets on so stern a material, and even the blows of the timber presently ceased, the assailants finding it difficult to make their battering ram work effectively from the narrow platform afforded by the steps on the exterior.

The prisoners congratulated themselves on their security, and again seating themselves on the cordage, renewed their council, and even jested upon the futile attempts of their enemies. An hour or more had passed away in most perfect quietness, and saving the occasional visits to the loop-holes of the tower, Lou had relapsed into a dreamy state of half wakefulness, while her uncle, with the caution of years, sat close to the door-way with his duck gun across his knee, and his ear to the crack.

"Don't you smell something strange, uncle?" said the girl, after a pause.

"No," whispered the old man. "What like?"

"I thought I smelt wood burning. What is that I see on the floor?"

Her uncle looked down on what seemed a carpet of lamb's wool, white and flaky, gradually spreading itself over the floor. Laidlaw leaned down his face until he could look out through the crack beneath the door. Then raising up his head suddenly, he stared at his niece, exclaiming in a whisper —"They have set fire to the door."

There was a long pause, and the two prisoners gazed at each other in silence. As they sat they could hear from without the crackle of the flames as they gathered volume, and then at intervals the whoop of the savages in mocking tones.

The thoughts that chased each other through the minds of the prisoners were stern and hurried. There was no water or other means of putting out the fire, and even had there been it was on the outside of the door and constantly supplied with fuel by the savages. In a little while the flames became perceptible through the crevices of the door as the panelling shrunk from the heat. The knots fell out, and through the openings left they could see the savages passing and repassing. Lou's mind likened them to devils in the flame of the pit, and her soul went up in an unsyllabled prayer for deliverance from a death to which only the torments of the lost bore any likeness.

Had Laidlaw been a man like the men that the wild scenes of those days often engendered, he would have been plotting against the savages, or at least been prepared for this emergency and capable of inflicting a salutary revenge; but he was mild and gentle, having outlived many of his friends and ambitions; he returned to gentle pursuits and dreamy musings to fill his vacant mind. His only attempt now was a trial of endurance without any retaliation upon the savages, and laying aside his fowling-piece he assisted his niece in carrying up to the lantern a few things that a protracted stay might render necessary. A few bags of biscuit and boxes of figs, a canvas sail and a rope were brought up, and two or three glass reflectors of heavy weight and much value, were lifted up, with great labour, to the topmost platform.

"I have forgotten my gun," said Laidlaw, descending for the last time the winding steps, blurred with smoke and dusky with the twilight, while Lou crouched down in the lantern to avoid being seen from the sands.

"And bring up some tobacco for your pipe, uncle," she called after him, down the stairs.

"I can't find the gun. Lou, did you see where I put it?" he called from below.

"Is it not leaning against the centre post?" she called.

The answer to her question was sent back up the confined tube of the tower, multiplied into infinite echoes by the hollow walls, in an Indian war-whoop.

The savages had effected an entrance from below. Where was her uncle? She listened, but there was no sound of struggle or pleading, no prayer or groan, only the war-whoop came up in the darkness, echoing and re-echoing from vermilion-coloured lips and stony walls. She leaned her head down the trap-door that communicated from the lantern to the stairs, calling, "Uncle, dear uncle, shall I come to you?" But no voice or sound replied; even the Indian yell died away. The fire had burned out, followed by a perfect hush, contrasting fearfully with the yells and tumult of a moment before. Lou listened and watched, but the tower was thick with smoke, and darkness had settled over all the world. She did not dare to go to the edge of the lantern, for doubtless the savages were watching her from below. She only fulfilled her woman's mission, and shutting and bolting the trap-door waited and hoped.

The darkness wrapped her as a mantle, not protecting her but pinion-ing her arms in helplessness. It seemed the greater from the contrast with the beacon light that usually shone from the lantern brightening even the distant sea. She struck a match and lit the great lamp of the lantern, and as its flash broke out on the night her heart grew lighter at its accustomed cheerfulness. She could once more see the white walls of her house, and the ranks of marching breakers that knelt along the beach, discharging their regular volleys of noise and foam. She laid down on the floor so as to be secure from any shot from without, and watched the narrow winding steps of the tower.

Where was her uncle? There had been no voice or sound of him since they had parted. There was but one opinion as to his fate; she could not think of it, and sternly shut it back lest she might be totally unnerved.

A few hours sped by, and a motion at the base of the tower indicated a new attempt on the part of the besiegers. The experiment developed itself in a cloud of smoke that gradually mounted the tower and found vent through the trap-door. Then a flame was seen below, and in a moment more the winding stairs were in a blaze. The fortress they dared not storm, was to be burned out. The girl looked around her as the smoke accumulated, and opened the windows and the door that led to the gallery to give it vent. The flames roared up through the aperture as through a hollow tree, above which the lantern, like the topmost boughs, came out against the night sky in bright relief or was wrapped in darkness as the flame or the smoke successively lighted or enveloped it. The girl cowered away from the flames as they came up the trap-door to the fullest extent of the tower. The smoke became denser and the stone beneath her warm. She wrapped a blanket around her and kept her face down to the floor. The fresh air that stole through the broken sash struggled with the smoke that curled around her. Her ear caught the whoop of the Indians exulting in their carnival, and an occasional shot that was fired at the lantern, more in triumph than with the intent to slay. She heard the surf, and the peevish cries of the sea-birds that circled around the unusual light. Her brain reeled with the smoke and she became insensible.

When she recovered her senses the morning had broken, and the world with its thousand happy tenants had awakened to the joys of another day. The slight wooden staircase in the tower had burned out, leaving the column of stone and mortar with its iron-ribbed lantern as strong as before. The girl looked down the column and found herself cut off from the earth. She looked out on the strand and there was no living being in sight. The lamp had gone out in the smoke. She looked out for her late enemies, but could see none. The world below her was beautiful to see, replete with rolling breakers, shells and sands, flowering palmettoes, and the long lagoon, with its little island, dreaming a hundred yards from shore.

CHAPTER 31

Besieging the Light-House

"And that unknowing what he did,
    He leaped amid a murderous band,
    And saved from outrage worse than death
    The lady of the land."

— *Coleridge*

THERE ARE SOME POSITIONS in which one is thrown so hopeless, and so complicated in the abundance of their misfortunes, that the heart gives up resistance and lamentation. Then, after a little, there arises a pride of superiority, and the heart grows greater from its conscious scaling of these disasters. They cease to afflict, and are the sources of a bitter pride.

So from her house of refuge by the sea the mind of the imprisoned girl ran over her lonely life, her position of disaster, and her feebleness against a nation of foes. Her mind recovered its tone, she became proud of herself, matching her feeble endurance against war, fire, and the girdling waves. She did not flaunt her new-found hardihood, but used the arm of the feeble, and kept concealed in the bottom of the lantern, yet proud of her own endurance and fortitude. She knew that Indian eyes were on the tower, and that the bushes, seemingly inhabited only by the cardinal birds, were sheltering her enemies as well. She peered out from the crevices of the tower, watching her foes or the passing sails that, unconscious of her fate, crept along the horizon, and the sea, in glassy undulations, murmured to the shore.

As noon rode in the dazzling air and the hollow tower still stood, blackened by the fire, yet seemingly deserted, the Indians, satisfied by the death-like stillness, stole from their hiding-places to examine their work of destruction. First one crept out, with his rifle in his hand, winding around different covers until he reached the base of the tower, and looked up its lofty cone. The embers still smouldered in its base, and up the darkened trunk he could see the square hole that led to the platform, and through it

266

the blue of the sky. Then another savage came out, and another, and they gathered together and talked long at the base of the tower. Lou saw them from where she lay, and could have thrown her lamp-scissors on their heads, but she kept quiet and concealed. The savages, tired of their siege, and satisfied that they had destroyed the only occupants of the light-house, collected together the spoils from the dwelling-house, and putting them in their canoes prepared to start. Lou watched them eagerly, thinking she might see her uncle a prisoner among them. She saw the patchwork coverlet from her bed go down wrapped around a painted chief. She saw some of the little mantle ornaments, her uncle's large brass compass, the family kettles and pewter plates. She saw many a little article of grace and comfort, endeared to her by gift or use, passed through brutal hands and stowed in the canoes lying in the lagoon, but her uncle was not there. The faint hope that had arisen in her soul faded away, and the mercury of her heart fell back with a cold chill.

The Indians paddled off fast, to get to the mainland, for the weather was changing; a cold wind was blowing, and they preferred the shelter of the main to their exposed camp on the Key. In a little while their canoes looked like a train of ducks gliding over the black waters of the bay, and the curling waves came in from seaward with a hollow sound, booming out at sea, and hissing on the sands. Far beyond the regular shore-breakers white spots on the ocean and curling ridges showed where the coral reefs reared their backs and made maëlstroms of boiling waves tangled with sea-weed and brightened with foam.

The sun set before its time in clouds. The air was all a haze. The gulls flew about hither and thither, like bits of white paper tossed on the winds.

"A hard night at sea," said Lou, gathering herself up and looking round her citadel. The wind blew up the trap-door with spatters of the salt water, and found egress through the shattered lantern. She drew some planks over the hole, and after a fashion stopped the broken windows with pieces of boards or glass. The activity calmed her mind. She saw she was safe if she could hold out until some one came to her relief, or until the store-ship returned again. There were a bag of crackers and several cans of lamp-oil safe from the flames stored in the lantern, but they formed a meagre diet. She trimmed her lamp as was her wont, from time to time stopping to watch the rising sea or scan the distant shore, where the Indians had disappeared. The night was a severe one for coasting vessels. Many a wreck would strew the Keys by the morrow, now that the good light was destroyed. Many a brave ship with its light hearts and cabins full of mirth

would "crash together the keel and the mast, to be tossed up aloft in the glee of the wave." A sense of duty and self-sacrifice came over her mind, strengthening her to action. "The ships shall have the benefit of the light as long I am here," spoke the girl; and so, when everything was made as secure in the lantern as her means admitted, she touched the wicks with turpentine, and then with a match. In an instant, like the contagion of a heroic deed, the bright light flashed over the seething main, in a train of splendour; and the mariner, who had been watching for that light from his reeling deck, saw it and blessed it aloud, though he wist not the enduring heart that made it burn.

Down among the tangled foliage of one of the islands close bordering the far shore was crouched a band of Indians. Over the fire cooked their supper. Their canoes, inverted, lay along the shore. Their blankets and the plunder of their foray were scattered around them. The dense hedge of palmetto with its fan-leaves, and the matted cane, bent over them, screening them from the wind, and though on the pulses of the gale they could hear the sobbing of the distant sea, they were secure from the tempest and from want, laughing low with humour, smoking their pipes, drying their leggings and stretching and basking like cats in the genial warmth and light of the fire. They too saw the bright flash of the light-house, as it stepped to its place in the heavens like the star over the cradle of Bethlehem. With their harshly uttered accents of surprise, they started to their feet and peered out from the foliage on the light they had thought darkened for ever. The whole temper of their meal was changed, and with diverted glances and low conference they ate their food and glowered at the star that shone so placidly in the horizon.

Still another party, besides the sailor on the sea and Indians at their camp, saw that star take its accustomed place in the dark.

Mike was coming down the same lagoon when the far-floating specks of the Indian canoes caught his eye and drove him to cover. He hid his little craft in the palmetto bushes on the land, and squatting beside it with his hound, the two watched the savages pass and land on the beach opposite to him. There were three canoes—that was the same number he had been tracking; there were no women with the party—that again tallied; here were nine men, and there had been nine in Tiger Tail's party. Had they sacked the light and left with the spoils? This seemed to be probable. This would be a likely result, in case the two inhabitants of the Key were attacked in such a manner that they could return but a single blow before they were overpowered.

"Or it might turn up," quoth Mike, to himself, "that they treed more'n they could ketch, and were goin' off for a time on a make-believe. Cum back, Yowler; don't show your ugly mug to them critters; they know you better'n their own squaws."

And the old dog obediently resumed his place at his master's side, and the couple quietly watched the open sound that had now become too rough to cross in a canoe.

"No, 'taint it," continued Mike, to himself. "They've been here four or five days. They wouldn't have sot there all that time and done nothing. Wall, wall, time'll show."

The hunter nibbled his jerked venison, giving a bit now and then to his dog, who sat with his head in his master's lap. He saw the screaming gulls come landward, and the darkness gather like a pavilion. He saw the light of the Indian fire, and the long reach of Key Biscayne like a log on the wrathful sea, and the breakers combing over either end.

When the lantern suddenly looked down at him with its tranquil eye, he sprang to his feet, exclaiming—"God is good! God is good to sinful critters. No daylight was ever so pretty to a lonesome bein'. Ha! they've got a long pull to make yet, before they can blow out that 'ere light."

When the morning came, Tiger Tail with his band came back to the island to complete his revenge, but Mike had already gone down along the lee-shore during the night, and was waiting for him.

The Indians, well knowing who was in the tower, made no secret of their approach. They landed just back of the house, and walked around the tower, and in and out the little building where Lou had so pleasantly lived. They entered the base of the tower, looking with eager eyes toward the aperture that led to the lantern. The sea was still rolling in its heavy billows; as they toppled over and danced in foam, the impetus of the waters behind them carried them up to the base of the tower, when they climbed up like a sheaf of white feathers, and then raced back down the sands to gain force for another attempt. The outer side of the tower was in a measure protected by the surf from the savages, and they confined their attack to that side that looked out toward the little island in the bay.

In the dwelling-house they found implements to aid them in their schemes. A beam was brought out and laid endwise against the tower. On this an Indian walked up and drove a spike into the plaster wall. He then mounted on the spike, the inclination of the tower permitting him to lean inward and drive another at such a height he could just reach it with his hand. With his hatchet he then cut out a stepping-place for his foot, and mounted on to the second spike, and then another, until he climbed up to the overhanging ledge of the tower under the lantern.

Thence throwing down his hatchet to his comrades he gradually extended one hand out until he could feel the edge of the over-hanging stonework. Then reaching out the other hand to the stone work, and dropping his feet from their support, he swung out pendent from his hands, and gradually raised himself up until he could see into the lantern.

Lou had been all this time not unconscious of the plots of her foes, but she did not dare to overlook the eaves to see what they were intending, and therefore could not tell precisely how the blow was to fall. She lay down on the floor and waited, trusting to the Providence that had kept her thus far to preserve her to the end.

While thus waiting and listening, her eyes caught sight of the head of the savage slowly rising to the level of the platform. The crest of eagle feathers, the circles of black and vermilion, and the glaring eye, had something in it of so paralysing a horror that she only gazed as she would have gazed in the dilating pupils of a lion, without making a motion of defence.

At this instant there came to the ear of the girl the crack of a rifle. The surf pounded so heavily on the beach, and the wind rustled so fiercely through the palmettoes, and wrestled with the cocoa-nut tree, that the report of the rifle could just be heard by the crouching girl in the lantern, and the crowd assembled on the strand thought the shot came from within the light-house.

But the Indian clinging to the tower sprang half his length above the ledge by the contraction of his arms alone. He writhed around so that his back turned toward the wall. His eyes searched the thickets and the little island that lay near by in the bay. He attempted to sound the war-cry, but the blood bubbled out of his mouth, and fell pattering on the astonished staring group below. One hand fell off from its grasp on the stone coping. He tried to reach it back again, but it wavered in the air half lifted. His filming eye caught sight of the sea-gulls that, drawn by the strange sights, balanced in the air above him, uttering their plaintive cries. He saw in them the spirits of the happy Hunting Grounds promised by his religion. His body swung around in the wind. The head fell back, and the fingers slipped their hold, then the limp corpse fell with a thud on the sands.

W. L. Sheppard

During the occurrence the savages stood mute looking on the unaccountable spectacle. When the body fell to the ground they paused a little, and then crept up to it, leaning over it and examining it. One pointed out with his finger the little blue spot under the arm that a rifle bullet makes. A guttural "ugh!" proclaimed their assent and surprise. They lifted up their dead comrade and retired to the dwelling-house, setting him up against its walls, and held a long consultation. They thought that the blow that had killed their comrade had come from the occupant of the light-house, and they watched for a chance to return it.

Lou crept up to the edge of the lantern and peered down through the crevices. She saw the dead warrior, and the council of the survivors, and their revengeful glances at the tower. She looked all around for the source of the rifle-shot, but could see no living or moving thing. The same crash of waves on one side, and the same monotonous line of coast and bay on the other. The little island stood off the shore, its palmetto bushes rustling and waving in the wind. The cocoa-nut tree bent and twisted, and far out at sea, past the Babel of noise and the tumbling waves, a happy white-sailed ship stood immovably on the horizon, passing from the north to some summer port of the West Indian islands.

A movement among the Indians announced the termination of the conference and another attempt on the tower. A young man came out with his rifle hung over his back like a sling. Like his predecessor, he was naked to the waist, only dressed in his leathern breeches, and as he walked he drew off his moccasins. Another Indian climbed up on the roof of the house, and with his rifle resting on the chimney seemed to keep guard over the lantern. The others scattered about with their guns in their hands, each one in a different direction, thus commanding the tower from all sides. The young man who had first advanced walked up to the cocoa-tree, and, keeping on the side farthest from the tower, commenced to ascend it.

The beleaguered girl saw at a glance the intent of the savage, for the tufted head of the tree where hung the huge cocoa-nuts was nearly on a level with the base of the lantern, and lying as close as possible, she would not be able entirely to hide herself from his shot.

She saw him mount slowly up, only his arms and legs exposed to her view, looking like a bronze serpent enlacing the tree. He had reached the top of the trunk, the long spinous leaves waved and tossed their bending fans above him and hid him from her view. He unslung his rifle from his back. There came a lull in the wind. The cocoa-tree resumed its upright position. Again sounded the crack of a rifle—it came from the islet in the bay—and the young Indian dropped motionless to the sands beneath, like the fruit of the tree when fully ripe.

There was no doubt in the minds of the savages now as to whence came the blow. They had heard the report of the rifle, and each one sprang off to a cover, and the one behind the chimney on the house-top jumped from his exposed position with a celerity that showed more fear than courage. In a moment more there was not a savage to be seen; only the two dead bodies lay on the beach.

CHAPTER 32

Mike and Tiger Tail Play Chess

"*Falstaff.* These nine in buckram that I told thee of, began
to give me ground.
"*Prince Henry.* O monstrous!"
— *King Henry the Fourth*

THERE ARE SOME PECULIARITIES in the Indian character that resemble those of a cat. The Indian is patient, and untiring in pursuit of prey, not seizing it by force but by surprise. He never openly attacks an equal, but waylays him, nor risks a life to take another, though the taking of that other may have been his sole occupation for days. The knowledge of these feline qualities of the savage gives to some backwoodsmen their great success in Indian warfare, and a reputation that, like Cœur de Lion's, is handed down from generation to generation among nations that had never heard of the great Crusader.

Mike was a philosopher in this lore. A saying of his was, "I know what an Injin's up to by his paint," meaning that his war-paint, his trappings, the arms he carried, the decoration of his dress, or its freshness, would show the errand on which he was bent.

So when the savages fell back from the tower Mike methodically loaded his rifle under the cover of the palmetto-bushes that covered the little islet, measuring the charge of powder in an alligator's tooth that hung at his girdle, and trimming off the spare corners of his greased patch after the ball was fitted as carefully as though he was shooting for a Christmas turkey, and then taking out his store of venison from his hunting-shirt, made his morning meal, as assured of a truce as though in his cabin. The islet he was concealed upon was scarcely twenty yards across, and yet so luxuriantly had the palmetto overgrown it that no single bit of sand could be seen. It looked like a floating garden. Under the fan-like leaves of the plants the hunter had made a pathway like an otter from the farther side to the landward edge, and thence he looked out on the light, a hundred yards across the open water and the long extended beach.

No boat could appear on the open water, or any approach be made to the light-house, without its being seen from the island. Mike knew that the Indians would not expose themselves either in the one way or the other, although they outnumbered him seven to one. That they were watching him he was perfectly assured, and he did not give them the opportunity of seeing him by any unwary motion. He merely stretched out an arm over the deep muzzled head of his hound, and waited.

From the other side of the narrow straits the Indians frowned on the island, consulted together, or passed from clump to clump to examine it more closely, carefully screening their bodies from the hunter, though careless as to all observation from the light-house. Among them, pre-eminent in gracefulness of figure, was one who wore on his breast a silver medal, like those given to Indians of distinction by the government of the United States as a reward, or inducement to fidelity. He had crawled down almost to the beach, and from behind some broken timber kept a steadfast watch of the island. Although they had seen neither the marksman, his trail, nor any of his signs, there was no doubt as to whom the island concealed. Mike's character was too well known to doubt whose daring act had cost the band two of their warriors. Even had they not known his intimacy at Far Away, or been warned by the diamond cut, his well-known monogram, that he had marked on their canoe. Tiger Tail would have given his rifle and squaw for the scalp Mike wore, and yet there slept the scout, almost in sight of him and his band, and they dared not go and take him.

Had a stranger looked on the scene he would have considered the beach a desolate ruin, never more to be inhabited. The lonely tower was blackened and marred, the place was deserted, and the two dead bodies lay on the sand, watched by vultures that, with braced wings, crept in slow circles like motes in the upper air. The storm of the previous night had passed away.

The descending sun sullenly set in the everglades, the wind lulled, and a gentle rain fell like a mist. The trees and light-house loomed large in the obscurity, and the white-reefed breakers on the reefs, spitting their frothy spume into air, could not be distinguished in the drifting scud that settled down on the sea. A tangled path would the ocean be for the ships that night.

Lou Jackson shivered on the stone flooring of the tower. The meagre diet of biscuit, the drink of rain water lapped up from the hollows of the stone, the excitement and terror, had begun to work on her system. Her hand trembled, her eye was sunken and brilliant, and her mind, excited unduly, ran riot with fancy, and became morbidly sensitive to the slightest indication of passing events. She knew that some one was near and had fired on the Indians. Who, or from where, she had not descried. She could see the bodies of the two Indians lying on the sands, and others walking about, and she knew she was still a hunted animal, and with the instincts of a quarry, hid as best her reason taught her.

But another thought came to her with the closing day and the darkening sea. She thought of the happy homes on the open main, and her mind took in the children's laugh, and the lighted cabin with its music and books, and the foretop with its hanging sailors prying about for Cape Florida light. Her own mother went to sea when Lou was yet a child; whether she went down crushed under toppling seas, whether captured by pirates, or whether she still floated over the waves watching for her native harbour, Lou did not know, only her feverish mind pictured her leaning over the taffrail, and saw her pale face looking for shore. When night came down, trailing her black robes heavy with sea fog, and shutting out the earth, the vision came stronger still. Her mother's voice calling to her in the wind to save her—the sea-bird, "lone watcher of despair," piped to her in plaintive cries for help. It was the call of the remembered voice. The feeling was so strong she felt her mother was careering past the reefs; she saw the ship among the spume, and started to save her. She arose from her hard bed, and taking her scissors and oil can, trimmed the great lamps and wiped dry the reflectors. She touched the wick with spirits, and then, striking a match, the fair light flashed out to sea, and the light-keeper again sank to her hiding-place. The darkness had protected her while trimming the lamps, and when the light came she sank so quickly to the floor, the Indians could as easily have shot one of the bale-fires that sometimes hung about the tower as her. As if in answer to her act of devotion a moment after, from so far at sea it looked like a thread of gold, a rocket went up into the air, parted its trident rays, and dropped again into darkness.

"Mother, mother!" called the girl, stretching her hands seaward toward the signal-light of the ship, "I am here"—but only the billows thundered back their responses, and her wavering mind flickered between reason and madness.

When the lamp shone out from the tower, the scout, satisfied of the safety, as he supposed, of Laidlaw and his niece, carefully backed out from his concealment, and drawing his canoe from under the rank foliage, noise-lessly embarked and disappeared in the darkness like a wraith. The fog and darkness concealed his movements from all observation. He knew that with the darkness he would be attacked by the savages, and that they would leave unmolested the tower until he was taken or driven from the neighbourhood. Having the first move, he moved away like a knight on the chess-board, with a great zig-zag that carried him far out into the sound, and then back to where he had seen the Indian canoes lying during the day-time.

This detour cost him much time, moving with the caution that he thought necessary. When he had floated into one of the narrow creeks, or ditches, that ran up into the beach, he left his canoe and the hound, and crept down the shore to where he had seen the Indians landing. Their canoes were gone. "Ha, I know'd it," said Mike to himself, "they've given over the fawn and are trailin' the painter now."

He crept up slowly from bush to bush toward the tower, and soon came out from the grove to the cleared land, and warily examined on every side for the rear-guard left by the enemy. There appeared to be none. "Seven agin one," said Mike, smiling to himself, "that's hardly fair play."

Then straightening himself up under some heavy foliage he looked long up into the lantern. There was no sound or motion from there, only the light burned on tranquilly, falling aslant on the heavy waves that crumbled over and hurried up the beach, simmering with the phosphoric fire that made them blue and white.

"Wall, wall, them folks are roostin' higher 'en turkey cocks. I wonder ef I could crawl up thar."

He crept along the house and found it sacked, and finally reached the foot of the tower. Drawing his hunting-knife he stepped inside, and felt around with his hands. Nothing but ashes and cinders met his hand. "Burned out the hollow tree," said he, and then looking up at the little glimmer of light that came down through the trap-door, he continued, "but didn't smoke out the coons."

Turning to go, his foot encountered something soft. He leaned down and felt it with his hands. It felt like a human body, and a taint of corrup-tion emanated from it. A fearful idea seized the hunter; he grasped the body with both hands and carried it to the door. There was just light enough to see that it was the body of a man. The hunter felt the head and it was scalped. He stood up for a moment and drew a long breath, repeating his favourite prayer of thanksgiving and praise, "God is good, God is good to sinful creeturs."

A stranger would have wondered what the man could have found in the mangled corpse to call forth so fervent an ejaculation of praise and of joy.

Then carrying back the body and placing it where he found it, he glided back to the bushes and was soon hid in his canoe under the mangrove roots that laced and interlaced the crumbling banks.

It was growing toward morning when the hunter saw the Indians returning. He saw the boats glide past without noise, seeking their former landing. From where he lay hid he counted the Indians as they passed —there were but six!

"Whare's that t'other one?" questioned he in a whisper. No one answered his question, and when the boats were out of sight Mike shot out into the misty water, and the strong long pushes of his paddle soon swept his canoe around opposite the island he had lain on during the day. The light from the lantern guided him so that he lost no time, and when the little islet could be discerned he halted, backed out a little, and softly let down a stone anchor attached to a string to keep his canoe from drifting from its place. Then throwing off his hunting-shirt, leggings and moccasins, and armed only with his knife, he cautiously let himself down into the water and floated toward the island. As he reached it he slowly drew himself up out of the water and wormed his way under the palmetto leaves toward the shoreward end of the island. In a moment more there was a guttural sound from the darkness, and the dense foliage was violently agitated as if two bodies were struggling beneath. The noise could not be heard on the shore for the sound of the surf. But backward and forward on the islet swayed the heavy leaves of the sea-rocket that reared its red head among the palmettoes, and the hound stretched his head shoreward from the boat and snuffed the air with quivering nostrils, and his eyes glowed like a lion's. Presently Mike crawled out again from the foliage, dragging down to the water's edge the pliant body of an Indian that he left under the leaves, and then he swam out and drew up his boat to the island and hid it where it had been before, under the tangled branches.

Then the red flush came out of the sea, and the morning wind, and like an army with banners, the great sea fog rolled up its masses and trailed away over the everglades, leaving the tower, and the beach, and the tumbling seas, rejoicing in the beauty and the joy of a Sabbath morning.

In a little while after daylight appeared, the warriors of Tiger Tail's band showed themselves among the coppices on the beach, carefully beating up every spot that might afford a cover for the scent they had spent the night searching for. They went into the ruined dwelling, and then into the light-house, and away down to where the point of land dwindled into the surf, and finally, as if satisfied with their search and assured of the flight of their foe, they resumed their positions around the tower, and one of them, laying his rifle down, prepared to make the ascent of the outer wall to the light that still burned dimly and fitfully in the lantern, like the morning star in the sky. The forest matador prepared himself for his task by laying aside his hunting-shirt that the Seminoles wore, contrary to the usual habit of dress among native tribes. He took off the necklace of coins with a pendent crescent of silver that ornamented his breast. He threw aside his wrought belt with its bullet-pouch and sheath, and putting his knife between his teeth, with a cat-like bound ran up the timber that still leaned against the tower, and carefully mounted the first of the iron spikes driven into the wall. His tight buckskin leggings were fringed with blue, his naked chest and arms glistened with sweat and the sunshine, and with the vermilion-coloured painting on his face and breast he resembled an ocelot climbing a tree. He found the ascent easy until he reached the top of the tower, where it curved out to form the little gallery that ran round the lantern. Here he paused for a moment, adjusting his feet and inserting a hand in a crevice of the wall to support him, while he reached out with the other to fix his hold in the ledge, and here he met the bolt of fate from Mike's rifle, that, with its ringing knell, proclaimed to the astonished band that not only was their comrade on the tower death-stricken, but that necessarily the outpost they had left on the island had first fallen before the same avenger.

Sometimes, when one is hunting squirrels, and has made his shot at some determined nut-cracker in a stately hickory, he will see the wounded animal shiver and drop the unopened nut it held in its teeth, then move on a little and lay flat on the limb, then one by one its feet relaxing their hold, until it slips from the cradling bough, still clinging by one paw, and when that loses its grasp, catching at a lower branch with the other, while on the forest leaves, with a slow patter, the red drops fall until the still wrestling animal hurtles from its retreat, crashing through the leaves to the earth beneath, never more to wake in the morning with its shrill bark.

So the Indian on the tower at the crack of the rifle shivered and dropped his hunting-knife from between his teeth, and reluctantly quitted his hold and fell to the earth below. His comrades had already fled to cover, and lying there in the sun he clenched the sand, gave a convulsive sob, and lay still for ever.

An hour passed by when Mike saw from his concealment the five Indians that remained crossing the sound in their boats. They had considered it safest to beat their retreat while they knew precisely where their foe was intrenched. They carried their dead with them, save the body of the one lying by Mike on the islet, and fled in the direction they were taking when the light in the lantern recalled them to complete their revenge.

The hunter watched their course until they faded into the distant shore, and then coming out of his retreat crossed over to the beach. For the first time since his arrival he seemed in a hurry. When he hailed the tower and called Lou Jackson by name his voice trembled, and when no answer came down to his repeated questions, he threw off his coat and climbed up in the same way so ineffectually tried by the savages.

Lou heard him call, and recognised his voice. She was lying on the stone floor, and her mind had returned with the soothing daylight, yet retained some of its wanderings, and she thought she was dreaming. The vision was so pleasant to her she held her breath that it might not go away. Other dreams had come to her and gone during the night, and left her alone to the terrors of death. She dreaded lest this one might also go. Presently she heard the brushing of garments against the outer wall, and the breathing of some one near her, and then she knew the vision was gone, and dreaded the spectre form she had before seen rising in the self-same place. She drew back in fear, and closed her eyes to shut out the coming Medusa head. She heard a sudden bound, as though something had swung itself upon the gallery, and then in her vision came the brown face of Mike the hunter, and she heard his low voice as he stooped over her, saying, as he lifted her in his arms—

"Lou, child, they haint put out the light yet."

She laid her face against his, and another light, warmer and brighter than any beacon, dawned in her heart.

his canoe as through a sewer. One such branch of the St. John's turned eastward and reached nearly to the coast. This was the course taken by the Indians when making their journeys from the interior to the sea, and it carried them so near Indian River, a broad inlet of the sea that margins the Atlantic, that they had but a very short carry to get across. Mike was following this outlet. He had seen old fires a day or two back, and thought them, judging by the brands, about as old as the interval of time which he had taken to reach there after Tiger Tail had passed, providing the chief had come this way immediately after visiting Lake George.

Mike examined the narrow passage up which he was paddling with the instinct of a tracker without any positive signs, merely led on by his suspicion. Every scratch on the canes he noticed, and floating bits of wood he picked up from the water to look at them, and then toss them back again. Where a flag had been broken, and half withered hung from its stem, he floated past with upraised paddle, calculating the number of days it would take a flag to wither that much.

At length a dint in the oozy bank he marked as made by the blade of a paddle, and marked it so exactly that when he saw another on the same bank he knew they were the blades of different paddles, and that there were more boats than one that had recently preceded him. By the inclination of the hole in the mud, he knew the direction of the stroke, and therefore the way the paddlers who left the marks were going. When there was an opening in the reeds he would raise himself to his feet and look out on the flatlands, watching the birds to see if they would indicate by their flight or their cries any passers in the desert.

Where the creek ran out, the scout examined warily the landing. There were no marks or signs of any kind. He searched long and closely, but could not see a token that a footstep had been there for a month.

"Queer, that!" he said, and paddling back to an out-of-the-way elbow, pulled in his canoe in the reeds, and stepped ashore, leaving his hound tied in the boat. He then crossed over from the low land to the higher rolling sand of the coast, but found no signs of passers. Extending his walk a couple of miles down, he came upon footsteps plainly marked in the sand, going from west to east.

"Ha!" said he, coming to a halt, and bringing his hand to the cock of his rifle. His eyes followed the signs back and forth, and he smiled drily. He felt the compliment to himself, implied in the pains taken by the savages to conceal their trail.